# MODERN HISTORY,

FROM THE FRENCH OF

# M. MICHELET.

WITH AN INTRODUCTION.

BY A. POTTER, D.D.

NEW YORK:
HARPER & BROTHERS, PUBLISHERS,
FRANKLIN SQUARE.
1855.

# INTRODUCTION.

The last thirty years have witnessed remarkable improvements among the scholars of Germany and France, in their methods of historical research and in their style of historical composition. In delineating the progress of events, the historian of these countries has become accustomed to embrace a much greater variety of topics than formerly. He has learned, too, to scrutinize the authenticity of facts more carefully, and to draw some of his most important information from sources which were once regarded either as unworthy of his notice, or as foreign from his inquiries. He has also learned to deal with facts, as significant of great principles, and to fix their historic value according as they represent more or less clearly and expressively the essential features of an age or the important revolutions of a system. In fine, these writers have been gradually imbodying in practice the fine idea that history is only philosophy teaching by example; and they have striven to make her lessons alike clear and impressive. The subscriber is not insensible of the difficulty of all such attempts, nor of the fallacies which have been perpetrated under the imposing title of the *Philosophy of History*. Still, every effort to make history more full, accurate, and instructive, merits applause, and it is an effort in which the two great nations just mentioned have been eminently successful. The learned and indefatigable Germans took the lead in it, and they have been followed with yet greater brilliancy, and with hardly inferior industry, by several French historians. The names of Guizot, Villemain, Mignet, Thiers, the two Thierrys, Sismondi, Barante, and Michelet, among the French, will at once occur to the student of history as justifying this remark. It has long been considered the reproach of English and American scholars, that so little has hitherto been accomplished towards diffusing the same spirit of research and the same just conceptions of historical study in two countries which, of all others, have the deepest interest in possessing them.

To assist in some slight degree towards removing this reproach, and to introduce to the knowledge of the public generally an elementary work conceived and executed after this new method, is the main object of the present translation. The author, M. Michelet, is one of the most learned, laborious, and elegant of that remarkable school, who have been engaged during the last twenty years, in France, in illustrating ancient and modern history. His intense devotion to his studies is said to have ruined his health, and will probably deprive the world of the full fruit of his researches.* With great philosophical sagacity, he combines what is so apt to be wanting in the German historians—a brilliant imagination, a clear and picturesque style, and great felicity of illustration. *Universal histories*, especially if in the form of abridgments, are usually meager and spiritless. The reader will find that Michelet, like his great predecessor Bossuet, is an exception. His summary is constantly relieved by reflections full of weight and vivacity, and his gen-

* His principal works are a *History of France* (unfinished); a *History of the Republic of Rome* (a translation of which is now preparing); *Memoirs of Luther* (compiled from his own writings); *Selections from Vico* (with notices of his Life and Writings); *Chronological Tables*, &c., &c.

eralities are made significant and interesting by examples as vivid as they are novel.

Another circumstance which gives interest to the work, while it calls, at the same time, for some caution in accepting its conclusions, is, that the author has been accustomed to survey history from a point very different from that occupied by English and American historians. He is a Frenchman, a monarchist, and a Roman Catholic; and, though more than usually free from prejudices, it is not to be expected that he should escape them entirely. To those who are sincerely desirous to take an enlarged and philosophical view of events, it must sometimes be grateful to neutralize the force of their own prepossessions by the aid of tolerant and enlightened minds, who have been formed under different systems of religion and law. It is due to the author to add that he is no bigot. A Roman Catholic, he still acknowledges with gratitude the inestimable blessings conferred on the world by the Protestant Reformation; a monarchist, his sympathies are still with the people; a Frenchman, and therefore bound, as he supposes, in common with all Frenchmen, to regard "his glorious country as the pilot of the great vessel of humanity,"* he has yet a heart and an understanding large enough to do justice, with few exceptions, to virtue and greatness, wherever he finds them.

It was the subscriber's intention to have animadverted in notes on some views of the author's which he regards as erroneous. The unexpected bulk, however, to which the volume has swelled prevents the execution of this design, and he therefore leaves this task to the discrimination of the reader or instructer.

While this work will be useful to general readers, its more immediate object is to furnish a good text-book in modern history for schools and colleges.† In Guizot's History of Civilization in Europe we have philosophy without facts. In most abridgments used in seminaries of learning, we have facts without philosophy. This work seems to have struck the golden mean so essential in a good text-book, and the subscriber has only to regret that the circumstances under which the translation was made, and the unavoidable interruptions to which he

* See Preface to Michelet's *Introduction à l'Histoire Universelle.*

† It has been adopted as a text-book by the Royal Council of the University of France.

has been subjected, have prevented its attaining greater precision and spirit. He trusts it will not be found altogether unworthy of its original or of its object.

It was also proposed, in the first instance, to add questions for the assistance of instructers and pupils. The want of room prevents this; but the subscriber may be allowed to remark, that if those questions had been prepared, they would not have superseded labour on the part either of teacher or scholar. Little faith is reposed in methods of teaching which relieve either of these parties from the necessity for exertion. It should rather be our object to awaken and encourage such exertion, and hence these questions would have been so framed as to provide the pupil with subjects for examination beyond the limits of his text-book. This volume will be found to contain many allusions and hints which must prove, unless explained, quite unintelligible to young students, and many brief notices, also, of events and revolutions which deserve to be investigated. The editor would suggest, that the student may, in many instances, be left with great advantage to prosecute these investigations, and work out the explanation of these hints for himself; proper books being pointed out, and the fruit of his inquiries being brought to the teacher for his examination and approval. Such a course would render the progress of a class through the book necessarily slow, but it would be a progress fraught with unspeakable advantages to the tastes and habits of the scholar.

In conclusion, the subscriber has only to express his hope that this work may contribute, in some degree, to diffuse among the young a taste for historical studies, and to promote in all its readers a generous and enlightened interest in the cause of freedom, humanity, and religion.

A. Potter.

*Union College, August,* 1843.

## CONTENTS.

## SECOND PERIOD.

## CHAPTER IX.

*Calvin—Reformation in France, England, Scotland, the Netherlands, to St. Bartholomew*, 1555–1572.



## CHAPTER X.

*Farther Events to the Death of Henry IV.*, 1572–1610—*Glance at the Situation of the Belligerant Powers after the Religious Wars.*

§ I. Death of Charles IX., 1574.



§ II. To the Death of Henry IV., and a Glance at the Belligerant Powers.



## CHAPTER XI.

*Revolution of England*, 1603–1649.



## CHAPTER XII.

*The Thirty Years' War*, 1618–1648.

## THIRD PERIOD.

# AUTHOR'S PREFACE.

In composing an abridgment, we ought particularly to consider for whom it is written. The present summary is addressed to the youthful public of our schools and colleges: it is intended to be committed to memory, and to serve as a text-book for the lessons of the professors.

If, however, it should fall into the hands of that part of the public for whom we do not write, we think they should be previously apprized of the object and form of our *Summary*, lest they should seek therein for that which does not appertain to it.

First, we have laid more stress upon the history of political events than upon the history of religion, institutions, commerce, letters, or the arts. We are not ignorant that the second is still more important than the first; but it is with the study of the first that we commence.

Facts and dates do not often occur in this little book; it is an abridgment, and not a chronological table like those we have published. The "*Chronological and Synchronological Tables*"* were a sort of storehouse

* See *Handbook for Readers* for a notice of these tables.

where a date might be looked for, and facts brought together and compared. In this summary our purpose was quite different: to leave, if possible, in the memory of pupils who should learn it by heart, a lasting impression of Modern History.

To attain this end, it would be necessary first to mark, in a comprehensive and simple division, the dramatic unity of the history of the last three centuries; afterward, to represent all the intermediate ideas, not by abstract expressions, but by characteristic facts, which should strike the imagination of youth. Few of these would be required, but they should be well selected, in order to serve as symbols for all others, so that the same facts would present to the child a succession of images—to the man, a chain of ideas. We speak of what we wished to do, not of what we have done.

The history of the nations of the north and east of Europe occupies comparatively little space in this abridgment. The narrow limits within which we were obliged to confine ourselves did not permit us to give to it the same development as to the history of those nations who have advanced at the head of European civilization.

# INTRODUCTION.

In the ancient history of Europe, two predominant nations occupy the scene in turns; there is, generally, unity of action and of interest. This unity, less apparent in the Middle Ages, reappears in Modern History, and is principally manifest in the revolutions of the System of Equilibrium.

The History of the Middle Ages and Modern History cannot be accurately divided. If we consider the History of the Middle Ages as terminating with the last invasion of the barbarians (that of the Ottoman Turks), Modern History will comprehend three centuries and a half, from the taking of Constantinople by the Turks to the French Revolution, 1453–1789.

Modern History may be divided into *three periods:* I. From the *taking of Constantinople to the Reformation of Luther*, 1453–1517. II. From the *Reformation to the Treaty of Westphalia*, 1517–1648. III. From the *Treaty of Westphalia to the French Revolution*, 1648–1789. The System of Equilibrium (*Balance of Power*), *prepared* in the first period, is *formed* in the second, and is *maintained* in the third. The last two periods subdivide themselves into five ages of the System of Equilibrium, 1517–1559, 1559–1603, 1603–1648, 1648–1715, 1715–1789.

## PRINCIPAL CHARACTERISTICS OF MODERN HISTORY.

1st. *The great states*, which are formed by the successive union of fiefs, *tend afterward to absorb the small states*, either by conquest or by marriage. The republics are absorbed by the monarchies, the elective by the hereditary states. Their tendency to absolute unity is arrested by the System of Equilibrium (Balance of Power). The marriages of sovereigns among themselves bring into Europe the connexions and rivalries of a family.

2d. *Europe tends to subject and civilize the rest of the world.* The colonial power of the Europeans only begins to be shaken towards the end of the eighteenth century—importance of the great maritime powers—commercial communications between all parts of the globe (hitherto nations had communicated more frequently by war than by commerce). Politics, which in the Middle Ages, and till the end of the 16th century, had been governed by religious interests, are more and more influenced among the moderns by the extension of commerce.

3d. *Difference between the Southern nations* (whose languages and civilization are of Latin origin) *and the Northern* (whose civilization and languages are Germanic). The Western people of Europe develope civilization and carry it to the most distant nations. The Eastern people (principally of Slavonic origin) are long engaged in shutting Europe against the barbarians; their progress also in the arts of peace is slower. It is the same with the Scandinavian nations, who are situated farthest from the centre of activity in the system of European civilization.

## FIRST PERIOD.

*From the taking of Constantinople by the Turks to the Reformation of Luther,* 1453–1517.

This period, common to the middle and modern ages, has fewer striking characteristics than the two following: the events in it present an interest less simple, and a combination less easy to seize. History is still occupied with the internal working of each state, which tends to imbody itself before it is connected with the neighbouring nations. The first essays at a system of equilibrium (balance of power) date from the end of this period.

The nations, already civilized in the Middle Ages, must be subdued by those who have preserved the exclusively military spirit of barbarous times. The inhabitants of Provence and Languedoc were thus overcome by the French; the Moors by the Spaniards; the Greeks by the Turks; the Italians by the Spaniards, the French, and the Germans.

*Internal Condition of the principal States.*

*The nations of Germanic and of Slavonic origin.*—Among the first alone, subject to a feudal system properly so called, a free citizenship, favoured by the progress of wealth and industry, is established; it supports the kings against the nobles.

In the middle of the 15th century, the feudal system has triumphed in the Empire; it has humbled the kings in Castile; it has prolonged its independence in Portugal, which was occupied with wars, and with the discoveries in Africa; also in the three kingdoms of the North, which had been in a state of anarchy since the Union of Calmar; in England, with the aid of the wars of the Roses, and at Naples, amid the quarrels of the houses of Aragon and Anjou. But in Scotland the kings already assail it; in France, Charles VII., conqueror of the English, prepares for its downfall by his institutions, and before the end of the century, the reigns of Ferdinand the Catholic and Ferdinand the Bastard, of John II. of Portugal, of Henry VII. and Louis XI., will establish the regal power upon the ruins of the feudal system.

Three states detach themselves from this group.

While the other states tend towards monarchical unity, Italy remains dismembered. The power of the dukes of Burgundy attains its summit, and falls into ruin, while the military republic of the Swiss is increasing in strength.

The two great Slavonic nations present a contrast, which foreshadows to us their destiny. Russia becomes *one*, and emerges from barbarism. Poland, though she thoroughly modifies her constitution, still clings to the anarchical form of a barbarian government.

*Relations of the principal states among themselves.*

The European commonwealth has no longer that unity of movement which religion gave to it at the era of the Crusades; its parts are not yet clearly separated, as they will be by the Reformation. It is now divided into several groups, whose limits are determined by the geographical position of the nations as much as by their political relations: England, with Scotland and France; Aragon, with Castile and Italy; Italy and Germany, with all the states (directly or indirectly); Turkey unites itself with Hungary; Hungary with Bohemia and Austria; Poland is the common bond of the East and of the North, of which she is the preponderating power. The three kingdoms of the North and Russia form two separate worlds.

The Western States, for the most part filled with internal commotions, are relieved from foreign wars. At the North, Sweden, subjected during sixty years to Denmark, breaks the Union of Calmar; Russia emancipates herself from the Tartars; the Teutonic order becomes a vassal of Poland. All the Eastern States are threatened by the Turks, who have nothing to fear from behind them since the taking of Constantinople, and who are only stopped by the Hungarians. The emperor, occupied with establishing the grandeur of his house, Germany with repairing the evils of the political and religious wars, seemed to forget the danger.

Detaching the history of the North and East, to follow without distraction the revolution of the Western States, we see England and Portugal, but especially Spain and France, reach an imposing grandeur, as well by their conquests in recently-discovered countries, as by the concentration of all national power in the hands of the kings. It is in Italy that those new powers are to unfold themselves by an obstinate struggle. It is necessary, then, to observe how Italy was opened to foreign nations, before she fostered the infancy of that struggle, of which she is to be the theatre in this and the following period.*

* The limits of this sketch do not permit us to carry forward the history of civilization in even course with political history. We shall con

## SECOND PERIOD.

*From the Reformation to the Treaty of Westphalia,*
1517–1648.

The second period of Modern History is opened with the rivalry of Francis I., Charles V., and Solyman: it is most eminently characterized by the Reformation. The house of Austria, whose colossal power could alone close Europe against the Turks, seems to have defended only to enslave it. But Charles V. encountered a triple barrier. Francis I. and Solyman withstand the emperor from motives of private ambition, and save the independence of Europe. When Francis I. is exhausted, Solyman seconds him, and Charles finds a new obstacle in the league of the Protestants of Germany. This is *the first stage or era of the Reformation, and*

tent ourselves here with noticing its points of departure in the 15th century.

The rise of the spirit of invention and discovery. In literature, the enthusiasm of learning arrested for a time the development of modern genius. Invention of printing (1436, 1452). More frequent use of gunpowder and of the compass. Discoveries by the Portuguese and Spaniards. Maritime commerce, centred till then in the Baltic (Hanseatic League) and in the Mediterranean (Venice, Genoa, Florence, Barcelona, Marseilles), is extended to every sea by the voyages of Columbus, Gama, &c., and passes into the hands of the Western nations towards the end of this period. Commerce by land; Lombard merchants; the Low Countries, and free cities of Germany, entrepôts of the North and South. Manufacturing industry of the same nations, especially of the Low Countries.

*of the System of Equilibrium (Balance of Power)*, 1517–1550.

1550–1600. *Second era of the System of Equilibrium, and of the Reformation.*

The Reformation has already spread itself in Europe, and particularly in France, England, Scotland, and the Low Countries. Spain, the only Western country that had remained closed against it, declared herself its adversary. Philip II. wishes to bring Europe back to religious unity, and to extend his dominion over the Western nations. During all the second period, and especially in this age, the wars are at once foreign and domestic.

1600–1648. *Third era of the System of Equilibrium (Balance of Power), and of the Reformation.*

The progress of the Reformation brings about, at length, two results, simultaneous, yet independent of each other: a revolution, whose catastrophe is a civil war, and a war, which presents to Europe the characteristics of a revolution, or, rather, of a European civil war. In England, the victorious Reformation becomes divided within itself, and its partisans are arrayed against each other. In Germany, it draws all the people into the vortex of war for thirty years. From this chaos issues the regular system of equilibrium, which is to prevail during the following period.

The Eastern and Northern States are no longer strangers to the political system of Western Europe, as in the former *period.* In the first age or era, Turkey takes her place in the balance of Europe; in the third, Sweden interposes still more decidedly in the affairs of the West. The second era brings the Slavonic States, through Livonia, in contact with the Scandinavian States, to which they have been hitherto strangers.

At the commencement of this period, the sovereigns reunite all the national strength in their own hands, bestowing internal repose and foreign conquest on the people in compensation for their privileges. Commerce is widely diffused, notwithstanding the system of monopoly which is organized at the same epoch.

## THIRD PERIOD.

*From the Treaty of Westphalia to the French Revolution,* 1648–1789.

In this period the moving power or motive is purely political: it is the *maintenance of the System of Equilibrium* (*Balance of Power*). It is divided into two parts, of about seventy years each: before the death of Louis XIV., 1648–1715; after the death of Louis XIV., 1715—1789.

I. 1648–1715. *Fourth age or era of the System of Equilibrium.*

At the commencement of the third period, as at that of the second, the independence of Europe is in danger. France occupies the political rank which Spain held, and exercises, in a greater degree, the influence of a superior civilization.

As long as Louis XIV. had for adversaries only Spain, already exhausted, Holland, an exclusively maritime power, and the Empire, divided by its negotiations, he dictated laws to Europe. England, at last, under a second William of Orange, resumes the part which she had played from the time of Elizabeth, that of principal antagonist to the preponderating power. In concert with Holland, she annihilated the pretensions of France to the sovereignty of the seas. In concert with Austria, she confines her within her natural limits, but cannot prevent her establishing a branch of the house of Bourbon in Spain.

Sweden is the first Northern power. Under two conquerors, she twice changed the aspect of the North, but she is too weak to obtain a lasting supremacy. Russia arrests her, assumes this supremacy, and retains it. The system of the North has little connexion with that of the Southern States of Europe, except by the old alliance of Sweden with France.

II. 1715–1789. *Fifth era or age of the System of Equilibrium* (*Balance of Power*).

The establishing of the new kingdoms of Russia and Sardinia mark the first years of the eighteenth century. Prussia is to be, with England, the arbiter of Europe, while France is weakened, and Russia does not yet attain her full strength.

During the eighteenth century there is less disproportion between the powers. The preponderating nation being insular, and essentially maritime, has no interest in relation to the Continent other than to maintain the balance of power. This policy she pursues in the three Continental wars between the Western States. Austria, mistress of the greatest part of Italy, might have seized the balance of power; England, her ally, permits her to be despoiled of Naples, which becomes an independent kingdom; France wishes to annihilate Austria; England saves the existence of Austria, but does not prevent Russia from weakening her, and becoming her rival. Austria and France wish to annihilate Prussia; England relieves her, as she had before relieved Austria—directly, with her subsidies, and indirectly, by her naval warfare against France.

On the ocean and in the colonies, the balance of power is broken by England. The colonial wars, which form one of the characteristics of this century, give her an opportunity to ruin the naval power both of France and Spain, and to assume a vexatious jurisdiction over neutrals. A most unexpected revolution shakes this colossal power. The most important colonies of England escape from her yoke, but she boldly faces all her enemies, lays the foundation of an empire in the East, as vast as that which she loses in the West, and remains mistress of the seas.

Russia grows as well by internal development as by the anarchy of her neighbours. For a long time she harasses Sweden, plunders Turkey, absorbs Poland, and advances herself in Europe. The system of the Northern States is mingled more and more with that of the States of the South and West. The revolutions and bloody wars which are about to break forth at the end of the fourth period, will blend into one single system all the European States.

# FIRST PERIOD.

## 1453–1517.

# SUMMARY

OF

# MODERN HISTORY.

## CHAPTER I.

### ITALY—WAR OF THE TURKS, 1453–1494.

Splendour of Italy: Venice, Florence, Rome, &c., &c.—Her real Decline.—Condottieri, Tyrannies, and Conspiracies.—Machiavellian Politics.—Threatening Conquest.—Turks, Spaniards, French.—Taking of Constantinople, 1453.—Attempt of John of Calabria upon the Kingdom of Naples, 1460–1464.—Diversions of the Albanese Scanderbeg, of Hunniades, and of Matthias Corvin in Hungary.—Project of the Crusade, which fails by the Death of Pius II., 1464.—Venice calls upon the Turks.—Taking of Otranto, 1480.—The Venitians call upon Réné of Anjou.—The Pope calls upon the Swiss.—Savanarola fortells the Conquest of Italy.

*Italy—Venice.*—In the midst of a feudal barbarism, of which the fifteenth century still bore the traces, Italy exhibited the spectacle of an old civilization. She impressed strangers by the venerable authority of religion, and by all the pomp of opulence and of the arts. The Frenchman or German who crossed the Alps, admired in Lombardy that skilful agriculture, and those innumerable canals, which make the valley of the Po one vast garden. He beheld with astonishment, rising out of the lagoons of the Adriatic, the wonderful Venice, with her palaces of marble, and her arsenal, which, it was said, employed fifty thousand men. From her ports three or four thousand vessels sailed every year, some for Oran, Cadiz, and Burges ; others for Egypt or Constantinople. The *mistress*, Venice, as she called herself, ruled by her *proveditors* in almost every port, from the extremity of the Adriatic to that of the Black Sea

*Florence — Rome.* — Farther off was ingenious Florence, secure (under the Comos and Lorenzos) that she would forever be a republic. At once princes, citizens, merchants, and men of letters, the Medicis received by the same vessels the tissues of Alexandria, and the manuscripts of Greece. At the same time that they revived Platonism by the labours of Ficino, they erected, by the aid of Brunelleschi, the cupola of St. Mary, facing which Michael Angelo wished his tomb to be placed. The same enthusiasm for letters and the arts existed at the courts of Milan, Ferrara, Mantua, Urbino, and Bologna. The Spanish conqueror of the kingdom of Naples imitated Italian taste ; and for making a treaty of peace with Cosmo de Medicis, he only demanded a handsome manuscript of Livy. In Rome we find erudition itself seated in the chair of St. Peter, in the persons of Nicholas

V. and Pius II. This universal cultivation of letters seemed to have humanized the feelings. In the most bloody battle of the fifteenth century, there were not a thousand men killed.* The combats were scarcely more than tournaments.

*Condottieri.* — In the mean time, an attentive observer might easily see signs of the decline of Italy. The apparent gentleness of manners was but a growing enervation of national character. The wars, from being bloodless, were only of longer duration, and more ruinous. The *Condottieri* traversed Italy in undisciplined troops, always ready to join the opposite standard for the least increase of pay ; war had become a lucrative game between the Piccinini and the Sforza. In every place there were little tyrants, extolled by the learned and detested by the people. Literature, to which Italy herself ascribed her glory, had lost the originality of the fourteenth century ; to Dante and Petrarch had succeeded Philelphus and Pontanus. Nowhere was religion less regarded. Nepotism afflicted the Church, and deprived it of the respect of the people. The usurper of the domains of the Holy See, the Condottieri Sforza, dated his letters *è Firmiano nostro invito Petro et Paulo.*†

*Conspiracies.*—The expiring genius of Italian

* Machiavelli, Storie Florentine, i., vii. † Id. Ibid., book v

liberty still made fruitless efforts by conspiracies. Porcaro, who believed himself the subject of Petrarch's prophetic verses, attempted to re-establish a republican government in Rome. At Florence the Pazzi, and at Milan the young Olgiati, with two others, stabbed both Julian de Medicis and Galeas Sforza in a church (1476–1487). The madmen believed that the liberty of their degenerated country depended on the life of one man.

*Lorenzo de Medicis — Inquisitors of the State,* 1454.—The two governments of Florence and of Venice passed for the wisest of Italy. Lorenzo de Medicis caused his verses to be sung to the Florentines, conducted in person through the streets of the city pedantic and sumptuous masquerades, and yielded himself blindly to that royal munificence which was the admiration of men of letters and the precursor of the bankruptcy of Florence. At Venice, on the contrary, the coldest self-interest seemed the only law of the government. There were no favourites, no caprice, and no prodigality. But this government of iron subsisted only to contract more and more the unity of power. The tyranny of the Ten was not sufficient, there must be created in the very bosom of this council Inquisitors of State (1434). This dictatorship made the affairs of the Republic successful abroad, but it was by draining the sources of its internal prosperity. From 1425 to 1453, Venice had enlarged her territory by four provinces, while her revenues were diminished more than one hundred thousand ducats. In vain she endeavoured to retain, by sanguinary measures, the resources which were escaping from her.* The time was not far distant when Italy was to lose at once her commerce, her riches, and her independence. There was only wanting another invasion of the barbarians to wrest from her the monopoly of commerce, and of those arts which were to be hereafter the patrimony of the world.

*Turks — French — Spaniards.*—Who are to be the conquerors of Italy? the Turks, the French, or the Spaniards? This is what no foresight may determine. The popes, and the greater part of the Italians, dreaded, above all, the Turks. The great Sforza, and Alphonso the Magnanimous, thought only of closing Italy against the French, who laid claim to Naples, and might demand Milan.† Venice, believing herself invincible in her lagoons, negotiated without distinction with one and another, sacrificing sometimes to secondary interests her honour and the safety of Italy.

* If we may believe the MS. published by Mr. Daru (vol. vii.), as containing the statutes of the Inquisitors of State, these inquisitors caused the mechanic to be put to death who carried to another country and branch of industry which was useful to the commonwealth.

† Sismondi, History of the Italian Republics, p. x., pg. 28.

*Constantinople*, 1453. — Such was the situation of that country when she heard the last cry of distress from Constantinople (1453). Separated already from Europe by the Turks and by her schism, this unhappy city saw before her walls an army of 300,000 barbarians. At this critical moment, the Western nations, accustomed to the complaints of the Greeks, paid little attention to them. Charles VII. achieved the expulsion of the English from France; Hungary was disturbed; the phlegmatic Ferdinand III. was occupied in erecting Austria into an archduchy. The possessors of Pera and Galata,* the Genoese and the Venitians, were calculating the greatness of their loss, instead of preventing it. Genoa sent four vessels; Venice deliberated whether she should renounce her conquests in Italy, to preserve her colonies and her commerce.† In the midst of this fatal hesitation, Italy sees the fugitives from Constantinople landing upon all her shores. Their recitals filled Europe with shame and terror; they bewailed the Church of St. Sophia changed into a mosque, Constantinople pillaged and deserted, and more than sixty thousand Christians dragged into slavery; they described the prodigious cannons of Mohammed, and that appalling moment, at early

* Suburbs of Constantinople, inhabited by the Greeks, Armenians, &c.

† Daru, Hist. of Venice, part ii., b xvi, and "Pièces Justificatives," t. viii.

morn, when the Greeks beheld, at awakening, the galleys of the infidels traversing the land,* and descending into their harbour.

*John of Calabria*, 1460–1464.—Europe was roused at last. Nicholas V. preached the Crusade; all the Italian States were reconciled at Lodi (1454). In other countries multitudes of men took the cross. At Lille the Duke of Burgundy exhibited at a banquet a picture of the desolate Church, and, according to the rites of chivalry, vowed to God, the Virgin, the ladies, and "*le faisan*," that he would fight against the infidels. But this ardour was of short duration; nine days after having signed the treaty of Lodi, the Venitians made another with the Turks; Charles VII. would not permit the Crusade to be preached in France; the Duke of Burgundy remained in his dominions, and the new attempt of John of Calabria upon the kingdom of Naples occupied all the attention of Italy.

*Scanderbeg.*—The true and only champions of Christianity were the Hungarian Hunniade and the Albanian Scanderbeg. The latter, whose barbarous heroism recalls fabulous times, struck off, it is

* It is said that the sultan transported his fleet in one night to the harbour of Constantinople, by sliding the vessels upon planks smoothed over with grease.—See Cantimir and Saadud-din, *Histoire Ottomane*, MS., transl. by M. Galland, cited by M. Daru, *Hist. de Venise*, 2d edit., Pièces Justificatives, vol. viii., p. 194–6.

said, with a single blow the head of a wild bull. He was seen, like Alexander, whose name the Turks applied to him, to leap alone within the walls of a besieged city. Ten years after his death, the Turks divided his bones among them, believing that they would become invincible. To this day the name of Scanderbeg is chanted in the mountains of Epirus.

*Hunniades*, 1456—*Mathias Corvin.*—The other *Soldier of Jesus Christ* (Hunniades), the *white knight* of Wallachia, the *devil* of the Turks, as he was also called,* arrested their progress, while the movements of Scanderbeg forced them backward. At the time the Ottomans attacked Belgrade, the bulwark of Hungary, Hunniades passed through the army of the infidels, to throw himself into that city; he repulsed during forty days the most furious assaults, and was celebrated as the saviour of Christendom (1456). His son, Mathias Corvin, whom the gratitude of the Hungarians raised to the throne, opposed his *garde noire*, the first regular infantry which that people ever had, to the janizaries of Mohammed II. The

* The first title is that which was always assumed by Scanderbeg; the second, that by which Hunniades is generally designated among his contemporaries (Comines, vol. vi., ch. xiii.); the third was given him by the Turks, who pronounced his name to their children, to frighten them (M. de Sacy, in the "Biog. Universelle," art. Hunniade), as the Saracens formerly threatened theirs with Richard Cœur de Lion

reign of Mathias was the glory of Hungary. While he fought successively the Turks, the Germans, and the Poles, he founded in his capital a university, two academies, an observatory, a museum of antiquities, and a library, which was then the most considerable in the world. This rival of Mohammed II. spoke, like him, several languages, and, like him, he was the friend of literature, while he retained the usages of the barbarians. It is said that he had accepted the offer of a man who engaged to assassinate his father-in-law, the King of Bohemia, but he rejected, with indignation, the proposition to poison him: "*Against my enemies*," said he, "*I will employ only steel.*" It is to him that the Hungarians owe their Magna Charta (Decretum majus, 1485. See chapter iii.) A Hungarian proverb suffices for his eulogy: "*Since the time of Corvin there is more justice.*"

*Pius II.*, 1464.—Pope Pius II. and the State of Venice were leagued with this great prince, when Servia and Bosnia, subjugated by the Turks, opened to them the road to Italy. The pontiff was the soul of the Crusade; he had appointed a rendezvous at Ancona to those who would go with him to fight the enemy of the faith. The accomplished secretary of the Council of Basle, the most polished mind of the age, and the most subtle of diplomatists, becomes a hero in the chair of St.

Peter. The noble idea of the salvation of Christendom seemed to have given him a new soul. But his strength was inadequate. This venerable man expired upon the shore, in sight of the Venitian galleys which were to have borne him to Greece (1464).

*Paul II.—Venice tributary to the Turks,* 1479.—His successor, Paul II., abandoned this generous policy. He armed against the heretical Bohemians the son-in-law of their king, this same Matthias Corvin, whose valour should have been exercised only against the Turks. While the Christians thus weakened themselves by their divisions, Mohammed II. swore solemnly in the Mosque, which had been the Church of St. Sophia, the extermination of Christianity. Venice, deserted by her allies, lost the island of Negropont, which was taken by the Turks in sight of her fleet. In vain Paul II. and the Venitians sought allies, even to the extremity of Persia; the schah was defeated by the Turks, and the taking of Caffa shut from the Europeans, for a long time, all communication with the Persians. The Turkish cavalry spread themselves in the Friouli as far as Piave, burning the crops, the woods, the villages, and the palaces of the Venitian nobles. At night the flames of this conflagration were visible even as far as Venice. The Republic abandoned the unequal struggle, which she had sustained alone during fifteen years, sacrificed Scutari, and submitted to a tribute.

*Death of Mohammed II.*, 1480–81.—Pope Sixtus IV., and Ferdinand, king of Naples, who had rendered no assistance to Venice, accused her of having betrayed the cause of Christendom. After having favoured the conspiracy of the Pazzi, and then declared open war with the Medicis, they turn their restless policy against the Venitians. The vengeance of Venice was cruel. At the same time that Mohammed II. made an attack upon Rhodes, they learned that a hundred Turkish vessels, under the escort of the Venitian fleet, had passed into Italy; that Otranto was already taken, and its governor sawn asunder. Great was their dismay, and the event would perhaps have realized their worst fears, if the death of the sultan had not arrested for some time the progress of Mohammedan conquest.

*Savanarola.*—The Italians thus saw strangers interposing in their quarrels. The Venitians, after having drawn in the Turks, took into their service René, the young Duke of Lorraine, who was heir to the claims of the house of Anjou upon the kingdom of Naples. Since 1474, Sixtus IV. had called for the aid of the Swiss. The *barbarians* were accustomed to pass the Alps, and they related in their own country the wonders of beautiful

Italy; some celebrated her luxury and her wealth, others her climate, her wines, and the delicious fruit.* Then the prophetic voice of the Dominican Savanarola was raised in Florence, who thus denounced upon Italy the chastisement of Babylon and Nineveh: "O Italy! O Rome! says the Lord, I will deliver you into the hands of a people who shall destroy you from among the nations. The barbarians shall come up against you, like hungry lions, . . . and behold, the dead shall be so many that they that bury shall run through the streets, and shall cry, 'Who hath any dead?' and the one shall bring his father, and another shall bring his son. . . . O Rome! I say again unto thee, repent! O Venice! O Milan, repent!"†

But they persisted. The King of Naples entrapped his rebellious subjects in the snare of a perfidious treaty. Genoa remained a prey to the factions of the Ardoni and the Tregosi. Lorenzo de Medicis on his deathbed refused the absolution to which Savanarola had annexed the freedom of Florence as a condition. At Milan, Ludovic the Moor imprisoned his nephew, preparatory to poi-

* See the merry and amusing history composed by the loyal servant of the good *knight, without fear and without reproach.*—Vol. xv. of the Collection of Memoirs, p. 306, 334, 335.

† Savanarola, Prediche quadragesimali (1544, in —12): predica vigesima prima, p. 211, 212. See also Petri Martyris Anglerii Epistol., cxxx., cxxxi., etc.: "Wo to thee, Mother of the Arts, O beautiful Italy," &c., &c. 1493.

soning him. Roderic Borgia assumed the tiara, under the name of Alexander VI. The inevitable moment had now arrived.

---

## CHAPTER II.

### THE WEST—FRANCE AND THE LOW COUNTRIES—ENGLAND AND SCOTLAND—SPAIN AND PORTUGAL IN THE SECOND HALF OF THE 15TH CENTURY.

BEFORE they disputed for the possession of Italy, it was necessary that the great powers of the West should be free from feudal anarchy, and should unite all the national strength in the hands of the kings. The triumph of monarchical power over feudalism is the subject of this chapter. With feudalism perish the privileges and the liberties of the Middle Ages. These liberties perished, like those of antiquity, because they were privileges. Civil equality could only be established by the triumph of monarchical power.*

The instruments of this revolution were churchmen and civilians. The Church, recruiting its ranks only by election, in the midst of the universal hereditary system which was established in the Middle Ages, had raised the conquered above the

* Equality makes rapid progress at the very moment that the political liberties of the Middle Ages are expiring. Those of Spain were overthrown by Charles V. in 1521, and in 1528 the Cortes of Spain permitted every citizen to wear a sword, *that they might defend themselves against the nobles.*—See Ferreras, part xii.

conquerors the sons of the citizens, and even of the serfs, above the nobles. In their last struggle against aristocracy, the kings demanded statesmen and counsellors from the Church. Duprat, Woolsey, and Ximenes, who were all cardinals and prime ministers, rose from obscure families. Ximenes had commenced by teaching law in private.* The churchmen and the civilians were both imbued with the principles of the Roman law, which was much more favourable to monarchy and to civil equality than the feudal customs.

The features of this revolution present some difference in the different nations. In England it is prepared and accelerated by a terrible war, which exterminates the nobles ; in Spain it is complicated by the struggle of religious creeds. But everywhere it offers one common characteristic : the aristocracy, already conquered by royal power, endeavours to lessen its influence by overturning reigning families, to substitute in their places the rival branches. The means employed by the two parties were odious, and often atrocious. Policy in its infancy can only choose between violence and perfidy ; see at a later period the death of the Earl of Douglas, the Dukes of Braganza and of

* Gomecius, fol. ii.—Giannone remarks that, under Ferdinand the Bastard, the Roman laws prevailed at Naples over the Lombard laws, by the influence of the professors, who were at the same time both magistrates and lawyers (book xxviii., chap. v.).

Viseu, above all, that of the Earl of Mar, and of the Dukes of Clarence and Guienne. Yet posterity, deceived by their success, has exaggerated the talents of the princes of this epoch (Louis XI., Ferdinand the Bastard, Henry VII., Iwan III., &c., &c.). The most skilful of all, Ferdinand the Catholic, is only a fortunate impostor in the eyes of Machiavel.*

## § I. FRANCE, 1452–1494.†

End of the English Wars.—Feudalism: Houses of Burgundy, Brittany, Anjou, Albret, Foix, Armagnac, &c.. — Grandeur of the Duke of Burgundy.—Advantages of the King of France: first perpetual Tax, first standing Army, 1444.—Death of Charles VII., accession of Louis XI., 1461.—Death of Philip the Good, Duke of Burgundy, accession of Charles the Bold, 1467.—League for the *Public Good*.—Treaties of Conflans and St. Maur, 1465.—Conference of Peronne, and Captivity of the King, 1468.—Second League of the great Vassals dissolved by the Death of the Duke of Guienne, Brother of Louis, 1472.—Invasion of Edward IV., Treaty of Peguigny, 1475.—Charles the Bold turns against Germany, then against the Swiss; his Defeat at Granson and at Morat, 1476.—His Death, 1477.—Mary of Burgundy marries Maximilian of Austria.—Louis XI., Master of Anjou, of Maine, of Provence, of Artois, and of Franche Compté, 1481–82.—His death; Regency of Anne of Beaujeu, 1483.—Pretensions of the States, 1484.—Humiliation of the Grandees.—Charles VIII. prepares for the Expedition into Italy.

*State of France.*—When the retreat of the English permitted France to recover herself, the

* See Machiavel, Familiar Letters, April, 1513, May, 1514.

† Principal authorities: vol. ix., x., xi., xii., xiii., xiv., of the collection of *Memoirs relative to the History of France*, edition of Mr. Pelitot, particularly the volumes which contain the Memoirs of Comines' History of the Dukes of Burgundy by M. de Barante, part vii., and following.

husbandmen, descending from the castles and fortified cities, where the war had confined them, found their fields untilled and their villages in ruins; the disbanded troops continued to infest the public roads, and to levy upon the peasantry. The feudal barons who came to aid Charles VII. to expel the English, were kings upon their own territories, and acknowledged no law, either human or divine. A count of Armagnac styled himself *count by the grace of God*, caused the officers of Parliament to be hung, married his own sister, and *beat his confessor when he refused to absolve him.** The Duke of Burgundy during three years asked bread from his prison windows, until his brother caused him to be strangled.

*Power of the great Vassals.*—The oppressed people turned all their hopes towards the king. It was from him that they expected some alleviation of their misery. The feudal system, which in the tenth century had been the salvation of Europe, had now become its scourge. This system, since the wars with the English, seemed to regain its ancient strength. Without mentioning the Counts of Albret, Foix, Armagnac, and many other nobles,

* Papers relating to the Trial of John IV., count of Armagnac, cited by the authors of the *Art of verifying Dates.* It was John V who married his sister.

the houses of Burgundy, of Brittany, and of Anjou vied with royalty in its splendour and power.

Provence, a heritage of the house of Anjou, was a rallying-point for the population of the South, as Flanders was for that of the North; to this rich province were joined Anjou, Maine, and Lorraine, thus surrounding on every side the king's domains. The spirit of ancient chivalry seemed to have taken refuge in this heroic family; the world was filled with the exploits and misfortunes of the King René and of his children. While his daughter, Margaret of Anjou, maintained the rights of the red rose in ten battles, John of Calabria, his son, took and lost the kingdom of Naples, and died at the moment when the enthusiasm of the Catalonians had raised him to the throne of Aragon. Aspirations so vast, and wars prosecuted at such a distance, destroyed the power of this house in France. The character of its chief, also, was not adapted to sustain an obstinate struggle against the royal power. The good René, in his last years, was almost entirely occupied with pastoral poetry, painting, and astrology. When told that Louis XI. had taken Anjou from him, he was painting a beautiful gray partridge, and did not suspend his work.

The true head of feudalism was the Duke of Burgundy. This prince, richer than any king in Europe, united under his government French prov inces and German states, an innumerable nobility and the most important commercial cities in Europe. Ghent and Liege could each furnish forty thousand infantry. But the elements which composed this great power were too various to agree well together. The Hollanders would not obey the Flemings, nor the Flemings be subservient to the Burgundians. An implacable hatred existed between the nobility of the castles and the people of the mercantile towns. These proud and opulent cities united the industrious spirit of modern times with the violence of feudal customs. The moment that the least attempt was made upon the privileges of Ghent, the deans of the guilds sounded St. Roland's bell, and planted their banners in the market-place. Then the duke, with his nobles, mounted their horses, and battles and torrents of blood followed.

*Strength of the King.*—The King of France, on the contrary, was generally supported by the cities. In his dominions, the lower classes were much better protected against the higher. It was a citizen, Jacques Cœur, who lent him the money necessary to reconquer Normandy. The king in every place repressed the license of the soldiers. Since 1441, he had cleared the kingdom of disorderly bands (*compagnies*) by sending them against the Swiss, who gave them their due at the battle of

St. James. At the same time he established the Parliament of Toulouse, extended the jurisdiction of the Parliament of Paris, notwithstanding the objections of the Duke of Burgundy, and limited all the feudal tribunals. In seeing an Armagnac exiled, an Alençon imprisoned, the natural son of a Bourbon thrown into the river, the nobles learned that rank was no protection from the law. A revolution so happy, made every innovation which was favourable to monarchical power most welcome. Charles VII. formed a standing army of fifteen hundred lancers, instituted the militia of free archers, who were to remain at home, and to perform their military evolutions on Sundays ; he laid a perpetual tax upon the people without the authority of the States-General, and there was not a murmur among them (1444).

The grandees themselves contributed to increase the royal power, which they disposed of by turns. Those who did not govern the king were contented to intrigue with the dauphin, and to excite him against his father. The face of all was changed, when Charles VII., who had retired into Burgundy, sunk under the troubles which his son had occasioned him (1461). At the funeral of the king, Dunois said to all the assembled nobility, "The king, our master, is dead ; let each one provide for himself."

*Louis XI.*, 1461.—Louis XI. possessed none of that chivalric disposition, in favour of which the French pardoned so many weaknesses in Charles VII. He liked negotiations better than battles, dressed himself meanly, and was surrounded by persons of low quality. He took a footman for his herald, a barber for master of ceremonies, and called the Provost Tristan his *gossip*. In his impatience to humble the nobles at his arrival, he dismissed all the ministers of Charles VII.; he took from the lords all influence in the ecclesiastical elections, by abolishing the Pragmatic Sanction;* he incensed the Duke of Brittany by endeavouring to deprive him of the rights of royalty; he provoked the Count of Charolais, a son of the Duke of Burgundy, by redeeming the cities of the Somme from his father, and by wishing to withdraw from him the gift of Normandy; finally, he dissatisfied all the nobles, by having no regard for their privileges of the chase, the most grievous offence, perhaps, which could be offered to a gentleman of that age.

*League for the Public Good.*—The dissatisfaction of the nobles did not show itself until the growing infirmities of the Duke of Burgundy had placed all the authority in the hands of his son,

* Pragmatic Sanction, the ordinance of Charles VII. of France, drawn up 1438, and on which rest the liberties of the Gallican Church.

the Count of Charolais, afterward so celebrated under the name of Charles the Bold. The Duke John of Calabria, the Duke of Bourbon, the Duke of Nemours, the Count of Armagnac, the Sieur of Albret, the Count of Dunois, and many others, then leagued themselves, for *the public good,* with the Duke of Brittany and the Count of Charolais. They had secret intelligence through their agents in the Church of Nôtre Dame, at Paris, and wore a rosette of red silk as a token of cognizance. To this coalition of almost the whole nobility, the king endeavoured to oppose the cities, and particularly Paris. He there abolished all the excise duties, and formed a council himself, composed of citizens, members of Parliament, and of the University; he confided the queen to the care of the Parisians, and wished her to give birth to his children in their city, *which, of all the cities in the world, he loved the most.** There was little effected in this attempt of the confederates. Louis XI. had time to overcome the Duke of Bourbon. The Duke of Brittany joined the principal army only after the battle of Montheri. The art of war was so entirely forgotten since the expulsion of the English, that, with an exception of a small number of troops, each army took to flight.* The king then entered into some deceptive negotiations,

* Comines, boek i., chap. iv.

and the threatened dissolution of the league decided the confederates to make a treaty with the enemy (at Conflans and at St. Maur, 1465). The king granted all their demands ; to his brother he gave Normandy, a province which, from itself alone, paid a third part of the royal revenues ; to the Count of Charolais, the cities of the Somme ; and to all the others he gave strong castles, seigneuries, and pensions. In order that the *public good* might not appear to be entirely forgotten, it was stipulated, for form's sake, that an assembly of notables should consult about it. The greater part of the other articles were not more seriously executed than the last; the king availed himself of the revolt of Liège and of Dinant against the Duke of Burgundy to retake Normandy, and had the principal articles of the treaty of Conflans annulled by the states of the kingdom (at Tours, 1466), and compelled the Duke of Brittany to renounce his alliance with the Count of Charolais then Duke of Burgundy.

*Conference of Peronne*, 1468.—Louis XI., who hoped, by the power of his address, to appease the Duke of Burgundy, went himself to meet him at Peronne (1468). The duke had just heard of the revolt of the people of Liège, who were excited against him by the emmissaries of the King of France. They had made their bishop, Louis of

Bourbon, a prisoner, murdered the archdeacon, and, in horrible sport, they threw his limbs about from one to another. So great was the fury of the Duke of Burgundy, that the king for a moment trembled for his life. He saw enclosed within the castle of Peronne the tower in which the Count of Vermandois had caused the death of Charles the Simple ; but he was happily relieved from apprehension. The duke was satisfied with making him confirm the treaty of Conflans and taking him before Liège to behold that city laid in ruins. The king, at his return, did not fail to have all that he had just sworn to annulled by the states.

*Death of the Duke of Guienne*, 1472.—There was now a more formidable league against him than that of the *public good.* His brother, to whom he had just given Guienne, and the Dukes of Brittany and Burgundy, had drawn to that place most of the lords who had been hitherto loyal. They asked aid of the King of Aragon, John II., who made claims to Roussillon, and of Edward IV., king of England, brother-in-law to the Duke of Burgundy, who felt that it was necessary for the safety of his reign to employ abroad the restless spirits of the English. The Duke of Brittany did not dissemble the views of the confederates. "I am so interested for the good of the kingdom of France," said he, "that, instead of one king, I would give her six." Louis XI., at this time, could not hope for the support of the cities, which he had just loaded with taxes. The death of his brother could alone break the league : his brother died. The king, who was regularly informed of the progress of his illness, ordered public prayers for the health of the Duke of Guienne, and, at the same time, he made his troops advance to seize his estates. He stopped the proceedings against the monk who was suspected of having poisoned the prince, and had it reported that the devil strangled him in his prison.

*Landing of Edward IV.*, 1475.—Louis XI., having thus disposed of his brother, repulsed John II. from Rousillon, Charles the Bold from Picardy, and arrested all his enemies within his kingdom.* But the greatest danger was not passed. The King of England landed at Calais, claiming, as was the custom, his *kingdom of France.* The Duke of Burgundy, instead of receiving the English at their arrival, and conducting them himself into a country where all was new to them, had gone to make war in Germany. In the mean time, the weather was

* He freed himself of the Duke of Alençon by imprisoning him (1472); of King Réné by depriving him of Anjou (1474); of the Duke of Bourbon by giving Anne of France (1473–74) to his brother, and by nominating him for his lieutenant in several provinces of the South (1475); and, finally, of the Count of Armagnac and Charles d'Albret (1473), the Duke of Nemours, and the Constable of St. Pol (1475–77) by causing them all four to be put to death.

unfavourable; though Edward had *lodged the citizens who followed him in good quarters, yet they were unaccustomed to such a life, and soon became weary of it; they had imagined that, having once crossed the Channel, they would have a battle within three days.*—(Comines, b. iv., ch. xi.) Louis had the address to make the king and his favourites accept of gifts and pensions, and laughed heartily at thus overcoming an army which came to conquer France.

*War of Charles the Bold against Germany.*—He had now nothing more to apprehend from Charles the Bold. This haughty prince had conceived the plan of establishing still more extensively the old kingdom of Burgundy, by uniting to his territories Lorraine, Provence, Dauphiny, and Switzerland. Louis XI. was careful not to interfere with him; he prolonged the truce, and "*let him go to knock against the Germans.*" The duke had undertaken to make the town of Neuss receive one of the pretenders to the archbishopric of Cologne; all the princes of the Empire, with an army of a hundred thousand men, assembled to watch his movements. He persevered for a whole year, and only left this unhappy siege to turn his army against the Swiss.

*Defeat of Granson,* 1476—*Defeat of Morat.*—This nation of citizens and peasantry, who for two centuries had been free from the yoke of the house of Austria, had always detested both its princes and its nobility. Louis XI., when dauphin, had proved the bravery of the Swiss at the battle of St. James, where sixteen hundred of them preferred death rather than to retreat before twenty thousand men. The Sire of Hagenbach, governor for the Duke of Burgundy, in the county of Ferrette, annoyed their allies, and did not scruple to insult them. "We will *flay the Bear of Berne*," said he, "*and take his skin of fur for a lining*." The patience of the Swiss became exhausted; they made an alliance with their ancient enemies, the Austrians, had Hagenbach beheaded and defeated the Burgundians at Hericourt. They endeavoured to appease the Duke of Burgundy; they showed him that he could gain nothing from a contest against them. "*There is more gold*," said they, "*in the spurs of your knights than you will find in all our cantons*." The duke was inflexible. Having invaded Lorraine and Switzerland, he took Granson, and caused all the garrison, which had surrendered on parole, to be drowned. In the mean time, the army of the Swiss advanced; the Duke of Burgundy imprudently went to meet them, and thus lost the advantage which the plain afforded to his cavalry. Posted upon a hill, which yet bears his name he saw them descending from the mountains, shouting "Granson! Granson!" while the whole valley echoed with the sound of those enormous trumpets, named by the Swiss the "Bull of Uri," and the "Cow of Unterwalden," and which, they said, they had received from Charlemagne. Nothing could check the confederates. In vain the Burgundians essayed to penetrate the forest of spears which constantly advanced towards them. The route was soon complete. The camp of the duke, his treasures, and his cannon became the spoils of the conquerors; the silver found among his treasures was shared without counting, and was measured out by hatfuls. But they knew not the value of all that they had gained. A soldier sold the great diamond of the Duke of Burgundy for a single crown. Yet Charles the Bold would learn no wisdom from misfortune. Three months after this loss he attacked the Swiss at Morat, and there met with a still more bloody defeat. At that battle the conquerors slew all the enemy, and raised a monument of the bones of the Burgundians. *Cruel as at Morat* was long a proverb with the Swiss.

*Defeat at Nancy*, 1477.—This last defeat was the ruin of Charles the Bold. He had drained his good cities of men and of money, and for two years his courtiers were constantly under arms. He now yielded to a melancholy, which bordered on derangement; he allowed his beard to grow, and would not change his clothing. Still he was obstinately bent on attacking the young Prince Réné, and on endeavouring to remove him from Lorraine. This prince, who had fought on the side of the Swiss, was vain of speaking their language, and even sometimes adopted their costume; he found them ready to aid him. The Duke of Burgundy, whose army was reduced to three thousand men, had little hope for the result of the battle; but he was reluctant, and ashamed *to fly before a child.* At the moment of the charge, the Italian Campo Basso, with whom Louis long since had contracted for the life of Charles the Bold, tore off the red cross, and thus commenced the defeat of the Burgundians, 1477. Some days after the battle, the body of the duke was found; it was borne in great pomp to Nancy; Réné sprinkled it with holy water, and taking the hand of his cousin, said, "*Fair cousin, God keep your soul! you have given us a good deal of trouble and difficulty.*" But the people would not believe in the death of a prince whose exploits had so long occupied all minds They confidently expected that he would soon appear to them again, and ten years afterward the merchants delivered goods without pay, on condition that they should receive double when the great Duke of Burgundy returned.

The fall of the house of Burgundy gave permanent strength to that of France. The proprietors of the three great fiefs of Burgundy, Provence, and Brittany, having died without male heirs, the French kings broke the succession to the first in 1477, secured the second by virtue of a will, 1481, and the third by a marriage, 1491.

*War against Maximilian.*—Louis XI. at first hoped to obtain the whole heritage of Charles the Bold by marrying the dauphin to his daughter, Mary of Burgundy. But the States of Flanders were not inclined to obey the French; they gave the hand of their sovereign to Maximilian of Austria, afterward emperor, and the grandfather of Charles V. Thus began the rivalry of the houses of France and Austria. Notwithstanding the defeat of the French at Guinegate, Louis XI. remained master of Artois and Franche Compté, which, by the treaty of Arras, were to be the dowry of Marguerite, daughter of the archduke, who was promised to the dauphin, Charles VIII.

*Charles VIII.*—When Louis XI. left his throne to his son, who was still a child (1483), France, which had suffered so much in silence, now raised her voice. The States, called together in 1484 by the regent, Anne of Beaujeu, wished to give their delegates the principal influence in the council of regency; to vote a tax for only two years, at the end of which they should be again called together and, lastly, to regulate the division of the tax themselves. The six *nations*, into which the states were divided, began to reproach each other, and wished to be formed into territories, like Languedoc and Normandy, when the dissolution of the assembly was pronounced. The regent, by her firmness, continued the policy of Louis XI. in regard to the grandees. She conquered the Duke of Orleans, who disputed the regency with her, and united Brittany to the crown, by marrying her son to the heiress of that duchy (1491). Thus the work of humbling the great vassals was accomplished. France attained that unity which was to make her formidable to all Europe, and the old servants of Louis XI. were followed by a generation young and ardent as their king. Charles VIII., impatient to give importance to his claims upon the kingdom of Naples, which he had inherited from the house of Anjou, appeased the jealousy of the King of England with money, gave up Roussillon to Ferdinand the Catholic, Artois and Franche Compté to Maximilian, thus sacrificing three of the strongest barriers of France. But the loss of a few provinces is of little importance to the future conqueror of the kingdom of Naples, and of the empire of the East.

## § II. ENGLAND, 1454–1509. SCOTLAND, 1452–1513.

*England:* Marriage of Henry VI. with Margaret of Anjou.—Death of Gloucester.—Loss of the French Provinces.—Richard of York, Warwick; Condemnation of the Ministers, Richard Protector, 1455.—Battles of Northampton and Wakefield; Death of Richard, his Son, Edward IV., 1461.—Defeat of the Lancastrians at Towton and at Exham, 1463.—Overthrow of Edward IV. at Nottingham, 1470.—Battle of Tewksbury, Defeat and Death of Henry VI., 1471.—Death of Edward IV., 1483.—Richard III.—Henry Tudor; Battle of Bosworth; Henry VII., 1485.—Increase of the Regal Power.—*Scotland:* Contest of James II. against the Aristocracy.—His Alliance with the House of Lancaster.—James III., 1460.—James IV., 1488.—Reconciliation of the King and Nobility.—Battle of Flodden.—James V., 1513.

*Henry VI.—Warwick.*—The French, who, during a century, had always been defeated by the English, had, at last, their turn. The English, driven from the French cities in every campaign by Dunois or Richmond, returned to their provinces with shame, and blamed their generals and their ministers for their defeat; it was now the quarrels of the uncles of the king, now the recall of the Duke of York, which had caused their disgrace. To the conqueror of Agincourt had succeeded the young prince Henry VI., whose innocence and gentleness were not formed to contend with these troublesome times, and whose feeble reason became completely deranged at the commencement of the civil war. While the annual revenue of the crown amounted to only £5,000 sterling,* several noble families had amassed royal fortunes by marriages, or from inheritance. It is said that the Earl of Warwick, one of the last and most illustrious examples of feudal hospitality, supported on his estates as many as 30,000 persons ;† when he kept house in London, his vassals and his friends consumed six oxen at a meal.‡ To this colossal fortune he added all the accomplishments of a chief of a party. But his courage was a stranger to the chivalric point of honour, for this chief, who was seen to attack a fleet of twice the size of his own,§ often fled without blushing, when he found his soldiers yield.‖ Without mercy towards the nobles, in battles he always spared the people. In review of his actions, how can we be astonished that he attained the surname of *King-maker?*

*Margaret of Anjou.*—The court, which was already too feeble to contend against such men, again aggravated, as if designedly, the discontent of the people. When the hatred of the English against France was imbittered by so many reverses, the court gave them a French queen. The fair Margaret of Anjou, daughter of King Réné of Provence, was to bring into England the heroic spirit of her family, but not its milder virtues. Henry

* Lingard, vol. v. of the Fr. translation, p. 259.

† Hume.

‡ Lingard, vol. v., p. 284.

§ Lingard, vol. v., p. 282.

‖ Comines, book iii., ch. vii

purchased her hand by yielding Maine and Anjou; and instead of receiving a dower, he gave one. A year had scarcely elapsed since this marriage, when the uncle of the king, the *good Duke of Gloucester*, whom the nation adored for his warlike spirit, was found dead in his bed. Bad tidings from France rapidly succeeded each other. While still indignant for the loss of Maine and Anjou, the news arrived that Rouen and all Normandy were in the hands of the French; their army found no resistance in Guienne; not a soldier was sent from England, not a governor endeavoured to oppose it, and in August, 1451, the city of Calais was all that belonged to the English on the Continent.

*York Protector*, 1455.—The national pride, so cruelly humbled, now began to seek a champion. All eyes were turned towards Richard, duke of York, whose claims, though long proscribed, were superior to those of the house of Lancaster. The Nevilles, and a great part of the nobility, rallied around him. The Duke of Suffolk, the queen's favourite, was their first victim. Afterward an impostor caused the revolt of the men of Kent, who were always the first for a revolution, conducted them to London, and beheaded Lord Say, another of Henry's ministers. At last Richard's own partisans came armed to St. Alban's, and demanded that Lord Somerset should be delivered to them who, after having lost Normandy, had become prime minister. Here was the first blood shed in that war which was to continue thirty years, to cost the lives of eighty-four princes, and to exterminate the ancient nobility of the kingdom. The Duke of York made a prisoner of the king, conducted him in triumph to London, and was satisfied with the title of *Protector* for himself (1455).

*His Death.*—In the mean time, Margaret of Anjou armed the northern counties, which were decided enemies to innovation. She was defeated at Northampton. Henry again fell into the hands of his enemies, and the conqueror, no longer dissembling his aim, made the Parliament declare him presumptive heir to the throne. He had thus attained the summit of his ambition, when he encountered near Wakefield the army which the indefatigable Margaret had again assembled. He accepted the combat, notwithstanding the inferiority of his forces, was conquered, and his head, decked by the queen with a crown of paper, was set upon the walls of York. Rutland, his son, who was scarcely twelve years of age, fled with his tutor; he was overtaken at the bridge of Wakefield, when the poor child, unable to speak, fell upon his knees; the tutor having pronounced his name, Lord Clifford exclaimed, "Thy father killed my father—thou must die, thou and all thy race," and stabbed him to the heart. This barbarity seemed to have opened an abyss between the two parties; from that time scaffolds were erected upon the fields of battle, and not a life among the conquered was spared.

*Edward IV.*, 1461—*Margaret in France*, 1463. —At this time the quarrels of the red and white rose (badges of the houses of York and Lancaster) became more systematic. Warwick had the son of the Duke of York proclaimed king by the populace of London, under the title of Edward IV. (1461). The child of a civil war, Edward permitted blood to flow without compunction; but he interested the people by the misfortunes of his father and his brother; he was only twenty years old, he loved pleasure, and was the handsomest man of the age. The Lancastrian party had only in their favour the long possession of the throne, and the oaths of the people. When the queen dragged towards the South a tribe of unbridled northern peasants, who were only paid by plunder, London and the richest provinces attached themselves to Edward, as their defender. Warwick speedily led the young king against her, as far as the village of Towton. It was there that, during a whole day and in a violent snowstorm, the two parties fought, with a fury rarely evinced even in civil war. Warwick, seeing that his party were giving way, killed his horse, and kissing the cross which formed the hilt of his sword, swore that he would share the fate of the last of his soldiers. The Lancastrians were precipitated into the River Cock. Edward forbade his army to give quarters to the vanquished, and 38,000 men were drowned and massacred. The queen, having no more resources, addressed herself to strangers, to the French; she had already given up Berwick to the Scotch; she went over to France, and promised Louis XI. to give him Calais as a pledge, to obtain thereby a feeble and odious assistance. But the fleet which carried her treasures was shattered by the tempest; she lost the battle of Exham, and her last hopes (1463). The unhappy Henry soon fell again into the power of his enemies. The queen at last arrived in France with her son, after encountering the greatest dangers.

After victory came the division of the spoils. Warwick and the other Nevilles had the principal share. But they soon saw their interest superseded by the relations of Elizabeth Woodville, a private gentlewoman, whom the imprudent love of Edward raised to the throne.* Then the *King-maker* thought of nothing but how to destroy his own

* According to a tradition generally received, Warwick had negotiated in France the marriage of the King of England with Bonne of Savoy, sister-in-law of Louis XI., during the time that Edward was married to Elizabeth Woodville. This tradition is not confirmed by the three principal contemporary historians.—*Lingard.*

work; he negotiated with France, caused a rebellion in the north of England, drew even the brother of the king, the Duke of Clarence, into his party, and made himself master of the person of Edward. England had for a moment two royal captives: but Warwick soon saw himself compelled to fly with Clarence, and to go over to the Continent.

*Edward IV. expelled*, 1470.—York could only be overthrown by the army of Lancaster. Warwick became reconciled with that same Margaret of Anjou who had caused his father to be beheaded, and returned to England in the vessels of the King of France. In vain Charles the Bold had warned the indolent Edward; in vain the people in their ballads chanted the name of the exile, and alluded in the rude plays of that age to his misfortunes, and to his virtues. Edward only roused himself on hearing that Warwick was approaching with an army of sixty thousand men. Betrayed by his own party at Nottingham, he saved himself so precipitately, that he landed almost alone in the territories of the Duke of Burgundy.

*Death of Warwick—Henry VI.*, 1471—*Edward IV.*, 1483.—While Henry VI. was leaving the Tower of London, and the King of France was celebrating the restoration of his ally in public fêtes, Clarence, who repented of the aid which he had rendered to the house of Lancaster, recalled his brother to England. Edward departed from Burgundy with means furnished secretly by the duke, and went on shore at Ravenspur, the very place where Henry IV. had landed to dethrone Richard II. No obstacle opposed his advance, and he declared, as he proceeded, that his intention was only to claim the Duchy of York, his family inheritance. He wore the ostrich feather (worn by the partisans of the Prince of Wales, son of Henry VI.), and made his followers cry, "Long life to King Henry!" But as soon as his army was strong enough, he dropped the mask, and prepared to dispute the throne with the Lancastrians upon the plain of Barnet. The treachery of Clarence, who went over to his brother with 12,000 men, and the embarrassment caused by their mistaking the sun, which Edward's party bore upon their arms, for the blazing star of their opponents, occasioned the loss of the battle, and the death of the Earl of Warwick. Margaret was attacked: before she could collect the troops which remained to her, she was vanquished, and taken, with her son, to Tewksbury. The young prince was conducted to the tent of the king. "Who has made you so bold as to enter my territories?" said Edward to him. "I came," proudly replied the young prince, "to defend my father's crown and my own inheritance." Edward, angry at the reply, struck him with his gauntlet in the face, and his brothers, Clarence and Gloucester (or perhaps their knights), threw themselves upon him, and killed him. It is said that on the same day that Edward entered London, Henry VI. was assassinated in the Tower by the hand of the same Duke of Gloucester (1471). From that time the triumph of the red rose was secured, and Edward had nothing more to fear except from his own brother. He anticipated Clarence by taking his life under some frivolous pretext; but, if we may believe common report, he was poisoned by Gloucester (1483). See above, his expedition to France.

*Richard III.*—Edward had scarcely left his throne to his young son, Edward V., when the Duke of Gloucester had himself proclaimed *Protector*. The queen-mother, who knew too well what protection she had to expect from a man whose appearance alone made one shudder, fled for refuge to Westminster, but the sanctity of the place was no barrier to Richard; she tremblingly placed her two children under his guardianship. But he could attempt nothing against them while their natural guardians were living, especially Lord Hastings, the personal friend of Edward IV. One day Richard entered the council-chamber with a smiling countenance; then suddenly changing his looks, he exclaimed, "What punishment do they deserve who conspire against the life of he protector? See into what a condition the wife of my brother and Jane Shore (who was the mistress of Hastings) have reduced me by their sorceries!" and he showed a withered arm, which had been in this state from his birth. Then addressing Lord Hastings, he said, "It is you who are the instigator of all this; by St. Paul, I will not dine until your head is brought to me." He struck upon a table, a crowd of soldiers entered the hall, dragged Hastings away, and beheaded him in the courtyard upon a piece of timber which they found there. The Parliament then declared the two young princes bastards, and the sons of a bastard. A Doctor Shaw preached to the people, "*that illegitimate slips would not be useful;*" a dozen workmen threw their caps in the air, crying "Live King Richard!" and he accepted the crown *to comply with the commands of the people.* His nephews were smothered in the Tower, and a long time after, the skeletons of two children were found under the stairway of the prison.

*Death of Richard III.*, 1485.—Nevertheless, the throne of Richard III. was not firm; there remained in a remote part of Brittany a scion of Lancaster, Henry Tudor, of Richmond, whose claims to the crown were unquestionable. He was, by his grandfather, Owen of Tudor, of Welsh origin. The Welsh invited him to England.* With the exception of the northern counties, where Richard had many partisans, all England waited for Richmond to declare themselves in his favour. Richard, not knowing on whom to rely, hastened the crisis, and advanced as far as Bosworth. Scarcely were the two armies in sight of each other, when Richard recognised in the hostile ranks the Stanleys, whom he believed to be on his side. He then bounded forward, the crown upon his head, crying "Treason! Treason!" killed two gentlemen with his own hand, overthrew the standard of the enemy, and opened the way even to his rival; but he was overwhelmed by numbers. Lord Stanley tore the crown from him, and placed it on the head of Henry. The body of Richard, stripped of everything, was thrown on a horse, the head hanging on one side, the feet on the other, and was thus conveyed to Leicester (1485).

*Henry VII., Tudor.*—Henry united the claims of the two rival houses by his marriage with Elizabeth, daughter of Edward IV. But his reign was a long time disturbed by the intrigues of the widow of Edward, and of his sister, the dowager Duchess of Burgundy. At first they raised against him a young baker, who passed himself for the

* Thierry, Hist de la Conquête de l'Angleterre par les Normands, vol. i., 2d edit.

Earl of Warwick, son of the Duke of Clarence. Henry having defeated the partisans of the impostor at the battle of Stoke, employed him as a scullion in his kitchen, and soon after, as a reward for his good conduct, he gave him the charge of his falconry. A more formidable rival afterward raised himself against him. This mysterious personage, who resembled Edward IV., took the name of the second son of that prince. The Duchess of Burgundy acknowledged him for her nephew, after a solemn examination, and publicly named him *The White Rose of England.* Charles VIII. treated him as a king. James III., king of Scotland, gave him one of his relatives in marriage, but his attempts were unsuccessful. He successively invaded Ireland, the north of England, the county of Cornwall, and was always repulsed. The inhabitants of this county, deceived in the hopes which they had formed at the accession of a prince from the Welsh race, refused to expose themselves for the Pretender. He was, notwithstanding his pretensions, made prisoner, and was compelled to read in Westminster Hall a confession signed by his own hand; in it he acknowledged that he was born at Tournay, of a Jewish family, and that his name was Perkin Warbeck. Another impostor, having assumed the name of the Earl of Warwick, Henry VII., to terminate all these troubles, had the true Earl of Warwick put to death: an unfortunate prince, whose birth was his only crime, and who, from his earliest years, had been shut up in the Tower of London.

*English Aristocracy.*—Such was the end of the troubles which had cost so much blood to England. Who was conquered in this long contest? Neither York nor Lancaster, but the English aristocracy, who were decimated by battles and wasted by proscription. Nearly a fifth of the estates in the kingdom (if we may believe Fortescue) had fallen by confiscation into the hands of Henry VII. What was still more fatal to the power of the nobles, was the law which permitted them to make over their estates by breaking the entails. The increasing want of luxuries, until then unknown, made them eagerly avail themselves of that permission which was to bring on their own ruin. To reside at court, they quitted their ancient castles, where they had reigned as sovereigns since the conquest. They discontinued those sumptuous entertainments and that hospitality by which they had so long retained the fidelity of their vassals. The *men of the barons* found the court-hall and the banquet-room deserted; they abandoned those who abandoned them, and returned to their homes *king's men.*—(*Abolition of the Law of Maintenance.*)

*Reign of Henry VII.*—The first care of Henry

VII., during all his reign, was the accumulation of a treasury; one could rely so little upon the future after so many revolutions! The exacting of feudal debts, the redeeming of feudal services, fines, confiscations—all means were good to him to attain his end. He obtained money from his Parliament to make war against France, and he procured money from the French to purchase peace, thus *gaining from his subjects by war, and from his enemies by peace.*—(*Bacon.*)

He sought also to support his throne by alliances with the best-established dynasties—gave his daughter to the King of Scotland, and obtained for his son the infant of Spain (1502–3). In his reign navigation and industry received their first impulse. He sent a Venitian, Sebastian Cabot, in search of new countries, who discovered North America, 1498. He granted to several cities the exemption from a law which forbade a father to place his son in apprenticeship unless he had an income of twenty shillings from real estate. Thus, at the moment when Henry VII. is establishing the unbounded power of the Tudors upon the downfall of the nobility, we see the beginning of the rise of that Commons which, in a century and a half, will overthrow the Stuarts.

*Scotland.*—The time was still far distant in which the other kingdom of Great Britain would become as regularly organized. Scotland contained many more elements of discord than England. First, its mountainous country had made it more easy to resist the conquered races. The sovereignty of the *Lowlanders* over the Highlanders, of the Saxons over the Celts,* was purely nominal. The latter scarcely knew any sovereigns but the hereditary chiefs of their clans. The principal of these chiefs, the Earl of Ross, the *Lord of the Isles*, was, with respect to the kings of Scotland, considered more as a tributary sovereign than as a subject. He was the secret or avowed friend of all the enemies of the king; the ally of England against Scotland, and of Douglas against the Stuarts. The first princes of this dynasty spared the Highlanders, from want of power to subdue them; James I. expressly exempted them from obeying any law, "*seeing*," said he, "*that their custom is to rob and kill each other.*"† Thus English civilization, which was gradually pervading Scotland, was arrested at the Grampian Hills.

*Douglas.*—The lords and barons to the south of these mountains were indefatigable adversaries to the royal authority, particularly the Lords Douglas; this heroic family had disputed the throne with

* The mountaineers always call the other Scots *Saxons.*

† Pinkerton, *Hist. of Scotland,* from the *accession of the house of Stuart* to that of Mary, with appendices of original papers.

the Stuarts ever since their accession to the dynasty, and had since gone to combat with the English in France, and had returned with the title of Counts of Touraine, as a trophy of their victory. In the family of the Stuarts even, the kings of Scotland had rivals; their brothers or their nephews, the Dukes of Albany, governed in their names, and harassed them with their ambitious pretensions. If to these troubles we add the singular circumstance of a succession of six minorities (1437–1578), we can comprehend why Scotland was the last kingdom to emerge from the anarchy of the Middle Ages.

After the French wars, the contest against the Douglases became more terrible, and the kings displayed more of violence than of ability in it. Under James II., William Douglas was enticed by Chancellor Crichton to the castle of Edinburgh, and after some pretended form of justice, was condemned to death (1440). Another William Douglas, the most insolent of all that bore the name, having been summoned by the same prince to Stirling, provoked him to the utmost by his outrageous language, and was stabbed by his own hand (1452). His brother, James Douglas, marched against the king at the head of 40,000 men, compelled him to fly into the North, and would have conquered him if he had not insulted the Hamiltons, who were.

until then, attached to his family. Douglas, deserted by his own party, was obliged to fly into England, and the war of the Roses just beginning, prevented the English from making use of this dangerous exile to embroil Scotland. The earls of Angus, a branch of the house of Douglas, received him, and were scarcely less formidable to the kings than the Earl of Douglas himself. Soon after the Hamiltons also rebelled, and became, with the Campbells (earls of Argyle), the most powerful lords of Scotland in the sixteenth and seventeenth centuries.

*James III.*, 1460.—In the reign of James III., Scotland extended her territories towards the north and the south by the acquisition of the Orcades and of Berwick; the reunion of the earldom of Ross to the crown destroyed forever the power of the *Lord of the Isles,* and yet no reign was ever more disgraceful; no prince ever shocked the opinions and customs of his subjects as did James III. What Scottish laird would deign to obey a king who, a stranger to the warlike amusements of the nobility, was always concealed in a strong castle, surrounded by English artists, and deciding upon peace and war after the counsel of a music-master, a mason, and a tailor? He had gone so far as to forbid the nobles to appear armed at his court, as if he was afraid to see a sword

Still, he might have been supported against the nobility by the commons or the clergy; but he estranged them both, by taking from the boroughs the election of their aldermen, and from the clergy the nomination of their dignitaries.

*His death*, 1488.—James III., who knew his own weakness, feared that his two brothers, the Duke of Albany and the Earl of Mar, might wish to supplant a king so deservedly despised. Influenced by the prediction of an astrologer, he decided to imprison them in the castle of Edinburgh. The Duke of Albany saved himself; the cowardly and base monarch thought to secure his repose by causing his younger brother to be bled to death. The favourites triumphed; Cochrane, the mason and architect, dared to take the spoils of his victim, and to assume the title of the Earl of Mar. Such was his confidence in the future, that, in putting some base money in circulation, he said, "Before my money shall be withdrawn, I shall be hung," and thus it was. The nobles seized the favourites in the presence of the king, and hanged them on the bridge of Lawder. Some time after, they attacked the king himself, and formed the most extensive conspiracy that had ever threatened the throne of Scotland (1488). The barons of the North and of the West still retained their loyalty, but James fled at the first encounter, and fell from his horse into a stream of water. He was carried into a neighbouring mill, and asked for a confessor; the priest who presented himself belonged to the enemy's party; he received the confession of the king, and then stabbed him.

*James IV.—His death*, 1513.—James IV., whom the malecontents raised to the throne, had a happier reign than his father. Instead of the humble duty of subjects to a king, the barons rendered homage to him, as the most brilliant knight of the kingdom. He completed the ruin of the *Lord of the Isles* by uniting the Hebrides to the crown; he established courts of royal justice throughout all the northern part of the kingdom. Neglected by the French, James IV. allied himself to the king of England, Henry VII. When Henry VIII. invaded France, Louis XII. implored the assistance of the Scotch; Anne of Brittany sent her ring to their king, thus designating him for her knight. James would have accused himself of disloyalty, had he not succoured a suppliant queen. All the ords and all the barons of Scotland followed him on this romantic expedition. But he lost much valuable time in the castle of Mrs. Heron, near Flodden, where he remained as if from enchantment, which was only broken by the arrival of the English army. He was conquered, notwithstanding his bravery, and all of his nobility were slain with him (1513). The death of twelve counts, of thirteen lords, of five eldest sons of peers, with a great number of barons, and ten thousund soldiers, delivered up Scotland, drained and exhausted for a century, to the intrigues of France and of England.

## § III. SPAIN AND PORTUGAL, 1454–1521.

Henry IV., King of Castile, 1454; Revolt of the Grandees in the Name of the Infant; Deposition of Henry; Battle of Medina del Campo, 1465. —John II., King of Aragon; Revolt of Catalonia, 1462–72.—Marriage of Ferdinand of Aragon and Isabella of Castile, 1469.—War against the Moors; Taking of Grenada, 1481–92.—Ferdinand and Isabella repress the Grandees and the Cities, relying on the Aid of the Inquisition, established in 1480.—Expulsion of the Jews, 1492.—Forced Conversion of the Moors, 1499.—Death of Isabella, 1504.—Ministry of Ximenes.—Conquest of Navarre, 1512.—Death of Ferdinand, 1516.—His Successor, Charles of Austria; Revolt of Castile, Murcia, &c., &c., 1516–1521.

The barbarians of the North and South, the Goths and Arabs, encountered each other in Spain. Arrested by the ocean in the Spanish Peninsula, they fight there, as in an enclosed field, during all the Middle Ages. Thus the spirit of the Crusades, which transiently agitated all the other nations of Europe, has formed the basis of the Spanish character, with its ferocious intolerance and its chivalrous pride exalted by the violence of African passions, for Spain still adhered to barbarism, notwithstanding the strait between them. On this side we again find the productions and families of Africa, and even its deserts.* A single battle delivered up Spain to the Moors, and it has required eight hundred years to subdue their power.

*Moors—Spaniards.*—The Christians had been masters since the 13th century; in the 15th, Mussulman population concentrated in the kingdom of Grenada, and, as if bounded by the sea, could move no farther; but we already see to which of the two nations the empire of Spain belonged; on the side of the Moors, a crowd of merchants, heaped together in the rich cities, made effeminate by the baths and the climate; peaceable husbandmen, employed in their rich valleys with the care of the mulberry-trees, and with the working of silk—a lively and ingenious people, who lived only for music and the dance, who loved gaudy and showy clothing, and were even dressed in their gayest garments for their graves; on the other side, a grave and silent people, clothed in brown and black, who loved nothing but war, and war of the most bloody kind; who left commerce and the sciences to the Jews, and knew not a more excellent title than Sons of the Goths, a race haughty in their independence, terrible in love and in religion.

* There is an adage in several parts of Old Castile, that the *lark that would traverse the country, must carry its grain with it.*—Bory de Saint Vincent, *Itinéraire*, p. 81. On the sterility and feeble population of Aragon, even in the Middle Ages, see Blancas, cited by Hallam, vol iv., p. 156.

With them there was no distinction of rank; the citizen did not pay for his privileges, and the peasant, who also bore arms against the Moors, felt his dignity as a *Christian*.

*Resistance to the Kings.*—These men, so formidable to the enemy, were scarcely less so to their kings. For a long time the king had only been as the chief of the barons; the King of Aragon sometimes prosecuted his subjects at the tribunal of the *justiza*, or grand justiciary of the kingdom. The spirit of resistance in the Aragonese had passed into a proverb, like the pride of the Castilians: "*Give a nail to an Aragon, and he will drive it with his head sooner than with a hammer.*" Their oath of obedience was haughty and threatening: "*We, who separately are as great as you, and who, united, may be greater than you, we make you our king, on condition that you will guard our privileges; if you do not, no!*"

*Jews.*—The kings of Spain also preferred to employ the *new Christians*, as they called the converted Jews and their children; they were more intelligent, and more submissive. The tolerance of the Moors had formerly drawn them into Spain, and since the year 1400 more than a hundred thou sand Jews had been converted. They made themselves necessary to the king by their skill and address in business, and by their knowledge of medicine and of astrology. It was a Jew who, in 1468, performed the operation for a cataract upon the King of Aragon. Commerce was in their hands; they had got by usury all the money of the country, and it was to them that the king intrusted the raising of the taxes. What titles to the hatred of the people! That hatred broke out several times in a terrible manner in the populous city of Toledo, of Segovia, and Cordova.

*The Grandees.*—The grandees, who saw themselves gradually put aside by the *new Christians*, and, in general, by men of inferior rank, became the enemies of the royal authority, which they could not dispose of to their own advantage. The nobles of Castile armed the infant Don Henry against his father, John II., and had the favourite of the king, Alvaro de Luna, beheaded. His immense property was confiscated, and during three days a basin was placed upon the scaffold, near his corpse, to receive the alms of those who were willing to contribute towards the expenses of his burial.

*Henry IV., King of Castile*, 1454—*Battle of Medina del Campo*, 1465.—When Henry IV. became king, he endeavoured to abridge the power of the grandees, which they had held since he was Infant of Spain, but at the same time he irritated the cities by raising the taxes on his own authority, and by daring to nominate deputies to the

Cortes.* He also was made contemptible by his connivance at the debaucheries of the queen, and by his own cowardice. The Castilians could not obey a prince who withdrew himself from the army at the moment of battle. The chief of the grandees, Carillo, archbishop of Toledo, Don Juan de Pacheco, marquis of Villana, and his brother, who possessed the grand-mastership of St. Jago and of Calatrava, opposed to the king his brother, Don Alonzo, who was still a child, and declared illegitimate the Infanta Donna Juana, who was believed to be the daughter of Bertrand la Cueva, the lover of the queen; they exposed the effigy of Henry upon a throne in the plain of Avila, and having stripped it of the royal ornaments, threw it down, to put Don Alonzo in its place. After an indecisive battle (Medina del Campo, 1465), the unhappy king, deserted by every one, wandered at random in his own kingdom, in the midst of castles and cities, which shut their gates against him, without any person condescending to arrest him. One evening, after a journey of eighteen leagues, he ventured to enter the city of Toledo; the alarm bell was sounded, he was obliged to fly, and not one of the horsemen who were with him would even lend him a horse.

*John II. of Aragon.* — Aragon and Navarre

* Mariana, *Teoria de las Cortes*, cited by Hallam, vol. i., p. 416–424.

were not more tranquil. John II., who had succeeded his brother, Alphonso the Magnanimous, inthe kingdoms of Aragon and Sicily, withheld from his own son, Don Carlos de Viarra, the crown of Navarre, which this young prince inherited from his mother (since 1441). His stepmother excited the father against his son for the advantage of her own children (Ferdinand the Catholic, and Leonora, countess of Froix). The never-ending factions of Navarre, the Beaumonts, and the Grammonts, prosecuted their private quarrels under the name of the two princes. Twice was the cause of justice vanquished in a pitched battle; twice did the indignation of Don Juan's subjects force him to set at liberty his unhappy son. Don Carlos having died from poison or grief (1461), his sister, Donna Blanca, inherited his rights. Her father intrusted her to her younger sister Leonora, who poisoned her in the castle of Orthey. Catalonia was already in rebellion; the horror of this double parricide gave a new excitement to their minds; the Catalonians, who could not have Don Carlos for their king, now worshipped him as a saint. They called to the throne, successively, the King of Castile, the Infant of Portugal, and John of Calabria, and they only submitted themselves after ten years of resistance (1472).

*Ferdinand and Isabella*, 1469–1479.—During

the period in which John II. was hazarding Catalonia, Ferdinand, his son, had gained Castile. The brother of Henry IV. being dead, the grandees had substituted in his place his sister Isabella. To support her against the king, they married her to the Infant of Aragon, who was, after her, the nearest heir to the throne (1469). Henry IV. soon died, in consequence of an entertainment given to him by his reconciled enemies (1474). When dying, he affirmed that Donna Juana was his legitimate daughter. Galicia, and all the country from Toledo as far as Murcia, had declared themselves for her. The King of Portugal, her uncle, Alphonso *the African*, was betrothed to her, and came with his knights, who had conquered Arzila and Tangier, to support her cause. The Portuguese and Castilians met for battle at Toro (1476). The Portuguese were vanquished, and the arms of Almeida, which were borne upon their standard, were hung in the Cathedral of Toledo. This check sufficed to discourage the Portuguese ; all the Castilian lords ranged themselves on the side of Ferdinand and Isabella ; the crown of Castile was secured to them, and the death of John II., who left Aragon to them (1479), enabled them to turn all the forces of Christian Spain against the Moors of Grenada.

1481–1492.—It was a common saying among

the Moors, that the fatal termination of their dominions in Spain had arrived. A Fakir troubled Grenada with his ominous predictions: they were sufficiently warranted by the state of the kingdom. Already, under Henry IV., Gibraltar had been lost. Some cities, strongly situated, but without ditches, having no exterior fortifications, and defended only by a wall, the thickness of which could afford no protection; a brilliant cavalry, prompt to charge or to fly; such were the resources of the people of Grenada. They could not rely upon Africa. The time was past when hordes of the Almohades and the Almoravides were able to overwhelm the Peninsula. The only aid which the Sultan of Egypt afforded them, was to send the guardian of the Holy Sepulchre to Ferdinand to speak to him in their favour, but he was soon drawn off from this distant affair by the fears which the Ottomans inspired.

*Taking of Grenada*, 1492.—Although the Christians and the Moors, every year alternately, infested the country of their enemy, burning the vines, olives, and orange-trees, a singular agreement existed between them: the truce was not to be considered as broken, even if one of the two parties should have captured a city or a town, provided it was taken possession of without the form of war, without banners and trumpets, and in less than three days. Zahara, which had been obtained in this manner by the Moors, was the pretext for the war. The Spaniards invaded the kingdom of Grenada, encouraged by their beautiful queen, whom alone the Castilians would obey. In this army we already see the future conquerors of Barbary and of Naples, Pedro of Navarre, and Gonsalvo of Cordova. In the course of eleven years, the Christians became masters of Alhama, the bulwark of Grenada; took Malaga, which was the entrepôt of the commerce of Spain with Africa, and Baca, which, it is said, contained one hundred and fifty thousand inhabitants; and at last came, with eighty thousand men, to lay siege to Grenada itself. This capital was a prey to the most furious discords. The son was armed against his father, and brother against brother. Bobadil and his uncle had divided the remains of this expiring sovereignty; the uncle sold his share to the Spaniards for a rich earldom. Bobadil, who was an acknowledged vassal of Ferdinand, remained; but, instead of directing the people, he followed the example of their obstinate fury. The siege lasted nine months. A Moor attempted to stab Ferdinand and Isabella; the camp was entirely destroyed by fire; but the queen, whom no event discouraged, ordered a city to be built in its place, and the town of Santa Fé, erected in twenty-four days, proved to the Mussulmen that the siege would never be raised.* At last the Moors opened their gates, upon the assurance that they should retain judges of their own nation, and the free enjoyment of their religion (1492).

*Columbus.*—In the same year Christopher Columbus gave a world to Spain.†

The kingdoms of Spain were reunited with the exception of Navarre, the sure prey of two great monarchies, between which nature herself seemed to have divided it in advance. But it was necessary that parts drawn together by force should of themselves form one body. The Castilians regarded the Aragonese with a jealous eye; they both saw continual enemies in the Moors, and in the Jews, who lived in the midst of them. Every city had its immunities, every grandee his prerogatives. All these obstacles must be overcome, these heterogeneous forces must be assimilated, before they could be turned towards conquest. Notwithstanding the ability of Ferdinand, notwithstanding the enthusiasm which Isabella inspired, this end was attained only after thirty years of effort. The means were terrible, commensurate with the energy of such a people; the price was the dominion of two worlds in the 16th century.

* Petri Martyris Angleri Epistolæ, 73, 91, &c. The author was an eyewitness of these events.

† Epitaph of Columbus.

*Cortes—Santa Hermandad.*—The Spanish Cortes, which alone were competent to regulate these conflicting elements, were the most ancient assemblies of Europe; but establishments formed in the anarchy of the Middle Ages had not that organization which alone could ensure their permanency. In 1480, only seventeen cities of Castile were represented; in 1520, not a deputy was sent to the Cortes from Galicia. Those of Guadalaxara alone voted for 400 boroughs or cities. It was nearly the same in Aragon. The rivalry of the cities perpetuated this abuse; in 1506 and 1512 the privileged cities of Castile repelled the claims of the others. Thus, to retain his power, Ferdinand had only to leave the field open to these rival pretensions. He obtained by the Holy Brotherhood of the cities (Santa Hermandad), and by the revolt of the vassals, the submission of the grandees; by the grandees, the submission of the cities; and by the Inquisition, the obedience of them both.* The violence of the grandees determined Saragossa to allow him to change her ancient municipal constitutions, a thing which she had always forbidden. The organization of the St. Hermandad, or Holy Brotherhood of the cities of Aragon, which would have terminated the private wars of the lords, was arrested by them (1488), and the king was compelled, in the Cortes of 1495, to postpone its establishment for ten years;

* In Galicia alone he destroyed forty-six castles.

but the people of Saragossa were so irritated at this, that, during a long time, the justiza of Aragon, who were not willing to take the oath of the Brotherhood, did not dare enter the city. Henceforth royalty was to inherit a great portion of the attachment of the people for that very magistracy which had so long been considered the rampart of the public liberties against the encroachments of kings.

Yet Ferdinand and Isabella would never have acquired absolute power, if the necessities of the crown had left them dependant upon the Cortes. They twice revoked the concessions of Henry IV.—concessions by which they themselves had purchased the submission of the grandees (1480–1506). The union of the three grand-masteries of Alcantra, of Calatrava, and of St. Jago, to their dominions, which they had the address to make the knights yield to them, gave them at once an army and immense wealth (1493, 1494). At a later period, the kings of Spain having obtained permission from the pope to sell the Bull of the Crusade, and the benefice of bishoprics (1508–1522), they became the richest sovereigns of Europe, even before they had drawn any considerable sum from America.

*Portugal.*—It was by similar means that the kings of Portugal established their power. They arrogated to themselves the privileges of the orders of Avis, of Saint Jago, and of Christ, for the purpose of placing the nobility in a state of dependance upon them. In a similar diet (at Evora, 1482), John II., successor to Alphonso the African, revoked the grants of his predecessors, took from the lords their power over life and death, and placed their domains under the royal jurisdiction. The indignant nobility appointed the Duke of Braganza for their chief, who called upon the Castilians to aid them; the king had him tried by a commission, and beheaded; the Duke of Vizen, the first cousin of Don Juan, and his brother-in-law, also conspired against the king, and the monarch stabbed him with his own hand.

*Inquisition in Spain.*—But what ensured the triumph of absolute power in Spain was its reliance upon that religious zeal, which was the national trait of the Spanish character. The kings leagued themselves with the Inquisition, that great and powerful hierarchy, the more terrible as it united the regular power of political authority with the violence of religious passions. The establishment of the Inquisition met with the greatest opposition from the Aragonese. Less in contact with the Moors than the Castilians, they were less exasperated against them: the greater part of the members of the government of Aragon were descended from

Jewish families. They remonstrated earnestly against the secret proceedings, and against the confiscations, which, they said, were contrary to the *fueros* of the kingdom. They even assassinated one of the Inquisitors, in hope of frightening the rest. But the new establishment was too conformable to the religious ideas of the greater part of the Spaniards not to withstand these attacks. The title of *Familiar of the Inquisition*, which secured exemption from municipal duties, was so much sought after, that in certain cities these privileged men exceeded in number the other inhabitants, and the Cortes were obliged to keep them in order.*

* Inscription placed by the Inquisitors, a short time after the establishment of the Inquisition, upon the castle of Triana, in a suburb of Seville: "Sanctum Inquisitionis officium contrà hæreticorum pravitatem in Hispaniæ regnis initiatum est Hispali, anno 1481, &c., &c. Generalis Inquisitor primus fuit Fr. Thomas de Torquemada. Faxit Deus ut in augmentum fidei usque sæculis permaneat, &c., &c. Exsurge, Domine; judica causam tuam. Capite nobis vulpes." Another inscription, placed in 1524 by the Inquisitors on their house at Seville: "Anno Domini 1481, sacrem Inquisitionis officium contrà hæreticos Judaizantes ad fidei exaltationem, hic exordium sumpsit; ubi, post Judæorum ac Saracenorum expulsionem ad annum usque 1524, divo Carolo, &c., &c., regnante, &c., &c., viginti millia hæreticorum et ultra nefandum hæreseos crimen adjurârunt; nec non hominum fere millia in suis hæresibus obstinatorum posteà jure prævio ignibus tradita sunt et combusta. Domini nostri imperatoris jussu et impensis licentiatus de La Cueva poni jussit, A.D. 1524."

It is worthy of remark, that many of the popes condemned the rigour of the Inquisition of Spain. Since 1445, Nicholas V. had forbidden any difference to be made between the old and new Christians. Sixtus IV., Innocent VIII., and Leo X. kindly received the numerous appeals which were made to their tribunals, and reminded the Spanish Inquisitors of the parable of the good shepherd. In 1546, when Charles the Fifth

*Expulsion of the Jews*, 1492. — After the conquest of Grenada, the Inquisition no longer limited itself to the prosecution of individuals. An order was proclaimed against all Jews, commanding them either to become converts within four months, or to depart from Spain, taking neither gold nor silver with them (1492). One hundred and seventy thousand families, forming a population of eight hundred thousand souls, sold their effects in haste, and fled into Portugal, to Italy, Africa, and as far as the Levant. *They were then seen to give a house in exchange for an ass, and a vineyard for a piece of linen or cloth.* An historian of the age relates, that he saw a crowd of these unhappy beings land in Italy, and die of famine and penury near the Mole of Genoa, the only place in that city where they were permitted to rest for some days.

*Inquisition in Portugal*, 1526.—The Jews who had retired into Portugal, were only received there by paying eight crowns of gold for each person; they were also obliged to depart from the kingdom within an appointed time, under the penalty of becoming slaves, a penalty which was most rigorously enforced, and yet it is said that the first Jews who arrived wrote to their brethren in Spain, " *The*

wished to introduce the Inquisition into Naples, Paul the Third encouraged the resistance of the Neapolitans, reproaching the Inquisition of Spain for not profiting by the examples of mildness which that of Rome had given them.

*land is good, the people are simple, and we have water; you may come, for all will belong to us."* Don Manuel, the successor of Don Juan, emancipated all those who had been made slaves. But in 1496 he commanded them to depart from the kingdom, leaving their children under fourteen years of age; the greater part preferred to receive baptism, and in 1507 Manuel abolished the distinction between *the old and new Christians.* The Inquisition was established at Lisbon in 1526, and from thence extended itself as far as the East Indies, where the Portuguese had landed in 1498. (See below.)

*Moors of Grenada.*—Seven years after the expulsion of the Jews (1499–1501), the King of Spain undertook, by means not less violent, to convert the Moors of Grenada, to whom the capitulation guarantied the free exercise of their religion. Those of the Albaydin (the most elevated part of Grenada) revolted first, and were followed by the savage inhabitants of Alpuxarros. The Gandules of Africa came to support them, and the king, having found the difficulty of reducing them, furnished vessels to those who were willing to go to Africa; the greater part, however, remained, pretending to become Christians.

*Death of Isabella*, 1504—*Ximenes.*—The reduction of the Moors was followed by the conquest of Naples (1501–1503), and the death of Isabella

(1504). This great queen was adored by the people of Castile, whose noble character she so well represented,* and whose independence she had defended against her husband. At her death the Castilians had but a choice among foreign masters. They must obey either the King of Aragon or the Archduke of Austria, Philip le Beau, sovereign of the Low Countries, who had espoused Donna Juana, the daughter of Ferdinand and Isabella, heiress to the kingdom of Castile. Such was their antipathy against the Aragonese, and particularly against Ferdinand, that, notwithstanding all his intrigues to obtain the regency, they joined themselves to the archduke, as soon as he landed in Spain. At first the conduct of Philip was popular; he arrested the violence of the Inquisition, which was ready to excite a general insurrection, but he deposed all the corregidors, and all the governors of cities, to give their places to his own Flemings; finally, he had Donna Juana confined as

* The principal part of the glory of this reign must be attributed to Queen Isabella. She evinced the greatest courage during the vicissitudes of her youth: when Ferdinand fled from Segovia, she undauntedly remained there; she would guard the Alhama, at the gates of Grenada, when her most valiant officers proposed a retreat. She consented reluctantly to the establishment of the Inquisition. She loved literature, and aided its advancement; she understood Latin, while Ferdinand could scarcely sign his name. Notwithstanding the objections of Ferdinand, she armed the fleet which discovered America. She defended the accused Columbus, consoled Gonsalva de Cordova in his disgrace, and gave liberty to the unhappy Americans.

insane, whose feeble reason was unsettled by jealousy. Philip soon died (1506). Yet Ferdinand would not have been able to govern Castile, had he not been supported by the confessor and minister of Isabella, the celebrated Ximenes de Cisneros, archbishop of Toledo, in whom the Castilians admired both the politician and the saint. He was a poor monk, whom the Archbishop of Grenada had given to Isabella for her confessor and counsellor. Great was the astonishment of the court when this man of the desert appeared there, *whose paleness and austerity reminded them of Paul and Hilarion.* Even in the midst of grandeur he rigorously observed the rules prescribed by St. Francis, travelling on foot, and begging for his daily nourishment. It was necessary to have an order from the pope to oblige him to accept the Archbishopric of Toledo, and to force him to live in a manner appropriate to the opulence of the richest benefice in Spain. He yielded, allowing himself to wear the most valuable furs, but they only covered the coarsest stuffs ; he ornamented his apartments with magnificent beds, while he continued to sleep on the floor. In this humble and austere life he retained the haughty dignity of the Spanish character, which was visible in all his actions ; the nobles whom he had crushed could not repress their admiration of his courage. An ordinance which was about to set Ferdinand and his son-in-law at variance, Ximenes dared to tear in pieces. One day, as he was crossing a place during a bull-fight, the infuriated animal broke loose and wounded some of his attendants, without making him quicken his pace.

*Moors of Africa—Navarre.*—The Castilians, thus finding in Ximenes the heroic spirit of their great queen, forgot that they obeyed Ferdinand, and the last years of this prince were marked by the conquest of Barbary and Navarre. The war with the Moors did not seem ended, inasmuch as those of Africa, being strengthened by a multitude of fugitives, infested the coasts of Spain, and found a sure refuge in the ports of Oran, of Penon de Velez, and in many other haunts. Ximenes projected an expedition against Oran, defrayed its expense, and conducted it in person. The capture of that city by Pedro of Navarre, of which he was an eyewitness, was followed by that of Tripoli, and by the subjection of Algiers, of Tunis, and of Fremecen (1509–1510). Two years after, the reunion of Navarre, which Ferdinand had taken by force from John of Albret, completed that of all the kingdoms of Spain (1512). Leonora, countess of Foix, had a month's enjoyment of this throne, which she had bought with her sister's blood. After the death of her son Phebus, the hand of

Catharine, her daughter, which had been solicited in vain for the Infant of Spain, was given by the French party to John of Albret, that her domains of Foix, Perigord, and Limoges might always be attached to France. As soon as the two great powers which were struggling in Italy came in close contact with each other, Navarre, from her geographical position, found herself divided between Ferdinand and Louis XII.

Ximenes was 80 years old when the dying king named him for regent until his grandson, Charles of Austria, should arrive (1516). He confronted with equal boldness enemies from without and within. He prevented the French from conquering Navarre by means as novel as they were daring: he had the walls of all the cities pulled down, except Pampeluna, and thus removed every stronghold, in case of an invasion. At the same time, he formed a national militia, made himself sure of the cities by giving to them the power to levy the taxes themselves (Gomecius, f. 25), and revoked the concessions which the late king had made to the grandees. When the latter came to claim those grants, and expressed some doubts as to the powers which had been given him, Ximenes answered, pointing from a balcony to a formidable train of artillery, "You see my powers!"

*Charles V. King*, 1516.—The Flemings gave

offence to Spain from the moment of their arrival. They disgraced the dying Ximenes, and nominated a stranger, a youth of twenty years, to replace him in the first seat of the kingdom. They established a tarif of all the offices, and if we may thus speak, put up Spain at auction. Charles assumed the title of king without waiting for the consent of the Cortes. He convoked the Cortes of Castile at some small place in Galicia, and demanded a second subsidy before they had paid the first; he procured it by force or bribery, and departed to take possession of the imperial crown, without disquieting himself, though he left a revolution behind him. Toledo had refused to send delegates to these Cortes; Segovia and Zamora put their deputies to death, and such was the horror they inspired, that there was not a person willing to plunder their houses, or to pollute themselves with the wealth of the traitors. In the mean time, the evil was disseminated over all Spain. Castile, and all of Galicia, Murcia, and the greater part of the cities of Leon and Estremadura, were in rebellion. The insurrection was not less furious in Valencia, but it bore a different character. The inhabitants had sworn a Hermandad against the nobles, and Charles, discontented with the noble, had the imprudence to confirm it. Majorca followed the example of Valencia, and was even willing to surrender herself to the French. In these two kingdoms the woollen-drapers were at the head of the Hermandad.

*John of Padilla.*—The *Communeros* first invaded Tordesillas, where the mother of Charles V. resided, and performed all their acts in the name of that princess. But their success was of short duration. They had demanded, in their remonstrances, that the lands of the nobles might be subject to taxes. The nobles abandoned a party whose victory would have been prejudicial to them. There was no union between the cities themselves. The old rivalry of Burgos and Toledo revived: the former submitted to the king, who secured to the city its commercial freedom. The only hope of relief for the distracted *Communeros* rested in the French army, which had invaded Navarre; but before they could effect a junction with it, they were overtaken by the *Leales*, and entirely defeated (1521). Don Juan of Padilla, the hero of the Revolution, sought death in the ranks of the enemy; but he was dismounted, wounded, taken prisoner, and beheaded the next day. Before his death, he sent to his wife, D. Maria Pacheca, the relics which he wore round his neck, and wrote his celebrated letter to the city of Toledo: "To thee, the crown of Spain, and the light of the world; to thee, who hast been free from the time of the Goths, and who hast given thy blood to secure thy liberty and that of the adjacent cities, thy legitimate son, John of Padilla, makes known, that by the blood of his body thine ancient victories are about to be revived, and renewed," &c., &c. The subjection of Castile was followed by that of the kingdom of Valencia, and of all the rebellious provinces. But Charles V., instructed by such a lesson, respected thenceforth the pride of the Spaniards; he affected to speak their language, resided much among them, and preserved in this heroic nation the instrument with which he hoped to subdue the world.

---

## CHAPTER III.

### THE EAST AND THE NORTH.—GERMAN AND SCANDINAVIAN STATES IN THE SECOND PART OF THE FIFTEENTH CENTURY.

Empire of Germany.—Preponderance and interested Policy of Austria.—Rise of Switzerland.—Decline of the Teutonic Order.—Cities of the Rhine, and of Swabia.—Preponderance and Decline of the Hanseatic League.—Elevation of Holland.—Wars of Denmark, Sweden, and Norway.—Enfranchisement of Sweden, 1433–1520.

*German States.*—If we consult the analogy of customs and of languages, we must include in the number of the Germanic States the Empire

Switzerland, the Netherlands, the three kingdoms of the North, and even England in several respects; but the political relations of the Netherlands and of England with France have obliged us to place the history of those powers in a preceding chapter.

*Germany.*—Germany is not only the centre of the Germanic System; it is a small Europe in the midst of the great one, where the varieties of population and of territory present themselves with a less decided diversity. We there find, in the 15th century, all forms of government, from the hereditary, or elective principalities of Saxony and Cologne, to the democracies of Uri and Underwaldt; from the commercial oligarchy of Lubeck, to the military aristocracy of the Teutonic Order.

This singular body of the empire, whose members were so heterogeneous and so unequal, and whose head was so powerless, seemed always ready to fall to pieces. The cities, the nobility, the greater part of the princes even, were almost strangers to an emperor whom the electors alone had chosen. Yet a common origin and language have maintained the unity of the Germanic body during centuries; add to this the need of mutual support, the fear of the Turks, of Charles V., and Louis XIV.

*Austria.*—This empire always remembered that

it had governed Europe, and from time to time resumed its rights in empty proclamations. The most powerful prince of the 15th century, Charles the Bold, had appeared to acknowledge them, by soliciting the royal dignity from the Emperor Frederic. These superannuated pretensions might become formidable, since the imperial crown had been settled upon the house of Austria (1438). Placed between Germany, Italy, and Hungary, in the very centre of Europe, Austria must prevail over the last two countries, at least by the spirit of perseverance and of obstinacy; unite with this that policy, more ingenious than heroic, which by means of a succession of marriages gave to the house of Austria the price of the blood of other nations, and subjected to it the conquerors with their conquests; she thus gained on the one side Hungary and Bohemia (1526), on the other the Netherlands (1481), and by the Netherlands Spain, Naples, and America (1506–1516), and by Spain, Portugal and the East Indies (1581).

*Imperial Power in the House of Austria.*—Towards the end of the 15th century, the imperial power was so fallen, that the princes of the house of Austria often forgot that they were emperors, while occupying themselves only with the interests of their hereditary estates. Nothing drew their attention from this policy, which must, sooner or later, restore to them the imperial power itself. Thus Frederic III., who was always beaten by the Elector Palatine, or by the King of Hungary, was deaf to the cries of Europe, which was alarmed by the progress of the Turks. But he erected Austria into an archduchy, and attached the interests of his house to those of the popes, by sacrificing to Nicholas V. the pragmatic of Augsburgh; he married his son Maximilian to the heiress of the Low Countries (1481). Maximilian himself became, by his insignificance and his poverty, the derision of Europe, travelling constantly from Switzerland to the Low Countries, and from Italy to Germany; imprisoned by the inhabitants of Bruges, beaten by the Venitians, and accurately noting his affronts in his *red-book*. But he inherited the States of Tyrol, of Goritz, and part of Bavaria. His son Philip le Beau, sovereign of the Netherlands, married the heiress of Spain (1496); one of his grandsons (treaty of 1515) was to marry the sister of the King of Bohemia and of Hungary.

*Constitution of the Empire*, 1495–1501.—While the house of Austria thus prepares its future grandeur, the empire endeavours to regulate its constitution. The *Imperial Chamber*, henceforth a permanent body (1493), must put a stop to private wars, and must substitute a government of laws for that state of nature which still prevails among the members of the Germanic body. The division of the parties will facilitate the exercise of this jurisdiction. A regency is destined to watch over it, and supply the place of the emperor (1500). The electors refuse for a long time to enter into this new organization. The emperor opposes the Aulic Council to the Imperial Chamber (1501), and these salutary institutions are thus weakened in their infancy.

This absence of order, this want of protection, had successively obliged the most distant subjects of the empire to form confederacies, more or less independent, or to seek for foreign support. Such was the situation of Switzerland, of the Teutonic Order, the Confederation of the Rhine and of Swabia, and of the Hanseatic League.

*Prussia.*—In the same epoch, we see the rise of Switzerland and the decline of the Teutonic Order. The second of these two military powers, a sort of vanguard, which the martial genius of Germany had carried even to the centre of the Slavonic States, was obliged to surrender to the King of Poland that Prussia which the Teutonic knights had conquered and Christianized two centuries before (treaty of Thorn, 1466).

*Switzerland.*—Switzerland, separated from the Empire by the victory of Morgarten and by the league of Brunnen, had confirmed its liberty by the defeat of Charles the Bold, which taught to feudal Europe the power of infantry. The alliance of the Grisons, the acquisition of five new cantons (Soleure, Bâsle, Schaffhausen, Appenzell, Fribourg, 1481–1513), had raised Switzerland to the summit of grandeur. The citizens of Berne and the shepherds of Uri saw themselves caressed by popes and courted by kings. Louis XI. substituted a Swiss guard in place of the free archers (1480). In the wars of Italy, they formed the best part of the infantry of Charles VIII. and of Louis XII. From the time that they crossed the Alps in the train of the French, they were welcomed by the pope, who opposed them to the French themselves, and they governed for a moment in the north of Italy (under the name of Maximilian Sforza). After their defeat at Marignan (1515), religious discords armed them against each other, and confined them closely to their mountains.

The two commercial powers of Germany did not form a body sufficiently compact to imitate the example of Switzerland, and render themselves independent.

*Cities of the Rhine and of Swabia.*—The league of the cities of the Rhine and of Swabia was composed of rich towns, among which those of Nuremberg, of Ratisbon, of Augsburg, and of Spire held the first rank. These are the cities which carried on the principal trade by land between the North and the South. The merchandise, arrived at Cologne, passed through the hands of the Hanseatics, who distributed it in all Northern Europe.

*Hanseatic League.*—The Hanseatic League, composed of twenty-four cities, comprised all the northern shores of Germany, and extended over those of the Netherlands. Until the sixteenth century it was the predominant power of the North. The great Hall of Lubeck, where the general assemblies of the Hanseatics were held, still attests the power of these sovereigns. They had united by innumerable canals the ocean, the Baltic, and the greater part of the rivers in the north of Germany; but their principal commerce was maritime. The Hanseatic counting-houses in London, in Bruges, in Bergen, and in Novogorod were in many respects similar to the factories of the Venitians, and of the Genoese in the Levant: they resembled a garrison. The clerks in them were not permitted to marry, for fear that they might instruct the natives in commerce and the arts.* They were only received into the offices after some cruel trials, which guarantied their courage, and business was almost everywhere transacted

* See Mallet, *Histoire de la Ligue Hanseatique*, Genoa (1805). The author has often been indebted to the labours of Sartorius.

with arms in their hands. If the agents of the Hanseatics carried to Novogorod or to London some Flemish cloth which was too coarse, too narrow, or too dear, the people rebelled, and often assassinated some of them. Then the merchants threatened to leave the city, and the alarmed inhabitants yielded everything. The inhabitants of Bruges having killed some of the Hanseatic men, the latter exacted as a condition of the re-establishment of their office in that city, that several of the citizens should make *l'amende honorable*, and that others should go on a pilgrimage to St. James of Compostella and to Jerusalem. The most terrible punishment which the Hanseatics could inflict on any country was never to return to it. When they had no establishment in Sweden, the inhabitants were in want of cloth, of hops, of salt, and of herrings; in the revolutions, the Swedish peasant always was in favour of those who furnished him with herrings and with salt. The Hanse Towns also exacted excessive privileges; in the greater part of the seaport towns in Sweden, at least one half of the offices were occupied by them.

Yet this great power did not rest upon a solid basis. The long line occupied by the Hanse Towns from Livonia to the Low Countries was narrow throughout, and everywhere intersected by foreign states or by enemies. The cities which composed it had different interests and unequal rights; some were *allies*, some *protégés*, and some *subjects*. Their commerce even, the source of their existence, was precarious. Being neither agriculturists nor manufacturers, they could only transport and sell foreign produce, and they were dependant upon a thousand accidents, political or natural, which no foresight could prevent. For instance, the herrings, which about the fourteenth century had left the coasts of Pomerania for those of Scandinavia, commenced in the fifteenth century to emigrate from the shores of the Baltic towards those of the Northern Ocean. The subjection of Novogorod, and of Plescow also, to the Czar Iwan III. (1477), and the capture of Bruges by the imperial army (about 1489), closed the two principal sources of their riches to the Hanseatics. At the same time, the progress of public order rendered the protection of the Hanse Towns useless to a great number of the Continental cities, particularly since the constitution of the empire was established (1495). The cities of the Rhine had never been willing to unite with them; Cologne, which had entered into their league, separated from them, and asked the protection of Flanders. The Hollanders, whose commerce and industry had grown up under the shade of the Hanse Towns, had no longer need of them when they became the subjects of the powerful houses of Burgundy and of Austria, and began to dispute with them the monopoly of the Baltic. At once agriculturists, manufacturers, and tradesmen, they had the advantage over a power entirely commercial. The Hanseatics, to defend their commercial interests against these dangerous rivals, were obliged to interpose in all the revolutions of the North.

*Denmark—Sweden—Norway.*—Christianity and civilization having passed from Germany into Denmark, and from thence into Sweden and Norway, preserved to Denmark for a long time the preponderance over the two other states. The Swedish and Norwegian bishops were the most powerful lords of those countries, and they were equally devoted to the Danes; but the kings of Denmark could only avail themselves of that preponderance by continual efforts and by frequent concessions to the Danish nobles, which placed them in a state of dependance upon them: these concessions were only made at the expense of royal authority and of the liberty of the peasants, which by degrees sunk into slavery. In Sweden, on the contrary, the peasants were not far below the ancient liberty of the Scandinavian nation, and they formed even a political order. This difference in its constitution explains the force with which Sweden shook off the yoke of the Danes. With regard to the Norwegians, whether the clergy had more influence among them than among the Swedes, or that they feared to obey Sweden, still they generally showed less repugnance to the Danish dominion.

*Revolutions of the North*, 1453–1520.—The celebrated union of Calmar, which seemed to promise so much of glory and of power to the three kingdoms of the North, had only made Sweden and Denmark subject to the yoke of the Danish and German princes, by whom they were surrounded. The revolution of 1433, like that of 1521, commenced among the peasants of Dalecarlia; Englebrecht was its Gustavus Vasa, and, like him, was supported by the Hanse Towns, whose monopoly the King of Denmark (Eric, the Pomeranian nephew of Margaret of Waldemar) combated by favouring the Hollanders. The union was re-established for some time by Christophe the Bavarian, the *king of bark*, as the Swedes called him, from his having been obliged to subsist on the bark of a tree; but after his death (1448) they expelled the Danes, and the Germans put themselves under the dominion of Charles Canutson, marshal of the kingdom, and refused to acknowledge the new king of Denmark and Norway, Christian, the first of the house of Oldenburg (from whence came, by the branch of Holstein Gottorp, the last dynasty of Sweden, and the present imperial house of Russia). The

Danes, strengthened by the reunion of Sleswick and Holstein (1459), twice re-established their authority over Sweden, with the aid of the Archbishop of Upsal (1457–1465), and were twice expelled by the party of the nobility and the people.

At the death of Charles Canutson in 1470, Sweden appointed successively for *administrators* three lords of the name of Sture (Stenon, Swante, and Stenon). They were supported by the husbandmen, whom they recalled to the Senate. They fought with the Danes before Stockholm (1471), and took from them the famous banner of Danebrog, which they regarded as the palladium of the monarchy. They founded the University of Upsala at the same time that the King of Denmark instituted that of Copenhagen (1477–1478). In fine, if we except a short period, during which Sweden was obliged to acknowledge John II. successor to Christian I., they preserved its independence until 1520.

## CHAPTER IV.

### EAST AND NORTH—SLAVONIC STATES AND TURKEY IN THE SECOND PART OF THE FIFTEENTH CENTURY.

Progress of the Turks, 1411–1582.—Podiebrad, King of Bohemia; Matthias Corwin, King of Hungary, 1458.—Wladislas, of Poland, reunites Hungary and Bohemia.—Poland under the Jagellons, 1386–1506.—Contest of Russia with the Tartars, the Lithuanians, and the Livonians, 1462–1505.

*Slavonic States.*—The conquest of the Grecian Empire by the Ottoman Turks may be considered as the last invasion of the barbarians, and the termination of the Middle Ages. It was a nation ot Slavonic origin, situated on the route of the barbarians of Asia, who shut them out from Europe, or at least that arrested them by powerful diversions. Russia, which had already exhausted the fury of the Tartars in the fourteenth century, again becomes formidable to them under Iwan III. (1462). A first league, composed of Hungarians, Wallachians, and Moldavians, is formed, like a reserve of the Christian army, to protect Germany and Poland against the invasion of the Turks. Poland, with no enemies in her rear, has just subdued Prussia, and penetrated to the Baltic (1454–1466).

*Causes of the Progress of Turkey.*—I. The following causes explain the rapid progress of the Ottoman conquest during the fifteenth century: 1st, their fanatical and military spirit; 2d, their disciplined troops, opposed to the feudal militia of the Europeans, and to the cavalry of the Persians and the Mamelukes; the appointment of janizaries; 3d, the particular situation of the enemies of the Turks; in the East, the political and religious feuds of Persia, the feeble basis of the power of the Mamelukes; in the West, the discords of the Christian world: Hungary protects it on the side of the land, and Venice on the side of the sea; but both are weakened, one by the ambition of the house of Austria, the other by the jealousy of Italy and of all Europe; the inefficient heroism of the knights of Rhodes and of the princes of Albany.

*Bajazet II.*, 1481.—In the first chapter we have seen Mohammed II. completing the conquest of the Grecian Empire, failing in his invasion of Hungary, but seizing the sovereignty of the sea, and making Christendom tremble. At the accession of Bajazet to the throne (1481), the scene changed, and terror seized the sultan: his brother Zizim, who had disputed the throne with him, fled for refuge to the knights of Rhodes, and became, in the hands of the King of France, and afterward of the pope, a pledge for the West. Bajazet paid considerable sums to Innocent VIII. and to Alexander VI., that they might retain his brother a prisoner. This unpopular prince, who had commenced his reign by beheading the Vizier Achmet (the idol of the janizaries, the old general of Mohammed II.), was influenced, despite of himself, by the military ardour of the nation. The Turks first turned their arms against the Mamelukes and the Persians ; defeated by the Mamelukes at Issus, they prepared the destruction of the conquerors by depopulating Circassia, where the Mamelukes recruited.

After the death of Zizim, having no longer a civil war to fear, they attacked the Venitians in Morea, and threatened Italy (1499–1503) ; but Hungary, Bohemia, and Poland put themselves in motion, and the accession of the Sophis renewed and regulated the political rivalry of the Persians and Turks (1501). After this war, Bajazet disaffected the Turks by a peace of eight years ; he wished to abdicate in favour of his son Achmet, but was dethroned and put to death by his second son Selim. The accession of the new prince, the most cruel and martial of all the sultans, spread terror both over the West and the East (1512) ; no one knew on whom he would fall first, Persia, Egypt, or Italy.

*Hungary and Bohemia.* — II. Europe would have had nothing to fear from the barbarians if Hungary, united to Bohemia in a permanent way, had held them in sufficient respect; but the former attacked the latter in her independence and religious creed. Thus weakened by each other, they were fluctuating in the fifteenth century between the two powers, Slavonic and German (Poland and Austria), which surrounded them. Reunited, from 1453 to 1458, under a German prince, again for some time separated and independent under national sovereigns (Bohemia until 1471, Hungary to 1490), they were once more reunited under Polish princes until 1526, the period in which they became decidedly subject to the dominion of Austria.

*Podiebrad and Matthias* 1458.—After the reign of Wladislas of Austria, which was rendered illustrious through the exploits of John Hunniade, George Podiebrad seized the crown of Bohemia, and Matthias Corvin, the son of Hunniade, was chosen King of Hungary (1458). These two princes successfully opposed the chimerical pretensions of the Emperor Frederic III. Podiebrad, in protecting the Hussites, incurred the enmity of the popes. Matthias gained a glorious victory over the Turks, and obtained the favour of Paul II., who offered him the crown of Podiebrad, his father-in-law.

The latter objected to the alliance of Matthias with the King of Poland, by which he was made to acknowledge the oldest son of Wladislas for his successor. At the same time, Casimir, the brother of Wladislas, attempted to take the crown of Hungary from Mathias by force. Matthias, thus pressed on all sides, was obliged to renounce the conquest of Bohemia, and to content himself with the provinces of Moravia, Silesia, and Lusacia, which should return to Wladislas if he survived Mathias (1475–1478).

The King of Hungary compensated himself at the expense of Austria. Under the pretence that Frederic III. had refused him his daughter, he twice invaded his dominions, and kept possession of them. With this great prince the Christian world lost its principal defender, and Hungary her conquests and her political preponderance (1490). Civilization, which he had endeavoured to introduce in this kingdom, was delayed for several centuries. We have already mentioned (chapter i.) what he did for literature and for the arts. By his *Decretum Maujs*, he regulated military discipline, abolished judicial combats, and forbade his subjects to appear armed at the fairs and in the market-places ; he ordered that punishment should no longer be extended to the relatives of a criminal, that their property should no longer be confiscated, and that the king should not accept of mines of gold, of salt, &c., &c., without recompensing the proprietors of them.

*Wladislas.*—Wladislas of Poland, the King of Bohemia, having been elected King of Hungary, was attacked by his brother, John Albret, and by Maximilian of Austria, both of whom claimed that crown. He appeased his brother by the cession of Silesia (1491), and Maximilian, by entailing the house of Austria upon the kingdom of Hungary, in case he should leave no male heirs (see 1526). Under Wladislas, and under his son Louis II., who, when yet a child, succeeded him in 1516, Hungary was ravaged with impunity by the Turks.

*Poland.*—III. Poland, reunited to Lithuania since 1386 by Wladislas Jagellon, the first prince of that dynasty, was, in the fifteenth century, the preponderating power in the Slavonic States. Covered on the side of the Turks by Wallachia, Moldavia, and Transylvania, the rival of Russia for Lithuania, of Austria for Hungary and Bohemia, she contended with the Teutonic Order for Prussia and Livonia. The principal source of her weakness was the jealousy of two nations of different languages, who of themselves composed the body of the state. The Jagellons, Lithuanian princes, would have wished their country independent of Polish laws, and that it might regain Podolia. The Poles, on the other hand, reproached Casimir IV. with passing the autumn, the winter, and the *spring in Lithuania.*

*Treaty of Thorn,* 1466. — Under Casimir, the second son of Wladislas Jagellon (fifth of the name), the Poles protected the serfs of Prussia against the tyranny of the Teutonic knights, and forced upon the latter the treaty of Thorn (1466), by which the order lost the western part of Prussia, and became the vassal of Poland for Eastern Prussia. Who at that time would have said that Prussia would some day dismember Poland? At the same time the Poles gave a king to Bohemia and to Hungary (1471–1490). The three brothers of Wladislas, John Albret, Alexander, and Sigismund I., who were successively elected kings of Poland (1492, 1501, 1506), made war against the Wallachians and the Turks, and obtained brilliant advantages over the Russians. Lithuania, separated from Poland at the ascension of John Albret to the throne, was definitely reunited to her by Alexander.

*Government of Poland.*—Towards the year 1466, the continuance of the war, bringing back the same wants, introduced a representative government into Poland; but the pride of the nobility, which alone was represented by its nuncio, maintained the anarchical forms of barbarous times; they continued to exact *unanimous consent* in their deliberations. Furthermore, on important occasions, the Poles remained faithful to their ancient customs, and one could see, as in the Middle Ages, numberless armed Polish noblemen deliberating in an open field, sword in hand.

*Russia.* — IV. In the fifteenth century, the Russian population presents to us three classes: the *children of the Boyards** (descendants of the conquerors); the free peasants, farmers of the former, and whose condition was gradually approaching slavery; and, finally, the slaves.

The grand-duchy of Moscow was constantly threatened, in the West by the Lithuanians and the Livonians, in the East by the Tartars of the great horde of Kasan and of Astrachan; she found herself enclosed by the commercial republics of Novogorod and of Plescow, and by the principalities of Twer, of Vereia, and of Rezan. In the North many savage and pagan nations were spread over the country. The Muscovite nation, though still barbarians, were at least settled in permanent abodes, and must destroy the wandering tribes of the Tartars. The grand-duchy, as an hereditary state, must sooner or later prevail over the elective states of Poland and Livonia.

* A name given to the Russian nobles.

1462–1505 — *Iwan III.*—To oppose the great horde, he made an alliance with the Tartars of Crimea; to oppose the Lithuanians, he allied himself with the Prince of Moldavia and Wallachia, with Matthias Corvin, and with Maximilian. He separated Plescow and Novogorod, which could resist him only by making common cause. He weakened gradually the Republic of Novogorod, made himself master of it in 1477, and exhausted it by forcing its principal citizens away. Made powerful by the alliance with the Khan of Crimea, he imposed a tribute on the Kazanais, refused that which his predecessors paid to the great horde, which was soon destroyed by the Nogais Tartars (1480). Iwan reunited Twer, Vereia, Bostof, Yaroslof; he made war for a long time against the Lithuanians, but Alexander, having reunited Lithuania to Poland, allied himself with the knights of Livonia; and the Czar, who, since the destruction of the great horde, had cared less for his allies of Moldavia and Crimea, lost all his ascendency; he was defeated at Plescow by Plettemberg, master of the knights of Livonia (1501), and the year of his death (1505) Kasan revolted against the Russians.

*Iwan IV.* — Iwan first took the title of Czar. Having obtained from the pope the hand of Sophia Paleologue, a refugee at Rome, he placed on his arms the double eagle of the Grecian Empire. He allured, and retained by force, Grecian and Italian artists. He was the first who assigned fiefs to the *children of the Boyards*, under condition of a military service; he introduced order in the finances, established posts, united into a code (1497) the ancient judicial institutions, and vainly endeavoured to distribute among the *children of the Boyards* the estates of the clergy. Iwan had laid the foundations of Iwangorod in 1492 (where, later, Petersburgh was built), when the victories of Plettemberg shut from the Russians during two centuries the passage to the Baltic.

---

## CHAPTER V.

### FIRST WARS OF ITALY, 1494–1516.

Louis the Moor calls for the Aid of the French.—Charles VIII. invades Italy.—League against the French.—Battle of Formosa, 1495.—Louis XII. invades Milan, 1499.—War with the Spaniards of Naples.—Defeat of the French at Garigliano, 1503.—Alexander VI. and Cæsar Borgia.—Julius II.—Revolt of Genoa against Louis XII., 1507.—Italy, the Empire, France, Hungary, conspire against Venice.—*Holy League* against France, 1511–12.—Victories and Death of Gaston of Foix.—Bad Success of Louis XII., 1512–14.—Francis I. invades Milan.—Battle of Marignan, 1515.—Treaty of Noyon, 1516.

When, in this age, we traverse the maremmes* of Sienna, and when we find in Italy so many

* Unhealthy tracts of country.

other traces of the wars of the sixteenth century, an inexpressible sadness comes over us, and we execrate the barbarians who commenced this desolation. This desert of the maremmes was made by a general of Charles V.; these ruins of burned palaces are the work of the landsknechts of Francis I.; these disfigured paintings of Guillo Romano still attest that the soldiers of the Constable of Bourbon had their stables in the Vatican. But let us not accuse our forefathers hastily. The wars of Italy were neither the caprice of a king nor of a nation. During more than half a century, an irresistible impulse had led all the people of the West, as formerly those of the North, beyond the Alps. Their calamities were almost as cruel, but the result was the same: the conquerors were raised to the civilization of the conquered.

*Louis the Moor calls for the Aid of the French.*—Alarmed by the threats of the King of Naples, whose granddaughter had married his nephew, John Galeas (see chap. i.), Louis the Moor resolved to support his usurpation by the aid of the French. But he was far from knowing what power he had drawn into Italy. He was himself seized with astonishment and terror when he beheld (September, 1494) this formidable army descending from the Mount of Geneva, which, from the variety of the costumes, arms, and languages, resembled an invasion of all the nations of Europe—French, Biscayans, Bretons, Swiss, Germans, and even Scotch; that invincible gendarmerie, those heavy brass cannons, which the French had made as movable as their armies. A war entirely new for Italy commenced. The ancient tactics, which in battle required one squadron to follow another, were at once overcome by the impetuosity of the French, and the calm courage of the Swiss. The war was no longer an affair of martial discipline; it was to be terrible, inexorable; the conqueror understood not even the prayer of the conquered. The soldiers of Charles VIII., full of distrust and hatred towards a country where they feared to be poisoned at every repast, massacred, in regular order, every prisoner.*

*Savanarola.*—At the approach of the French, the old governments of Italy dissolved themselves. Pisa delivered herself from the Florentines, and Florence from the Medicis. Savanarola received Charles VIII. as the *scourge from God*, sent to punish the sins of Italy. Alexander VI., who, until then, had negotiated at the same time with the French, the Aragonese, and the Turks, heard with dismay the word of censure and degradation, and concealed himself in the castle of St. Ange.

* At Montefortino, at Mount St. John, at Rapallo, at Sarzana, at Toscanella, at Fornoo, at Gaete.

He delivered up, with trembling, the brother of Bajazet II., supposed by Charles VIII. to be necessary to him, in order to conquer the Empire of the East; but he delivered him poisoned. In the mean time, the new King of Naples, Alphonso II., fled to a convent of Sicily, leaving his kingdom to be defended by a monarch of 18 years. The young Ferdinand II. was abandoned at St. Germano, and saw his palace pillaged by the populace of Naples, always furious against the vanquished. The French soldiers no longer fatigued themselves by wearing armour, but pursued their conquest leisurely in their morning attire, without any trouble other than to send their quartermasters before them to prepare their lodgings. The Turks soon saw the *fleurs de lis* waving at Otranto, and the Greeks taking up arms.*

The partisans of the house of Anjou, plundered for sixty years, had thought to conquer with Charles VIII.; but this prince, who cared little for the services which they had been able to render to the kings of Provence, exacted no restitution from the opposite party. He dissatisfied all the nobility by announcing his intention to limit the feudal jurisdiction, after the example of those of France. He nominated French governors for all the cities and fortresses, and thus decided several cities to

* Comines, book vii., chap. xvii.

raise again the standard of Aragon. At the end of three months the French were wearied with the Neapolitans, the Neapolitans weary of the French; they had forgotten their projects upon the East, and were impatient to return, to relate to the ladies of their own country their brilliant adventures.

*Formosa*, 1493.—In the mean time, a league, which was almost universal, was formed against Charles VIII., who must hasten to regain France, if he did not wish to be made a prisoner in the kingdom which he had come to conquer. In again descending the Apennines, he met at Formosa the army of the allies, composed of forty thousand men; the French had only nine thousand. Having in vain demanded a passage, they forced it, and the enemy's army, which endeavoured to arrest them, were put to flight by a few charges of the cavalry. Thus the king re-entered France gloriously, having justified all his imprudence by one victory.

*Death of Savanarola.* — The Italians, believing themselves delivered, called Savanarola to account for his sinister predictions; and his party, that of the *Piagnoni* (Feuillants), who had freed and reformed Florence, beheld all his influence overthrown. The friends of the Medicis, whom they had bitterly persecuted, and the Pope Alexander VI., whose excesses Savanarola had attacked with great freedom, seized the occasion to destroy a faction which had exhausted the capricious enthusiasm of the Florentines. A Franciscan monk wishing, he said, to prove that Savanarola was an impostor, and that he possessed neither the gift of prophecy nor of miracles, offered to pass through a burning fire with him. On the appointed day, when the pile was arranged, and all the people in expectation, the two parties made some difficulty, and a violent rain completed the ill-humour of the people. Savanarola was arrested, tried by the commissioners of the pope, and burned alive. When the sentence was read to him, by which he was cut off from the Church, " From the Church militant," said he, hoping thenceforward to belong to the Church triumphant (1498).

Italy discovered that there was but too much truth in these prophecies.

*Louis XII.*, 1498—*Division of the Kingdom of Naples.*—On the same day of the ordeal by fire of Savanarola, Charles VIII. died at Amboise, and left the throne to the Duke of Orleans (Louis XII.), who joined to the claims of his predecessor upon Naples those which his grandmother, Valentine Visconti, gave him upon Milan. As soon as his marriage with the widow of Charles VIII. had secured the reunion of Brittany, he invaded Milan in concert with the Venitians. The two hostile armies were partly composed of Swiss; those of Ludovic refused to fight against the banner of their canton, which they saw in the army of the King of France, and deserted the Duke of Milan. But in returning to their mountains, they took possession of Bellinzona, which Louis XII. was obliged to yield to them, and which became to them the key of Lombardy. Milan being taken, Louis XII., who could not hope for the conquest of Naples while opposed by the Spaniards, divided that kingdom with them by a secret treaty. The unfortunate Don Frederic, who then reigned, called the Spaniards to his aid, and when he had led Gonzalvo di Cordova into his principal fortresses, the treaty of transfer was notified to him (1501). This odious conquest only engendered war. The two nations contended for the salt-tax which was levied on the travelling flocks that in the spring passed from the Puglia into the Abruzzo, and which was the surest revenue in the kingdom. Ferdinand amused Louis XII. by a treaty until he had sent sufficient re-enforcements to Gonzalvo, who was blocked up in Bartella. The military skill of the *great captain*, and the discipline of the Spanish infantry, obtained advantages everywhere over the brilliant courage of the French troops. The valour of Louis d'Ars and of D'Aubigny, the exploits of Bayard, who, it is said, defended a bridge against an army, could not prevent the French from being beaten at Seminara and at Cerignola, nor from being driven a second time from the kingdom of Naples by their defeat at Garigliano (December, 1503).

*Death of Alexander VI.*, 1503. — Louis XII. was still master of a great part of Italy, sovereign of Milan and lord of Genoa, ally of Florence and of the Pope Alexander VI., who relied on none but him.* He extended his influence over Tuscany, Romagna, and the State of Rome. The death of Alexander VI., and the ruin of his son, were events scarcely less fatal to him than his defeat at Garigliano. The Italian power of Borgia, which raised itself between the possessions of the French and those of the Spaniards, was as the advance guard of Milan.

Cæsar Borgia deserved to be the ideal of Machiavel, not for having shown himself more perfidious than the other princes of that epoch: Ferdinand the Catholic could disprove that; not for having been the assassin of his brother, and the lover of his sister; he could not surpass his father in de-

* *Cæsar Borgia of France, by the grace of God Duke of Romagna and of Valentinois*, &c., &c. (passport of the 19th of October, 1502). He said to the ambassador of Florence, the *King of France, our common master* (10th January, 1503). Legation of Machiavel with Cæsar Borgia.

pravity or cruelty; but for having made a science of crime; for having established a school and given lessons in infamy.* In the mean time the hero of the system, by his bad success, pronounced its most memorable condemnation. The ally of Louis XII. and standard-bearer of the Church, he employed during six years all the resources of cunning and of courage. He believed that he was working for his own aggrandizement; he said to Machiavel that he had foreseen everything; at the death of his father he hoped to be made pope, through the influence of eighteen Spanish cardinals, who had been appointed by Alexander VI.; in the Roman States, he had gained the lower class of nobles, destroyed the higher; he had exterminated the tyrants of Romagna; he had attached to himself the people of that province, who were happy under his vigorous and skilful administration. He had foreseen everything except the event of his being ill at the period of his father's death, and this event happened. Both the father and the son, who, it is said, had invited a cardinal with the intent of putting him to death, drank the poison which they had prepared for him. "This man, so wise, seems to have lost his reason," then

* Machiavel says somewhere, *He has sent one of his pupils.* Hugues de Moneade, a general of Charles V., boasted to have been the pupil of that school.

wrote Machiavel (November 14, 1503). Forced by the new pope, Julius II., he abandoned all the fortresses that he possessed, and then delivered himself up to Gonzalvo de Cordova, believing *that another's word was better than his own.* (Letter of 4th November.) But the general of Ferdinand the Catholic, who said that "the robe of honour ought to be of a loose tissue," sent him to Spain, where he was imprisoned in the citadel of Medina del Campo.

*Julius II.*—Julius II. followed up the conquests of Borgia from motives less personal. He wished to make the pontifical state the predominant state of Italy, to deliver all the peninsula from the *barbarians*, and to constitute the Swiss the guardians of Italian liberty. Employing by turns both spiritual and temporal weapons, this intrepid pontiff consumed his life in the execution of this incongruous project; the barbarians could only be driven away by the assistance of Venice, and Venice must be humbled, in order to make the Church the preponderating power of Italy.

Julius II. at first wished to give liberty to his countrymen, the Genoese, and encouraged their revolt against Louis XII. The nobles, favoured by the French government, ceased not to insult the people; they went everywhere armed with poignards, on which they had engraved, "*I chastise* *the low-born.*" The people revolted, and chose a dyer for their doge. Louis XII. soon appeared under their walls with a brilliant army; the Chevalier Bayard ascended without difficulty the mountains which covered Genoa, and cried aloud to them, "Knights of the yardstick, merchants, defend yourselves with your measure-sticks, and throw down the pikes and lances, which you are not accustomed to."* The king, unwilling to ruin so rich a city, caused only the doge and a few of the citizens to be hung, burned the privileges of the city, and constructed a fortress which commanded the entrance of the port (1507).

*League of Cambray*, 1508.—The same jealousy of monarchies against republics, of the poor against industrious opulence, soon armed the greater part of the princes of the West against the ancient rival of Genoa. The government of Venice had known how to profit by the faults and the misfortunes of all the other powers; it had gained from the fall of Ludovic the Moor, from the expulsion of the French from Naples, and from the ruin of Cæsar Borgia. So much success excited the fears and the jealousies of the Italian powers themselves, who ought to have desired the grandeur of Venice. "Your lordships (Machiavel wrote to the Floren-

* Champier, *The Deeds, together with the Life of the worthy Chevalier Bayard*, &c.

tines) have always told me that it was Venice which threatened the liberty of Italy."* From the year 1503, M. de Chaumont, lieutenant of the king in Milan, said to the same ambassador, "It will so happen that the Venitians will now have no occupation but fishing; and for the Swiss, we are sure of them" (22d January). This conspiracy against Venice, which existed since 1504 (treaty of Blois), was renewed in 1508 (league of Cambray, 10th December) by the imprudence of Julius II., who wished, at any price, to recover some of the cities of Romagna. The pope, the emperor, and the King of France, proposed to the King of Hungary to enter into a confederation, for the purpose of retaking Dalmatia and Esclavonia. The Dukes of Savoy and of Ferrara, and even the Marquis of Mantua, were also willing to aid in the overthrow of a power which they had so long feared. The Venitians were defeated by Louis XII. at the bloody battle of Aignadel (1509), and the balls of the French batteries flew even to the Lagunes. In this perilous moment, the decision of the Senate of Venice did justice to its reputation for wisdom. They declared that they wished to save the provinces from the miseries of war; they absolved them from the oath of fidelity, and promised to in-

* Legation to the Emperor, February, 1508. See, also, the Legation to the Court of France, February 13, 1503.

demnify them for all their losses at the return of peace. Whether from attachment to the Republic, or from hatred of the Germans, the peasants of Verona would sooner permit themselves to be hung than abjure St. Mark, and cry *Vive l'Empereur.* The Venitians gained a victory over the Marquis of Mantua, retook Padua, and defended the city against Maximilian, who besieged it with 100,000 men. The King of Naples and the pope, whose claims were satisfied, made peace with Ven ice; and Julius II., who only thought to drive the *barbarians* from Italy, turned his impetuous policy against the French.

*Holy League.*—The projects of the pope were greatly assisted by the injudicious economy of Louis XII., who had reduced the pay of the Swiss, and who would no longer permit them to procure provisions from Burgundy and Milan. The error of Louis XI. was now perceived, who, in substituting the mercenary infantry of the Swiss for his free archers, had placed France in the power of strangers. It became necessary to replace the Swiss by the German Landsknechts, who were recalled by the emperor on the eve of the battle of Ravenna. In the mean time, the pope had commenced the war; he summoned the Swiss into Italy, and made them enter into the *Holy League* against France, Ferdinand, Venice, Henry VIII., and Maximilian

(1511–12). While Louis XII., doubtful whether he could defend himself against the pope without sinning, consulted the learned doctors, and assembled a council at Pisa, Julius II. besieged Mirandola in person, lodged himself, with his trembling cardinals, under the fire of the city, and made his entrance there through the breach.

*Gaston of Foix.* — The ardour of Julius II., and the policy of the allies, were for an instant disconcerted by the sudden appearance of Gaston of Foix, the nephew of Louis XII., at the head of the French army. This young man, 22 years of age, arrived in Lombardy, gained three victories in three months, and died, leaving behind him the memory of the most impetuous general Italy had ever known. At first he intimidated or won the Swiss to his cause, and made them return to their mountains; he saved Bologna, which was besieged, and, favoured by the snow and a hurricane, he rushed with his army into the city (7th February). On the 18th he was before Brescia, which had been retaken by the Venitians; on the 19th he had taken it by storm; on the 11th of April he died a conqueror, at Ravenna. In the terrific rapidity of his success, he spared neither his own troops nor the vanquished. Brescia, during seven days, was delivered up to the fury of the soldiery; and it is said that the conquerors massacred 15,000 persons, men, women, and children. Truly, the Chevalier Bayard had few imitators.

Gaston, on his return to Romagna, attacked Ravenna, in order to force the army of Spain and the pope to accept battle.* The cannonade having commenced, Pedro de Navarre, who had formed the Spanish infantry, and relied on them for victory, kept them lying flat on their faces, expecting, with cold-blooded indifference, that the cannon-balls would cut to pieces the gendarmerie of the two armies. The Italian soldiers lost all command of themselves, and were beaten by the French. The Spanish infantry, after having sustained the combat with an obstinate valour, retreated slowly. Gaston, furious with indignation, precipitated himself, with twenty soldiers, upon them, penetrated into their ranks, and there found his death (1512).

From that time success no longer attended Louis XII. The Sforza were re-established at Milan, and the Medicis at Florence. The army of the king was beaten by the Swiss at Navarre, by the English at Guinegate. France, attacked in front by the Spaniards and Swiss, beset in the rear by the English, beheld her two allies of Scotland and of Navarre vanquished and plundered. (See chap. ii.)

* See the letter of the Chevalier Bayard to his uncle, vol. xvi. of the Collection of Memoirs.

The war had no longer an object. The Swiss reigned at Milan under the name of Maximilian Sforza; France and Venice were humbled; the emperor was exhausted, Henry VIII. discouraged, Ferdinand satisfied with the conquest of Navarre, which opened to him the frontier of France. Louis XII. concluded a truce with Ferdinand, abjured the Council of Pisa, left Milan to Maximilian Sforza, and espoused the sister of Henry VIII. (1514). (See, later, his administration.)

*Francis I.*, 1515—*Marignan.*—While Europe believed that France was prostrated, and, as it were, superannuated with Louis XII., she displayed unexpected resources under the young Francis I., who had just succeeded him (1st of January, 1515). The Swiss, who supposed that they had guarded all the passages of the Alps, heard with terror that the French army had opened a way through the valley of Argentière. Two thousand five hundred lancers, ten thousand Biscayans, and twenty-two thousand Landsknechts passed through a defile which had never been entered except by the hunters of the chamois. The French army advanced, while negotiating, as far as Marignan; there the Swiss, whom the French thought they had gained over, threw themselves upon their invaders with their pikes, eighteen feet long, and with broadswords in both hands, without artillery, without cavalry, and employing no other military resource but bodily strength, they marched in front of the batteries, the discharges of which carried away whole files of their troops, and sustained more than thirty charges from those great war-horses, covered with steel like the soldiers who mounted them. In the evening they had broken the line of the French army. The king, who had fought most bravely, saw but a small number of his men around him. But during the night the French collected their dispersed troops, and the battle was renewed in the morning, more furiously than ever. At last the Swiss, hearing the war-cry from the Venitians, the allies of France, *Marco! Marco!* were persuaded that all the Italian army had arrived; they closed their ranks, and retreated, but with so proud an air that no one dared to pursue them.* Having obtained from Francis I. more money than Sforza was able to give them, they appeared no more in Italy. The pope also made

* *Letter of Francis I. to his Mother.* "All night we remained in the saddle, the lance in hand, the helmet on the head .... and because I was the nearest to our enemies, I was obliged to keep watch, so that they did not surprise us in the morning ... and believe, madame, that we have been 28 hours on horseback, without eating or drinking. For two thousand years there has never been seen so fierce and so cruel a battle; they say that that of Ravenna was but trifling compared to this ... and let no one say that the gens d'armes are armed hares, for ... Written in the camp of St. Brigide, Friday, 14th September, 1515."—17th vol. of Collection of Memoirs.

a treaty with the conqueror, and obtained from Francis the concordat which abolished the pragmatic sanction. The alliance of the pope and Venice seemed to open to Francis I. the way to Naples. The youthful Charles of Austria, sovereign of the Netherlands, who had just succeeded his grandfather, Ferdinand the Catholic, in Spain, had need of peace to regulate his vast heritage. Francis I. enjoyed his victory, instead of completing it. The treaty of Noyon gave a moment of repose to Europe, and allowed the two rivals time to prepare for a more terrible conflict (1516).

# SECOND PERIOD.

## FROM THE REFORMATION TO THE TREATY OF WESTPHALIA.

## 1517–1648.

M

# SECOND PERIOD.

## INTRODUCTION.

If we regard only the series of wars and of political events, the sixteenth century is an age of blood and ruin. It opens with the devastation of Italy by the merciless troops of Francis I. and of Charles V., and the frightful ravages of Solyman, who annually depopulated Hungary. Then follow those terrible struggles of religious creeds, in which the war was one not only of nation against nation, but of city against city, and of man against man ; when it intruded even to the domestic fireside, and raged between father and son. They who should leave history at this crisis, would believe that Europe was about to fall into a state of profound barbarism. But far otherwise : the delicate plant of the arts and of civilization grew and gathered strength amid those violent shocks which seemed ready to destroy it. Michael Angelo painted the Sixtine Chapel the very year of the battle of Ravenna. The youthful Tartaglio rises from the destruction of Brescia to become the restorer of mathematics. The grand epoch of law among the moderns, the age of L'Hôpital and Cujacius, was also that of the massacre of St. Bartholomew.

The peculiar characteristic of the sixteenth century, and that which distinguished it so decidedly from the Middle Ages, was the *power of opinion*, which at that period truly became the *sovereign of the world*. Henry VIII. dared not repudiate Catharine of Aragon without consulting the principal universities of Europe. Charles V. sought to prove his faith by the persecution of the Moors, while his armies made a prisoner of, and ransomed the pope. Francis I. raised the first funeral pile which was ascended by the Protestants of France, in order to excuse to himself and his subjects his connexion with Solyman and with the Lutherans in Germany. Even these acts of intolerance were so much homage rendered to *public opinion*. Princes then courted the praises of those most unworthy to bestow renown. The Kings of France and Spain vied with each other in their eagerness to obtain the favour of Paul Jove, and of Peter Aretinus.

While France is slowly following Italy in the more elegant developments of intellect, two nations of a profoundly serious character relinquish to them the letters and arts, as trifling toys or profane amusements. The Spaniards, a politic people, inflamed with the lust of conquest, draw their strength, as the Romans did formerly, from their attachment to old maxims and ancient creeds. Occupied in conquering and governing Europe, they relied in all speculative matters upon the authority of the Church. While Spain inclines more firmly to a political and religious unity, Germany, with its anarchical constitution, surrenders itself to every variety of opinions and of systems. France, placed between both, will in the sixteenth century be the principal field of battle, where these two opposing spirits will contend. The conflict will be the more violent and lasting, in proportion as the forces are more equal.

---

## CHAPTER VI.

### LEO X., FRANCIS I., AND CHARLES V.

Francis I., 1515.—Charles V., Emperor, 1519.—First War against Charles V., 1521.—Disaffection of the Duke of Bourbon, 1523.—Battle of Pavia, 1525.—Captivity of Francis I.; Treaty of Madrid, 1526. —Second War, 1527.—Peace of Cambray, 1529.—Public Alliance of Francis I. with Solyman, 1534.—Third War, 1535.—Truce of Nice, 1538.—Renewal of Hostilities, 1541.—Battle of Cerisoles, 1544.—Treaty of Crespy; Death of Francis I. and Henry VIII., 1547.—Internal Situation of France and Spain; Reformation; First Persecutions, 1535.—Massacre of the Vaudois, 1545.

*Francis I. and Charles V.*—However severely

we may judge Francis I. and Leo X., we must guard against comparing them with that ignoble generation of princes who closed the preceding age (Alexander VI., Louis XI., Ferdinand the Catholic, James III., &c., &c.). In their faults even there was at least some glory, some grandeur. They certainly did not make the age in which they lived, but they showed themselves worthy of it; they loved the arts, and the arts at this day still speak for them, and demand an offering of thanks to their memory. The price obtained by selling the indulgences which roused Germany to resistance, paid for the paintings of the Vatican, and for the construction of St. Peter's. The extortions of Duprat are forgotten; but the royal establishment for printing, the College of France, remain.

Charles V., surrounded by his statesmen and his generals, between Lannoy, Pescaire, Antonio de Leyva, and as many other illustrious warriors, presents himself to us under a graver aspect. We see him constantly traversing Europe, to visit the widely-separated parts of his vast empire, speaking to each people in their own language, making war by turns upon Francis I. and the Protestants of Germany, upon Solyman and the barbarians. He was the true follower of Charlemagne, and the defender of the Christian world. In him the statesman predominated over the warrior. He presents to us the first model of the sovereigns of modern times ; Francis I. is but a hero of the Middle Ages. When the empire became vacant by the death of Maximilian I. (1519), and the Kings of France, of Spain, and of England claimed the imperial crown, the electors, fearing to become subjects of foreign power, offered the crown to one of their own number, Frederic *Le Sage* (the wise), elector of Saxony. This prince caused it to be given to Charles V., and merited his surname by the wisdom of his choice. Charles V. was the one of the three candidates whose power would be most inimical to the liberty of Germany, but he was also the most capable of defending it against the Turks. Selim and Solyman were reviving at this time the fears which had disturbed Europe in the time of Mohammed II. The master of Spain, of the kingdom of Naples, and of Austria, was alone able to close the civilized world against the barbarians of Africa and Asia.

Thus, with their competition for the imperial crown, broke out the bloody rivalry of Francis I. and Charles V. The former claimed Naples for himself, and Navarre for Henry of Albret ; the emperor demanded the imperial fief of Milan and the duchy of Burgundy. Their resources might pass as equal. If the empire of Charles was larger, it was not so compact as that of

France. His subjects were richer, but his authority was more limited. The French gendarmerie had not less reputation than the Spanish infantry. The victory would accrue to him who could engage the King of England in his party. Henry VIII., not without reason, took for his motto, *Whom I defend is Master*. Both gave a pension to his prime minister, Cardinal Wolsey, and both demanded his daughter Mary in marriage; one for the dauphin, and the other for himself. Francis I. obtained an interview with him near Calais, but, forgetting that he had still need to gain him, he eclipsed him by his grace and his magnificence.* Charles V., more artful, had anticipated that interview by visiting Henry VIII. in England. He had gained Wolsey by permitting him to hope for the papal crown. The negotiation was also much more easy for him than for Francis I. Henry VIII. was already indisposed towards the King of France, who governed Scotland by the Duke of Albany, his protégé and his subject,† to the prejudice of Margaret, the widow of James IV., and sister of the King of England. By an alliance with Charles

* The place of this interview was called the *Field of the Cloth of Gold.*

† Pinkerton, vol. ii., p. 135. The regent himself, in his despatches, calls the King of France *my master*, and he valued the great possessions which he had in France much more than the regency of the kingdom of Scotland.

V., too, he hoped to recover a part of those domains which his ancestors had formerly possessed in France.

Everything succeeded with the emperor. He gained Leo X., and he had afterward the merit of raising to the papal chair his preceptor, Adrian of Utrecht. The French, who penetrated into Spain, arrived too late to aid the insurgents (1521). The Governor of Milan, Lautrec, who, it is said, had exiled nearly half of the inhabitants of Milan, was driven from Lombardy. It was the same thing again the following year; the badly-paid Swiss demanded *discharge or battle,* and brought defeat on themselves at Bicoque. The money designed for the troops had been disposed of by the queen-mother, from hatred to the general.

*The Constable of Bourbon.*—At the moment when Francis I. expected to enter Italy, an internal enemy placed France in the greatest danger. He had bestowed favours on the Constable of Bourbon, one of those who had contributed most to the victory of Marignan. Charles, count of Montpensier, and dauphin of Auvergne, held from his wife, the granddaughter of Louis XI., the dukedom of Bourbon and the earldoms of Clermont, Marche, and other domains, which made him the greatest lord of the kingdom. At the death of his wife, the queen-mother, Louise of Savoy, who had wished to unite herself to the constable, but who had received a refusal, now desired his ruin, as she could not marry him. She contested his title to that rich inheritance, and obtained through her son, that the property should be put in sequestration. Bourbon, enraged, resolved to join the emperor (1523). A century before, this revolt would have involved no idea of disloyalty. The most accomplished chevaliers of France had entered into the *League for the Public Good.* More recently, in Spain, Don Pedro de Giron, discontented with Charles V., had been seen to renounce to his face all obedience to him, and to take the command of the *Communeros.* But here was no question of a revolt against the king; at that epoch it was impossible in France. This was a conspiracy against the very existence of France, which Bourbon was plotting with strangers. He had promised Charles V. to attack Burgundy as soon as Francis I. had passed the Alps, and to excite a rebellion in five provinces, of which he believed himself master; the kingdom of Provence was to be re-established in favour of the constable, and France, shared between Spain and England, would cease to exist as a nation. He soon enjoyed the misfortunes of his country. As general of the armies of the emperor, he saw the French fly before him at Brigassa; he beheld the Chevalier

Bayard mortally wounded, lying at the foot of a tree with his face towards the enemy, and said to him "that he felt great pain at seeing him in this state, who had been so virtuous a chevalier." Bayard replied, "Sir, pity me not, for I die a man of honour. But I pity you, who fight against your king, your country, and your oath."

Bourbon believed that, at his first appearance in France, his vassals would rank themselves with him under the imperial banners. Not a being moved. The Imperialists were repulsed at the siege of Marseilles, and only saved their exhausted army by a retreat, which seemed more like a flight. Instead of overthrowing the Imperialists in Provence, the king preferred to precede them into Italy.

*Pavia*, 1523. — At an epoch of military science and tactics, Francis I. believed himself still in an age of chivalry. He made it a point of honour not to retreat, even to conquer. With an obstinate courage, he maintained the siege of Pavia (1523). He gave no time to the badly-paid Imperialists to disperse of themselves. He weakened his army by sending a detachment of 12,000 soldiers towards Naples. His superiority consisted in his artillery; he wished to decide the victory by the gendarmerie, as at Marignan; he precipitated himself before his artillery, and rendered it useless. The Swiss fled; the Landsknechts, with their colonel, the *White Rose*,* were entirely destroyed. Then all the weight of the battle fell upon the king and his gendarmerie. The old heroes of the wars of Italy, Parlisse, and Tremouille, were laid prostrate; the King of Navarre, Montmorency, the *Adventurous*,† and a great many others, were made prisoners. Francis I. defended himself on foot; his horse had been killed under him, and his armour, which we still have, was all indented by the force of bullets and lances. Happily, one of the French gentlemen, who had revolted with Bourbon, perceived him, and saved his life; but he would not surrender himself to a traitor, and he sent for the viceroy of Naples, who received his sword on his knees. According to tradition, he wrote in the evening a single word to his mother: "*Madame, all is lost except our honour!*"‡

*Captivity of the King — Treaty of Madrid.*— Charles V. knew well that *all was not lost;* he did not exaggerate his success; he felt that France was strong and entire, notwithstanding the loss of

* The Duke of Suffolk. † The Marshal de Fleuranges.

‡ See the letter, in which Charles V. informs the Marquis de Denia of the captivity of Francis I. (Sandoval, pt. i., b. vii. § 11, p. 487, fol., Antwerp, 1581), and the letter of Louise de Savoy, written to the emperor in favour of her son, and that of Francis I. to the different orders of the state, and the Act of Abdication, vol. xxi., p. 69, 71, and 84 of the *Collection of Memoirs*.

an army. He hoped only to draw from his prisoner an advantageous treaty. Francis I. had arrived in Spain, judging from his own feelings that it would be sufficient for him to see *his good brother* in order to be sent back honourably to his kingdom. But he did not find it so. The emperor ill treated his prisoner to obtain from him a richer ransom. In the mean time, Europe evinced the highest interest in behalf of this *soldier king*.* Erasmus, the subject of Charles V., dared to write to him in favour of his captive. The Spanish nobles demanded that he might be a prisoner on parole, and offered themselves as his security. But it was only at the expiration of a year, when Charles V. feared that his prisoner might escape from him by death, and when Francis I. had abdicated in favour of the dauphin, that he decided to release him, making him sign a most disgraceful treaty. The King of France renounced his pretensions to Italy —promised to do justice to the claims of Bourbon— to yield Burgundy—to give his two sons as hostages, and to ally himself by a double marriage with the family of Charles V. (1526).

At this price Francis was free. But he did not leave that fatal prison as he had entered it; he left behind that noble frankness of character, that

* The expression of Montluc, speaking to Francis I. himself, vol. xxi., p. vi.

heroic confidence which, until then, had formed his glory. Even at Madrid he had secretly protested against the treaty. Reinstated as king, it was not difficult for him to elude it. Henry VIII., alarmed at the victory of Charles V., had allied himself with France. The pope, Venice, Florence, Genoa, even the Duke of Milan, who, since the battle of Pavia, had all been in the power of the imperial armies, now regarded the French only as liberators. Francis I. caused the States of Burgundy to proclaim that he had no authority to give up any part of France; and when Charles V. claimed the performance of the treaty, accusing him of perfidy, he replied that he *lied from his throat*, and challenged him to *meet him in the field*, at the same time proffering to the emperor a choice of weapons.

*Taking of Rome*, 1527.—While Europe was expecting a terrible war, Francis I. thought only how to make a compromise with his allies, in order to alarm Charles V., and ameliorate the conditions of the treaty of Madrid. Italy remained a prey to the most hideous war which had ever dishonoured humanity; it was less of a war than a long chastisement inflicted by a ferocious soldiery upon a disarmed people. The badly-paid troops of Charles V. would neither obey him nor any other power; they even ruled their generals. During ten entire months Milan was abandoned to the barbarity of the Spaniards. As soon as it was known in Germany that Italy was thus delivered up to pillage, thirteen or fourteen thousand Germans passed the Alps, commanded by George Frondsberg, a furious Lutheran, who wore a chain of gold on his neck, with which he said he designed to strangle the pope. Bourbon and Leyva led, or, rather, followed this army of brigands. It gathered, as they proceeded, a crowd of Italians, who practised the vices of the barbarians, though they could not imitate their valour. The army took the road through Ferrara and Bologna; it was on the point of entering Tuscany, and the Spaniards swore only by the *glorious pillage of Florence*. A more powerful impulse, however, led the Germans, as it had formerly their predecessors, the Goths, towards Rome. Clement VII., who had made a treaty with the Viceroy of Naples, seeing the army of Bourbon approach, seemed to blind himself, or, rather, appeared to be fascinated by the very greatness of the danger. He discharged his best troops at the approach of the Imperialists, believing, perhaps, that Rome disarmed would inspire them with some respect. On the morning of the 6th of May, Bourbon commenced the assault (1527). He wore a white uniform, that he might be more easily distinguished by his own, and by the enemy's men.

In such an odious enterprise, success alone could restore his self-esteem. Perceiving that his German foot-soldiers but slowly aided him, he seized a ladder and mounted it, when a ball struck his loins; he felt that the blow was fatal, and ordered his attendants to cover his body with his cloak, and thus to conceal his fall. His soldiers but too well avenged his death. From seven to eight thousand Romans were massacred the first day; nothing was spared, neither convents nor churches; not even St. Peter's. The streets were strewed with relics, and with the ornaments of the altars, which the Germans threw away, after having stripped them of the gold and silver. The Spaniards, still more rapacious and cruel, renewed every day, during nearly a year, the most frightful atrocities of the victory; everywhere was heard the cry of miserable beings whom they tortured even to death, to make them confess if they had concealed any money. Often they tied them in their houses, that they might find them again when they wished to renew their torture.

*Lautrec—Doria.*—Great was the indignation of Europe when it heard of the pillage of Rome, and of the captivity of the pope. Charles V. ordered prayers for the deliverance of the pontiff, who was more a prisoner of the imperial army than of the emperor. Francis I. believed this a favourable moment to introduce those troops into Italy, which some months sooner might have saved Rome and Milan. Lautrec marched towards Naples, while the imperial generals negotiated with their soldiers, to induce them to leave Rome ; but, as in the first wars, they gave them no money. The plague destroyed the French army. Yet nothing was lost as long as they preserved an intercourse with France by sea. Francis I. most imprudently displeased the Genoese Doria, the first mariner of the age. *It seems*, said Montluc, *that the sea dreads this man.* They kept from him the ransom of the Prince of Orange ; they did not pay the mariners of his galleys, and they appointed to his prejudice an admiral of the Levant; and what irritated him still more was, that Francis I. did not respect the privileges of Genoa, and wished to transport to Savona the commerce of that city. Instead of compensating him for these various grievances, the king gave orders to arrest him. Doria, whose engagement with France had just expired, offered himself to the emperor on condition that his country should be independent, and again govern in Liguria. Charles V. offered to acknowledge him for Prince of Genoa, but Doria preferred to be the first citizen of a free city.

*Treaty of Cambray*, 1529.—In the mean time, the two nations desired peace. Charles V. was alarmed at the progress of the Reformation, and by the invasion of the terrible Solyman, who had just encamped before Vienna. Francis I., whose resources were exhausted, thougnt only how to restore his wasted kingdom at the expense of his allies. He wished to redeem his children, and to retain Burgundy. Even when at the point of signing the treaty, he protested to his allies of Italy that he would not separate his interests from theirs. He refused permission to the Florentines to make a separate peace with the emperor, and he signed the treaty of Cambray, by which he abandoned them, the Venitians, and all his partisans, to the vengeance of Charles V. (1529). This wretched treaty forever banished the French power from Italy. From that time the principal theatre of war will be everywhere else: in Savoy, in Picardy, in the Netherlands, and in Lorraine.

*Charles V. in Africa*, 1535.—While the Christian world hoped to enjoy some tranquillity, a plague, until then unknown, depopulated the shores of Italy and of Spain. Towards this period, the corsairs of Barbary began to make the *treaty des blancs.* The Turks first devastated the countries which they intended to invade; it was thus that they made almost a desert of Southern Hungary, and of the western provinces of the ancient Grecian Empire. The Tartars and the infidels of the Barbary States skirmishing troops of the Ottoman power, contributed, the one in the East, the other in the South, to this system of depopulation. The knights of Rhodes, whom Charles V. had established on the island of Malta, were too weak to clear the sea of those innumerable vessels with which Barbarossa, the Dey of Tunis, and the Admiral of Solyman had covered it. Charles V. resolved to attack the pirate in his own retreat (1535). Five hundred vessels transported to Africa an army of thirty thousand men, composed in great part of veteran troops, who had been engaged in the wars of Italy. The pope and the King of Portugal had enlarged this fleet. Doria had joined his galleys to it, and the emperor himself, with the élite of the Spanish nobility, embarked in it. Barbarossa had not forces enough to oppose the most formidable armament which the Christian world had sent against the infidels since the Crusades. Goletta was taken by assault, Tunis surrendered itself, and 20,000 Christians delivered from slavery, and brought back to their country at the expense of the emperor, caused all Europe to bless the name of Charles V.

*Alliance of Francis I. with Solyman.*—The conduct of Francis I. presents a painful contrast. He had just declared his alliance with Solyman, when he made a treaty with the Protestants of Germany, and with Henry VIII., who had repudiated the aunt of Charles V., and had abandoned the Church. Neither of them afforded the aid which he had expected from them. Solyman had gone to lose his janizaries in the boundless plains of Asia. Henry VIII. was too much occupied with the religious revolution in his own kingdom, which proceeded with so much violence. The confederates of Smalcalde had no confidence in a prince who caressed the Protestants at Dresden, and burned them in Paris. Francis I. was not deterred from renewing the war; he invaded Savoy, and threatened Milan (1535). The Duke of Savoy, alarmed by the claims of the mother of the King of France (Louise of Savoy), had espoused the sister-in-law of Charles V. The Duke of Milan, accused by the emperor of making a treaty with the French, endeavoured to exculpate himself from the charge by having, on some trifling pretext, the ambassador of Francis I. beheaded. Charles V. announced in Rome, in the presence of the envoys from all the Christian world, that he was assured of victory, and declared that, "if he had not more resources than his rival, he would go that moment, with his arms tied, a cord around his neck, and throw himself at the feet of Francis and implore his pity." Before commencing the campaign, he shared between his officers the domains and the grand dignities of the crown of France.

*Provincial Legions.*—In fact, all the world believed that Francis I. was lost. They knew not what resources France had within itself. Since 1533, the king had decided to concentrate the military strength of France in the infantry, and in a national infantry. He remembered that the Swiss had caused the loss of the battle of Bicoque, and perhaps that of Pavia; that the landknechts had been withdrawn by the emperor on the eve of the battle of Ravenna. But thus to give arms to the people was, they said, running a great risk.* In an ordinance on the privileges of the chase, passed in 1517, he had forbidden any subject carrying arms under the severest penalty; yet now he decided to form seven provincial legions, each of 6000 men, and drawn from the frontier provinces. These troops were still undisciplined, when the armies of Charles V. entered at the same time into Provence, Champagne, and Picardy. As Francis I. did not rely upon their valour, he resolved to arrest the enemy by devasta-

* At the first sound of war, King Francis organized the legionaries, which was a very good expedient, had it only been followed up; for this is the true way to secure having always a good army on foot, as the Romans did, and to keep the people disciplined, although I know not if this be a benefit or an evil. The question is not a small one: Shall I prefer to trust myself to my countrymen, or strangers? (Montluc, vol. xx., p. 385). The Memoirs of Montluc and De Tavanes show that some gentlemen were placed in each legion, and that the bravest were those containing the most.

ting the country. All of Provence from the Alps to Marseilles, and from the sea to Dauphiny, was laid waste with inflexible severity, by the Marshal Montmorency; villages, farms, mills, were all burned, and not an appearance of cultivation remained. The marshal, established in an impregnable camp between the Rhone and Durance, was quietly waiting for the destruction of the emperor's army, which was before Marseilles. Charles V. was compelled to retreat, and was obliged to consent to a truce, of which the pope was the mediator (truce of Nice, 1538). A month after, Charles and Francis met at Aigues-Mortes; and these princes, who had treated each other so outrageously, one of whom accused the other of having poisoned the dauphin, now exchanged every assurance of fraternal affection.

*Feebleness of Charles V.* — The only cause of the truce was the exhausted power of the two rivals. Charles V. endeavoured to gain the Cortes of Castile by authorizing a permanent deputation in imitation of that of Aragon, and by renewing the law which excluded strangers from offices of the government; yet he was not able to obtain money either in 1527, or in 1533, or in 1538. The city of Ghent had taken up arms rather than pay a new tax. The administration of Mexico was not yet organized; Peru, as yet, belonged only to those who had conquered it, and who desolated it by their civil wars. The emperor had been obliged to sell a great part of the royal domains ; he had contracted a debt of seven millions of ducats, and could find no bank which would loan at 13 or 14 per cent. This penury excited towards 1539 a revolt, which was almost universal in the armies of Charles V. They rebelled in Sicily, pillaged Lombardy, and threatened to deliver Goletta to Barbarossa. The means to pay the arrears due to the soldiers, and to disband the greater part of them, had to be found, and at any price.

*Feebleness of Francis I.*—The King of France was scarcely less embarrassed. Since the reign of Charles VIII., the wealth of the nation had been rapidly developed through the effects of its internal tranquillity, but the expenses exceeded by far the resources. Charles VII. had 1700 armed men. Francis I. had 3000, without counting 6000 light-horsemen, and often twelve or fifteen thousand Swiss. Charles VII. levied less than two millions of taxes ; Louis XI. five millions, and Francis I. near nine millions. Since 1484,* the kings had not assembled the States-General to supply these expenses. They had substituted for them the assemblies of the notables (1526), and more frequently had raised money by ordinances, which

* Once only at Tours in 1506, and then only to annul the treaty of Blois.

they made the Parliament of Paris register. Louis XII., the *father of the people*, first diminished the taxes, and farmed them out (1499); but towards the end of his reign he was obliged to increase the duties, to make loans, and to alienate the royal domains (1511–1514). Francis I. established new taxes (particularly in 1525), sold and multiplied judicial offices (1515, 1522, 1524), founded the first perpetual revenue upon the *Hôtel de Ville*, transferred the royal domains (1532–1544), and instituted the Royal Lottery (1539).

In this facility of ruining himself Francis I. had the advantage over Charles V. He availed himself of it when the emperor had failed in his great expedition against Algiers (1541–1542). Two years before, Charles V., passing through France, when on his way to repress the revolt of Ghent, had amused the king with a promise to give to his second son, the Duke of Orleans, the investiture of Milan. The Duchess d'Etampes, who governed the king, seeing his powers weakened, and fearing the enmity of Diana of Poictiers, the mistress of the dauphin, made great efforts to procure for the Duke of Orleans an independent establishment, where she might also find an asylum at the death of Francis I. Add to this principal cause of the war the assassination of two French envoys, who, crossing Italy to go to the court of Solyman, were killed in Milan by the order of the imperial governor, who seized their despatches. Francis relied upon his alliance with the Turks, and upon his treaty with the Protestant princes of Germany, of Denmark, and of Sweden; he attached William, duke of Cleves, particularly to himself, by making him espouse his niece, Jeanne d'Albret, who afterward became the mother of Henry IV.; he invaded, at almost the same time, Roussillon, Piedmont, Luxembourg, Brabant, and Flanders. Solyman joined his fleet to that of France; they bombarded the castle of Nice in vain. But the odious spectacle of the crescent united to the *fleurs de lis* alienated all the Christian world from the King of France. Even those who, until now, had favoured him, became regardless of the interests of Europe, in order to unite themselves with Charles V. The empire declared itself against the alliance with the Turks. The King of England, who had been reconciled to Charles since the death of Catharine of Aragon, joined the party against the King of France, who had given his daughter to the King of Scotland. Henry VIII. defeated James V. (1543); Charles V. overthrew the Duke of Cleves (1543); and having nothing more to fear in the rear, they both agreed to invade the dominions of Francis I. France alone, with all against her, displayed an unexpected vigour;

she fought with five armies, and astonished the confederates by the brilliant victory at Cerisoles; the infantry gained that battle, lost by the gendarmerie. Charles V., badly supported by Henry VIII., and recalled by the progress of Solyman in Hungary, signed, at thirteen leagues from Paris, a treaty, by which Francis renounced his claims to Naples, Charles his to Burgundy. The Duke of Orleans was to take possession of Milan (1545). The King of France and Henry VIII. soon proclaimed peace, and they both died in the same year (1549).

The long contest between the two great powers of Europe is not yet terminated; but, for the future, it is combined with religious interests, which we cannot comprehend without tracing the progress of the Reformation in Germany. We will stop here, and take a retrospect of the past, and examine what has been the internal situation of Spain and of France during the rivalry of Francis I. and Charles V.

*Spain.*—In Spain, royalty was speedily verging towards that absolute power which it had attained in France. Charles V. imitated the example of his father, and made several laws without the sanction of the Cortes. In 1538, the nobles and the prelates of Castile, having rejected the general tax of the *Sisa*, which would have been raised upon the sale of provisions by retail, the King of Spain ceased to convoke them, alleging that they had no right to vote taxes which they did not pay. The Cortes were composed of but thirty-six deputies, sent by eighteen cities, which alone were represented. The nobles repented too late of having joined the king, for the purpose of overthrowing the *Communeros*, in 1521.

The power of the Spanish Inquisition increased more rapidly as Charles V. became more alarmed at the commotions in Germany, and more apprehensive for the political consequences of religious innovations. The Inquisition was introduced into the Netherlands in 1522, and if the Neapolitans had not most obstinately resisted, it would have been established among them in 1546. After having withdrawn from the Inquisition the right of exercising the royal jurisdiction (in Spain 1535–1543, in Sicily 1535–1550), it was again given to them. Since 1539, the inquisitor-general, Tabera, had governed Spain in the absence of the emperor, in the name of the Infante, afterward Philip II.

The reign of Francis I. was the most brilliant era in the history of royal power in France before the ministry of the Cardinal Richelieu. He commenced by concentrating in his own hands the ecclesiastical power by means of the Treaty of the

Concordat (1515), limited the ecclesiastical jurisdiction (1559), organized a system of police, and silenced the Parliaments. The Parliament of Paris had been weakened under Charles VII. and Louis XI. by the formation of the Parliaments of Grenoble, Bordeaux, and Dijon (1451, 1462, 1477); under Louis XII. by the Parliaments of Rouen and Aix (1499, 1501). During the captivity of Francis I., the Parliament endeavoured to recover some importance, and commenced a prosecution against the Chancellor Duprat. But the king, after his restoration, forbade them to interfere with political affairs, and again deprived them of their influence by increasing the offices under government, and authorizing them to be sold.

Francis I. boasted that he had placed kings from henceforth *beyond control.* But the increasing agitation of men's minds which we remark under his reign, augured new troubles. That spirit of freedom which was now applying itself to religion was one day to enter with redoubled vigour into political institutions. First, the reformers made remonstrances against the manners of the clergy; the *Colloquia* of Erasmus, of which there were 24,000 copies, were quickly exhausted. The Psalms, translated by Marot, were adapted to the airs of romance and sung by gentlemen and ladies at the court, while the ordinance which required the statutes, to be hereafter written in French, enabled all the world to know and to discuss political affairs (1538). The court of Margaret of Navarre, and that of the Duchess of Ferrara, Réné of France, were the rendezvous of all the partisans of the new opinions. The greatest levity of mind and the most profound fanaticism, Marot and Calvin, met each other at Nerac. Francis I. had at first seen these commotions without apprehension. He had protected the first Protestants of France against the clergy (1523–1524). In 1534, when he wished to make a treaty with the Protestants of Germany, he requested Melancthon to present a conciliatory confession of faith. He favoured the revolution of Geneva, which became the focus of Calvinism (1535). Yet, since his return from Madrid, he had become more severe towards the Protestants of France. In 1527 and in 1534 the fermentation caused by the new doctrines being manifested by outrages towards the images of saints, and by placards affixed to the Louvre, several Protestants were burned by a slow fire, in presence of the king and of all the court. In 1535 he ordered the suppression of the printing offices, under pain of death; but upon the remonstrance of Parliament in the same year, he revoked that ordinance, in order to establish the censorship.

The end of the reign of Francis I. was marked

by a frightful event: the Vaudois, who were inhabitants of some of the inaccessible valleys of Provence and Dauphiny, had retained the doctrines of Arius, and were about to adopt those of Calvin. The strength of their positions in the midst of the Alps caused some apprehension, and in 1540 the Parliament of Aix ordered that the two principal points of their union, Cabriere and Merindol, should be burned. After the retreat of Charles V. (1545), the decree was executed, notwithstanding the expostulations of Sadolet, bishop of Carpentras. The president D'Oppede, Guerin the advocate of the king, and Pauline, the old envoy of the king to the Turks, penetrated into the valleys, and with barbarous cruelty exterminated all the inhabitants, and converted the whole country into a desert. This terrible catastrophe may be considered as one of the first causes of our civil wars

# CHAPTER VII.

## LUTHER — REFORMATION IN GERMANY — WAR OF THE TURKS, 1517-1555.

Luther attacks the Sale of Indulgences, 1517.—He burns the Pope's Bull, 1520.—Diet of Worms, 1521.—Secularization of Prussia, 1525.—War of the Peasants of Swabia, 1524-5.—Anabaptists.—Catholic League, 1524.—Protestant League, 1526.—War of the Turks; Solyman, 1521.—Invasion of Hungary, 1526.—Siege of Vienna, 1529.—Diet of Spire, 1529.—*Confession* of Augsburg, 1530.—League of Smallkalde, 1531.—Revolt of the Anabaptists of Westphalia, 1534.—Troubles and internal Wars of Germany, 1534-46.—Council of Trent, 1545.—War of Charles V. against the Protestants; Battle of Muhlberg, 1547.—Revolt of Maurice of Saxony, 1551.—Peace of Augsburg, 1555.—Death of Charles V., 1558.

All the governments of Europe had attained a monarchical unity, and the system of equilibrium (balance of power) was established among them, when the ancient religious unity of the West was broken by the Reformation. This event, the greatest of modern times, together with the French Revolution, separated one half of Europe from the Roman Church, and led to the greater part of the revolutions and wars which took place before the treaty of Westphalia. Since the Reformation, we find Europe divided in a manner which coincides with the division of races. The Roman race have remained Catholics. Protestantism reigns over those of the Germanic race, and the Greek Church among the *Slavonic* nations.

The *first* epoch of the Reformation presents Luther and Zwingle in opposition, the *second* Calvin and Socinus. Luther and Calvin retained a part of the dogmas of the Church, and of its hierarchy. Zwingle and Socinus reduced religion by degrees to deism. The pontifical monarchy was overthrown by the Lutheran aristocracy, and this is attacked by Calvinistic democracy. It was a reformation within the Reformation. During both the first and second periods, some ancient anarchical sects, who were composed partly of prophetic visionaries, arose, and gave to the Reformation the formidable aspect of a war against society ; these were the Anabaptists in the first period, the Independents and Levellers in the second.

The principle of the Reformation was essentially active and progressive. Divided even in its infancy, it spread itself over Europe under a hundred different forms. Repulsed in Italy, in Spain, in Portugal (1526), in Poland (1523), the privileges allowed to the Calistins contributed to its establishment in Bohemia: in England the remembrance of Wickliffe was its support, and it proceeded adapting itself to every degree of civilization, and conforming to the wants of every country. Democratic in Switzerland (1525), aristocratic in Denmark (1527), it associated itself with the royal power in Sweden (1529), and in the Empire with the cause of Germanic privileges.

## § I. ORIGIN OF THE REFORMATION.

*Reformation*, 1517—*Leo. X.*—In the memorable year 1517, from which we generally date the commencement of the Reformation, neither Europe nor the pope, nor Luther himself, had dreamed of so great an event. The Christian princes had leagued themselves against the Turks. Leo X. had invaded the duchy of Urbino, and raised to the highest pinnacle the temporal power of the Holy See. Notwithstanding the embarrassment of his finances, which obliged him to make a sale of indulgences in Germany, and to create at one time thirty-one cardinals, yet he lavished with prodigality the treasures of the Church upon artists and men of letters. He sent even to Denmark and Sweden in search of monuments of the history of the North. He authorized the sale of *Orlando Furioso** by the pope's letter, and received an eloquent epistle from Raphael upon the restoration of the antiquities of Rome. In the midst of these cares, he learned that a professor of the new University of Wittemberg, named Martin Luther, already known by having in the preceding year ven-

* Published in 1516

tured some bold *opinions* in matters of faith, had just attacked the sale of indulgences. Leo X., who himself corresponded with Erasmus, was not alarmed by these novelties; he replied to the accusers of Luther that he was a man of talents, and that the whole dispute was only a quarrel of monks.*

*Luther.*—The University of Wittemberg was founded by the Elector of Saxony, Frederic the Wise, and was one of the first in Germany where Platonism had triumphed over school divinity, and where literary instruction was associated with that of law, theology, and philosophy. Luther had at first studied law, afterward he became monk, and then, having taken the monastic habit in a fit of devotion, he had resolved to seek philosophy from Plato, and religion in the Bible. But he was less distinguished by his extensive knowledge than by a vivid and passionate eloquence, and, by a facility then extraordinary, of discoursing upon philosophical and religious subjects in his mother tongue; *it was this by which he carried away all the world.*† This impetuous spirit, once let loose, went farther than he had intended.‡ He attacked first the

* *Che fra Martino aveva bellissimo ingegno, e che coteste erano invidie fratesche.* † Bossuet.

‡ Luther, in his preface to the *Captivity of Babylon*, says, "In spite of myself, I am forced to become wise, from day to day, since masters so renowned attack me, now together, then separately. I have written for

abuse, then the principle of indulgences, afterward the intercession of saints, auricular confession, purgatory, the celibacy of the priests, and transubstantiation ; finally, the authority of the Church, and the character of her visible head. He was entreated to retract by the legate Cajetan, but in vain ; he appealed from the legate to the pope, from the pope to a general council ; and when the pope had condemned him he dared to retaliate, and solemnly burned on the square of Wittemberg the bull of condemnation and the volumes of the canon law (15th of June, 1520).

*Zwingle.*—An act so daring seized all Europe with astonishment. The greater part of the sects and heretics had formed themselves in secret, and would have been happy to remain unknown. Zwingle himself, whose preaching at the same

ten years on indulgences, but I now repent that I published this little volume. I was still wavering, from a superstitious respect for the tyranny of Rome ; I then believed that indulgences should not be condemned ; but since, thanks to Sylvester and other defenders of indulgences, I have learned that they are but an invention of the papal court to destroy faith in God, and get wealth from men. Finally came Eccius and Emser with their band, to teach me the supremacy and unlimited power of the pope. Not to show myself ungrateful towards such learned men, it becomes me to acknowledge that I have profited much by their writings. *I denied* that popery was of Divine right ; I admitted that it was of human origin. After having heard and read the subtleties by which these poor people would raise their idol, I am convinced that the papacy is the kingdom of Babylon and the power of Nimrod, the *strong huntsman.*"

period had withdrawn half the Swiss from the authority of the Holy See, did not announce himself with such boldness.* They imagined that something very great must belong to him who had constituted himself the judge of the head of the Church. Luther pronounced his own boldness and his success a miracle.

*Causes which favoured the Reformation.*—In the mean time, it was easy to perceive how many favourable circumstances encouraged the reformer. The pontifical monarchy, which alone had brought some harmony into the anarchical chaos of the Middle Ages, had successively been weakened by the progress of royal power and of civil order. The scandals with which a great proportion of

* Zwingle, a cure of Zurich, commenced preaching in 1516: the cantons of Zurich, of Basle, of Schaffhausen, of Berne, and the allied cities of St. Gaul and of Muhlhausen, embraced his doctrine. Those of Lucerne, Uri, Schwitz, Unterwalden, Zug, Fribourg, Sololhurn, and Valais, remained faithful to the Catholic religion. Glari and Appenzel were divided. The inhabitants of the Catholic cantons, democratic in their form of government, and dwelling almost altogether without the cities, retained their ancient forms of worship, and received pensions from the pope and from the King of France. Francis I. in vain offered himself as mediator between the Swiss; the Catholic cantons would not accept the proposed pacification; those of Zurich and of Berne cut off their supplies. The Catholics invaded the territory of Zurich, and gained a battle over the Protestants, in which Zwingle was killed, fighting at the head of his flock (battle of Cappel, 1531). The Catholics, more barbarous, more valiant, and less rich, would have conquered, but they were not able to support the war for so long a time as the Protestant cantons.—Sleidan. Müller, *Univ. Hist.*, vol. ii., p. 159.

priests afflicted the Church, daily undermined an edifice already shaken by the spirit of doubt and of contradiction. Two circumstances contributed to complete her ruin. First, the invention of printing gave to the innovators of the sixteenth century the means of communicating and propagating their tenets, which were wanted by those of the Middle Ages, and which enabled them to resist a power as strongly organized as that of the Church. Afterward the financial embarrassment of many of the princes induced them to avail themselves of a doctrine which placed the riches of the clergy at their disposal. Europe at that period presented a remarkable spectacle, in the disproportion between its wants and its resources, a result of the recent elevation of a central power in each state. The Church paid the balance. Several Catholic sovereigns had already obtained permission from the Holy See to exercise a part of its privileges. The princes of the North of Germany, whose independence was threatened by the master of Peru and Mexico, found their Indies in the secularization of ecclesiastical wealth.

*Germany necessarily the Birthplace of the Reformation.*—The Reformation had already been attempted several times: in Italy by Arnold of Brescia, by Waldus in France, and by Wickliffe in England. But in Germany it was to have a firmer foundation. The German clergy were richer, and, consequently, more envied. The Episcopal sovereignties of the Empire were given to the younger branches of noble families, who brought the violent and scandalous manners of worldly men into the ecclesiastical ranks. But the greatest hatred was against the court of Rome, against the Italian clergy, whose fiscal genius had exhausted Germany. From the time of the Roman Empire, the constant opposition between the North and the South seemed as if personified in Germany and Italy. In the Middle Ages there was some order in the combat; power and intellect, violence and politics, the feudal system and Catholic hierarchy, hereditary succession and elective government, were prizes in the contests of the Empire with the priesthood; the critical spirit, at its revival, prefaced an examination of opinions by an attack upon persons. In the fifteenth century, the Hussites forced some concessions by a war of thirty years. In the sixteenth, the connexion of the Italians with the Germans only served to augment their ancient antipathy. Led constantly into Italy by the wars, the men of the North were scandalized at the magnificence of the popes, and those pageantries with which worship delights to surround itself in Southern countries. The ignorance of the Germans increased their displeasure; they regarded as profane all that they could not comprehend, and when they repassed the Alps, they excited the horror of their barbarous fellow-citizens by describing to them the *idolatrous feasts of the new Babylon.*

*Diet of Worms,* 1521 — *Luther at Wartburg.*— Luther knew well the state of their minds. When he was summoned by the new emperor to the Diet of Worms, he did not hesitate to go there. His friends reminded him of the fate of John Huss. " I am legally summoned to appear at Worms," he replied, " and should I see conspired against me as many devils as there are tiles on the roofs, I would go there in the name of the Lord." A great number of his partisans insisted upon attending him, and he entered the city escorted by a hundred armed knights. Having refused to retract, notwithstanding the public request and the private solicitations of the princes and electors, he was exiled from the Empire a few days after his departure. Charles V. also declared himself against the Reformation. He was King of Spain ; he needed the influence of the pope in his affairs in Italy ; finally, his title of Emperor, and of First Sovereign of Europe, constituted him the defender of the ancient faith. Similar motives influenced Francis I. ; the new heresy was condemned by the University of Paris. The young King of England, Henry VIII., who made pretensions to theology, wrote a volume against Luther. But he found zealous defenders in the princes of Germany, especially in the Elector of Saxony, who seemed to have even put him forward. This prince had been the imperial vicar in the interregnum, and it was then that Luther had dared to burn the bull of the pope. After the Diet of Worms, the elector, thinking that affairs were not yet matured, resolved to preserve Luther from the effects of his own impetuosity. In returning from the Diet of Worms, when in the midst of the forest of Thuringen, Luther was carried off by some masked horseman, who concealed him in the castle of Wartburg. Shut up for nearly a year in this place of captivity, which, however, seemed to have governed all Germany, the Reformer commenced his translation of the Bible into the German language, and inundated Europe with his writings. These theological pamphlets, printed as soon as written, penetrated into the most distant provinces, and were read by families at their evening reunion; and the invisible preacher was heard throughout all the Empire. Never had writer so entirely understood the feelings of the people. His fierce audacity, his satirical jesting, his apostrophes to the higher powers of the world, to the bishops, to the pope, to the King of England, whom he treated *with a magnificent contempt of them and of Satan,* charmed and excited all Germany; and the burlesque parts of these popular dramas only rendered their influence more sure. Erasmus, Melancthon, and the greater number of learned men, pardoned the proud boasting and vulgarity of Luther for the violence with which he attacked the scholastic divinity of the schools. The princes applauded a reformation which conduced to their gain. Besides, Luther, while exciting the passions of the people, forbade the use of any other weapon than that of words. "It was the word," said he, "which, while I slept tranquilly and drank my beer with my dear Melancthon, has shaken popery more than prince or emperor ever did."

*Albert of Brandenbourg,* 1525.—But in vain did he flatter himself that he could restrain passions, once excited, within the boundaries of an abstract discussion; men were not slow in deducing from his principles more rigorous consequences than he wished. The princes had taken possession of ecclesiastical property; Albert of Brandenbourg, Grand-master of the Teutonic Order, secularized one state entirely; he espoused the daughter of the new King of Denmark, and declared himself the hereditary Duke of Prussia, under the Lord-paramount of Poland. This was a terrible precedent in an empire full of ecclesiastical sovereigns, who might be tempted to essay a similar usurpation (1525).

*Effect of the Reformation upon the people*, 1524—*Anabaptists*.—Yet this was not the greatest danger. The lower class of people and the peasants, who, for a long time, had been stupified under the weight of feudal oppression, heard the learned and the princes speak of liberty and of enfranchisement, and they applied to themselves sentiments which were not uttered for them. The demand of the poor peasants of Swabia will ever remain, in its rustic simplicity, a monument of courageous moderation.* By degrees, the constant hatred of the poor against the rich was revived, blind and furious, as in the *Jacquerie*, but already assuming a systematic form, as in the time of the *Levellers*. It was complicated with all the first principles of religious democracy which had been suppressed in the Middle Ages. Lollards, Beghards, a crowd of prophetic visionaries, were roused. The rallying-word was the necessity of a second baptism; the aim, a terrible war against established order, and every kind of order; a war against property, it was robbery for the benefit of the poor; a war against science, it destroyed the equality of nature, and tempted God, who had revealed all to his

* Diè 12 Artikel der Bauernschaft. See, at the end of Sartorius, Bauernkrieg, and in the German works of Luther, Wittemberg, 1569, vol. ii., p. 64.

saints; books and paintings were inventions of the devil. The fiery Carlostadt had already given the example, by rushing from church to church, breaking the images and destroying the altars. At Wittemberg the students burned their books before the eyes of Luther. The peasants of Thuringia, imitating those of Swabia, followed the enthusiast Muncer, overthrew Muhlhausen, called the workmen of the mines of Mansfeld to arms, and endeavoured to join themselves to their brethren of Franconia (1524). On the Rhine, in Alsace and in Lorraine, in Tyrol, Carinthia, and Styria, the people everywhere took arms. The magistrates of every place were deposed; the lands of the nobility were seized, and the people forced the nobles to exchange their titles and their clothes for common names and apparel like their own. All the Catholic and Protestant princes armed themselves against them; the heavy cavalry of the nobles crushed them in a moment, and they were treated like wild beasts.

### § II. FIRST STRUGGLE AGAINST THE REFORMATION.

The secularization of Prussia, and especially the revolt of the Anabaptists, gave to the Reformation a most threatening political character. The two opinions became two parties (Catholic at Ratisbon, 1524, and at Dessau; Protestant at Torgau,

1526). The emperor watched for the proper moment to overthrow one by the other, and, at the same time, to subject both Catholics and Protestants. He believed that the moment had arrived when the victory of Pavia made his rival a captive. But in the year following a universal league in the West was formed against him. The pope and all Italy, Henry VIII., his ally, declared war against him. At the same time, the election of Ferdinand to the thrones of Bohemia and Hungary drew the house of Austria into the civil wars of that kingdom, and (if we may thus speak) unmasked Germany, and placed her face to face with Solyman.

*Selim—Solyman,* 1521—*Siege of Vienna,* 1529. —The progress of the Ottoman barbarism, which daily approached nearer, complicated the affairs of Europe in a most alarming manner. The Sultan Selim, that rapid conqueror, whose ferocity made the Turks themselves tremble, had just doubled the extent of the dominion of the Osmanlis. This tiger, by three bounds, had seized Egypt, Syria, and Arabia. The brilliant cavalry of the Mamelukes had perished at the foot of his throne, in the great massacre at Cairo.* He had sworn to break the *red heads,*† in order afterward to turn the strength

* "Hi ! c'est Sultan Selim ! . . ." Allusion of an Arab poet to this massacre in Kantimir.

† The Persians are so called by the Turks.

of the Mohammedan nations against the Christians. A cancer, of which he died, absolved him from keeping this oath. *In the year* 926 *of the Hegira* (1521), *Sultan Selim passed to the Eternal Kingdom, leaving the empire of the world to Solyman.** Solyman the Magnificent girded on the sabre at Stamboul the same year that Charles V. received the imperial crown at Aix-la-Chapelle. He commenced his reign by the conquest of Belgrade and Rhodes, the two keys of Mohammed II. (1521–2). The conquest of Rhodes secured to the Turks the empire of the sea, in the eastern part of the Mediterranean. Belgrade opened Hungary to them. When they invaded this kingdom in 1526, the young king, Louis, could assemble only 25,000 men against 150,000. The Hungarians, who, according to the ancient custom, took off the spurs from him who bore the standard of the Virgin, were nevertheless defeated at Mohaez. Louis and his general, Paul Tomorri, bishop of Colocza, were killed in the defeat, and a great many other bishops, who bore arms during the constant perils of Hungary, lost their lives. Two kings were elected at the same time, Ferdinand of Austria and John Zapoly, waywode of Transylvania. Zapoly, obtaining no assistance from Poland, applied to the Turks themselves. The ambassador

* Epitaph of Selim.

of Ferdinand, the gigantic Hobordanse, who was celebrated for having vanquished, in single combat, one of the most valiant pachas, had dared to brave the sultan; and Solyman had sworn that, if he did not find Ferdinand at Buda, he would go to Vienna to seek him. In the month of September, 1529, the dark circle of an innumerable army enclosed the capital of Austria. Happily, a crowd of valiant men, Germans and Spaniards, were found there. Among them were Don Pedro de Navarre, and the Count of Salm, who, if we believe the Germans, had taken Francis I. at Pavia. At the end of twenty days, and of twenty assaults, Solyman pronounced an anathema against the sultan who should again attack that fatal city. He departed in the night, destroying all bridges behind him, strangling his prisoners, and on the fifth day he had returned to Buda. He consoled his wounded pride by crowning Zapoly, that unfortunate prince, who, at the same time, beheld from the windows of the citadel of Pesth 10,000 Hungarian prisoners, whom the Tartars of Solyman had surprised in celebrating the feast of Christmas, and whom they drove before them like flocks.

What was Germany doing while the Turks were breaking through all the ancient barriers, and while Solyman was dispersing his Tartars beyond Vienna? She was disputing about transubstantiation and about free-will. Her most illustrious warriors were seated in the diets, and were interrogating doctors. Such was the intrepid phlegm of that great nation—such its confidence in its own strength and numbers.

*Confession of Augsburg*, 1530—*League of Smalkalde*, 1530.—The war with the Turks and with the French, the taking of Rome, and the defence of Vienna, had so entirely occupied Charles V. and his brother, that the Protestants obtained toleration until the next council. But after the peace of Cambray, Charles V., seeing France exhausted, Italy in subjection, and Solyman repulsed, undertook to try the great cause of the Reformation. The two parties appeared at Augsburg. The disciples of Luther, who were designated by the general name of *Protestants*, since they had *protested* against the prohibition of innovation (Spire, 1529), wished to be distinguished from all the other enemies of Rome, whose excesses might bring reproach on their cause; from the Zwinglian Republicans of Switzerland, who were odious to the princes and the nobility; and, above all, from the Anabaptists, who were proscribed as the enemies of order and of society. Their confession, softened by the learned and peaceable Melancthon, who, with tears, addressed the two parties, was repulsed as heretical. They were commanded to renounce their errors upon pain of being put under the ban of the Empire (Augsburg, 1530). Charles V. seemed even ready to employ violence, and for a moment the gates of Augsburg were closed. The diet was scarcely dissolved when the Protestant princes reassembled at Smalkalde, and there concluded a defensive league, by which they were to form one body (December 31, 1530). They protested against Ferdinand's assumption of the title of King of the Romans. The contingents were settled; they applied to the Kings of France, of England, and of Denmark, to aid them, and they held themselves ready for a combat.

*Germany reunited by Solyman.* — The Turks seem again to be charged with the reconciliation of Germany. The emperor heard that Solyman had just entered Hungary at the head of 300,000 men, while the pirate Khair Eddyn Barbarossa, who was become Captain Pacha, had joined the kingdom of Tunis to Algiers, and was the terror of all the Mediterranean. Charles V. hastened to offer to the Protestants all that they had demanded: religious toleration, the preservation of secularized property until the next council, and admission to the Imperial Chamber.

*Defeat of the Turks.*—During the negotiation, Solyman was arrested for a month before a small and miserable town by the Dalmatian Juritzi. He endeavoured to gain time in going across the impassable roads of Styria, when the snow and ice already covered the mountains, but the formidable appearance of the army of Charles V. decided his retreat. Germany, reunited by the promises of the emperor, had made the greatest efforts. An army, composed of Italian, Flemish, Burgundian, Bohemian, and Hungarian troops, joined themselves to the imperial army, and brought a force of 90,000 foot-soldiers and 30,000 horsemen, of whom a great number were covered with iron.* Never, since the time of Godfrey d'Bouillon, had there been an army more European. The light cavalry of the Turks was soon surrounded and cut in pieces. The sultan only regained courage by going out from those narrow passages through which the Murr and Drave flow, and entering the plain of Waradin.

*Anabaptists of Munster — John of Leyden.*— Francis I. and Solyman now relieved each other in occupying Charles V. The sultan, after invading Persia, had gone to be crowned at Bagdad. The King of France attacked the emperor by making an assault upon his ally, Savoy. The decisive rupture between the Catholics and Protestants of Germany was delayed by this new war for twelve years, but the interval was not a period of peace.

* P. Zove, an eyewitness.

First, the Anabaptists broke out anew in Munster, under a more frightful form, and from the same anarchical phrensy, proceeded a strange government, a monstrous union of democracy and tyranny. The Anabaptists of Munster followed exclusively the Old Testament; they believed that, as Jesus Christ was of the race of David, his kingdom was to be of Jewish form. They acknowledged two prophets of God, David, and John of Leyden their chief, and two prophets of the devil—the pope and Luther. John of Leyden was a journeyman tailor, a daring and ferocious man, whom they had made their king, and who was to spread the kingdom of Jesus Christ throughout the world. The princes were beforehand with him.

*Council of Trent*, 1545.—The Catholics and the Protestants, who, during a short period, had formed one common cause against the Anabaptists, were afterward only more at enmity. They constantly spoke of a General Council; nobody desired it. The pope dreaded it; the Protestants challenged it in advance. The council (reunited at Trent, 1545) might bind the unity of the Catholic hierarchy more closely, but it could not restore the unity of the Church. The weapons of war alone could decide it. The Protestants had already driven the Austrians from Wurtemberg; they had dispossessed Henry of Brunswick, who took advantage of the judgments of the Imperial Chamber for his own profit. They incited the Archbishop of Cologne to imitate the example of Albert of Brandenburg, who had given them the majority in the Electoral Council.

*Battle of Muhlberg*, 1547.—When the war with France was terminated, Charles V. and his brother made a treaty with the Turks, and united themselves closely to the pope, in order to overthrow at the same time the religious and political liberties of Germany. The Lutherans, warned by the imprudence of Paul III., who proclaimed the war as if it had been a crusade, rose, under the Elector of Saxony and the Landgrave of Hesse, to the number of 80,000. Abandoned by France, England, and Denmark, who had excited them to the war, separated from the Swiss by their *horror of the blasphemies of Zwingle*, they were still strong enough if they had remained united. Charles V. diminished their numbers by taking from them, under the canons of Ingolstadt, Maurice, the young duke of Saxony, who had made a secret treaty with him, had betrayed the Protestant cause, and invaded the states of his father-in-law, the elector. Charles V. had now only to overthrow the isolated members of the league. Immediately after the death of Henry VIII. and Francis I. (21st January, 31st March, 1547), which event had deprived the Protestants of every hope of succour, he marched against the Elector of Saxony, and defeated him at Muhlberg, 24th April. The two brothers abused the power which that victory had obtained for them. Charles V. condemned the elector to death by a court-martial of Spanish officers, over whom the Duke of Alba presided, and deprived him of the cession of his electorate, which he transferred to Maurice. He retained the Landgrave of Hesse a prisoner, whom he had deceived by a cowardly stratagem, and showed that his victory was neither for the Catholic faith nor for the Constitution of the Empire.

Ferdinand imitated his brother. Since 1545 he had declared himself a feudatory of Solyman for the kingdom of Hungary, reserving all his forces for an attack upon Bohemia and Germany. He re-established the archbishopric of Prague, which had been so formidable to the ancient Hussites, and declared himself hereditary sovereign of Bohemia. In 1547 he endeavoured to raise an army without the authority of the States, in order to attack the Lutherans of Saxony, who were the allies of the Bohemians. That army was raised, but it was against the prince, who had violated his oaths. The Bohemians leagued themselves together for the defence of their constitution and of *their language.* The battle of Muhlberg delivered them to Ferdinand, who destroyed their privileges.

*Martinuzzi.* — Hungary had not less to complain of. The fatal war of Ferdinand against Zapoly had rendered this kingdom accessible to the Turks. All the national party, all those who would have neither the Turks nor the Austrians for masters, ranged themselves around the Cardinal George Martinuzzi (Uthysenitsch), who was tutor to the young son of Zapoly. This extraordinary man, who at twenty years of age still gained his living by attending to the fires in the royal palace of Buda, had become the master of Transylvania. The queen-mother calling the Turks to her aid, he treated with Ferdinand, who was at least a Christian; he caused the cry of war to be raised everywhere,* assembled in a few days 70,000 men, and at the head of his heiduques he conquered the city of Lippe, which the Austrians could not retake under the infidels. This success and this popularity alarmed the brother of Charles V. Martinuzzi had authorized the Transylvanians to repress the licentiousness of the German soldiers with arms. Ferdinand caused him to be assassinated, but this crime cost him Transylvania. The son of Zapoly was established there, and the

* Beeket's *History of Martinusius*, p. 324. A man on horseback, completely armed, and one on foot, holding a bloody sword, went throughout the country raising the cry of war, according to the ancient custom of Transylvania.

Austrians only preserved what they possessed of Hungary by paying tribute to the Ottoman Porte.

*Charles V.*—In the mean time, Charles V. oppressed Germany and threatened Europe. On the one side, he excepted from the alliance which he proposed to the Swiss, Basle, Zurich, and Schaffhausen, which he said belonged to the Empire; on the other side, he pronounced the sentence of outlaw against Albert of Brandenburg, who had become a feudatory of the King of Poland: he even disaffected Ferdinand, and separated the interests of the two branches of the house of Austria by endeavouring to transfer the succession of the Empire from his brother to his son. He had introduced the Inquisition in the Netherlands. In Germany, he wished to impose on the Catholics and Protestants his *Inhalt* (Interim), a conciliatory arrangement, which united them in one point, their hatred for the emperor. The Interim has been compared to the Establishment of Henry VIII., and not without reason; the emperor also assumed a privilege of the pope. When Maurice of Saxony, son-in-law of the landgrave, demanded the liberty of his father-in-law, which he had sworn to maintain, Charles V. declared to him that he absolved him from his oath.

But his most unfeeling act of arrogance was leading in his train the Landgrave and the venerable Elector of Saxony, as if to triumph in their persons over German liberty. Germany now, for the first time, saw strangers violate her territory in the name of the emperor: she was crossed in every sense by Italian mercenaries and by wild Spaniards, who laid Catholics and Protestants, friends and foes, equally under contribution.

*Maurice of Saxony—Pacification of Augsburg,* 1555.—To overthrow this unjust power, which seemed immovable, the young Maurice of Saxony, the principal instrument of the victory of Charles V., alone was competent. Charles V. had caused the Electorate of Saxony, and the place of the chief of the Protestants of Germany, to be transferred to a more able prince. Maurice found himself the sport of the emperor, who retained his father-in-law a prisoner. A number of little books and satirical prints, which circulated in Germany,* described him as an apostate, a traitor, and the scourge of his country. A profound dissimulation concealed the projects of Maurice: first he must raise an army without alarming the emperor; he engages to submit Magdeburg to the Interim, and to join the troops of the city to his own. At the same time, he made a secret treaty with the King of France. The emperor, having again refused liberty to the landgrave, received two manifestos

* Id., i., xxiii.

at the same time, one from Maurice in the name of Germany, which represented it to be plundered by the Spaniards, and outraged in the official history of Louis of Avilla ;* the other was from the King of France, Henry II., who styled himself Protector of the Princes of the Empire, and who placed a cap of liberty between two swords at the head of his manifesto.† While the French invaded the three bishoprics, Maurice marched rapidly towards Innspruck (1552). The aged emperor, sick and without troops, departed in the night, during a heavy rain, and was carried towards the mountains of Carinthia ; and had not a mutiny of his troops retarded Maurice, Charles V. would have fallen into the hands of his enemies. He was obliged to yield. The emperor concluded the convention of Passau with the Protestants, and the bad success of the war, which he continued against France, changed this convention to a definite peace (Augsburg, 1555). The Protestants professed their religion freely, retained the ecclesiastical property which they possessed before 1552, and were permitted to enter the Imperial Chamber. Such was the first victory of religious liberty ; the critical spirit, having thus obtained a legal existence, followed from this time a determined course through obstacles which were not able to retard it. (See

* Id., i., xxiv.

† Id. ibid.

farther on, the germes of war comprised in that peace.)

*Abdication of Charles V.*—The emperor, abandoned by fortune, "*who does not love old men,*"* resigned the Empire to his brother, his kingdom to his sons, and retired to end his days in the solitude of the monastery of St. Just. His own obsequies, which he celebrated while living, were but a too faithful picture of that eclipsed glory which he had survived.†

---

## CHAPTER VIII.

### THE REFORMATION IN ENGLAND AND THE NORTH OF EUROPE, 1521–1547.

### § I. ENGLAND AND SCOTLAND, 1527–1547.

Divorce of Henry VIII.—England separates herself from the Roman Church, March 30th, 1534.—*Pilgrimage of Grace.*—Persecution of Catholics and Protestants, 1540.—Attempts on Scotland, 1542.—Submission and Administrative Organization of Wales and Ireland.

THE Germanic States of the North, England, Sweden, and Denmark, followed the example of Germany; but in separating themselves from the Holy See, the last three states, influenced by the spirit of aristocracy, preserved in part the Catholic hierarchy.

* Saying of Charles V.

† A Spanish historian is said to have discovered proof, recently, that these alleged obsequies never took place.

*Henry VIII.*—The revolution effected by Henry VIII. ought not to be confounded with the true Reformation of England. That revolution only caused England to separate from Rome, and to confiscate the power and property of the Church for the benefit of the kings. Made, without conscience or conviction, by the king and the aristocracy, it was only the last term of that absolute power in which the English had indulged the crown, for half a century, in hatred of the anarchy of the Roses. The propagation of the ancient doctrines of Occam and Wickliffe rendered the higher classes indifferent to religious innovations. This official reform had nothing to do with that which operated at the same time among the lower orders of the people, through the spontaneous enthusiasm of the Lutherans, Calvinists, and Anabaptists, who came in crowds from Germany, the Netherlands, and Geneva. This Reformation soon predominated in Scotland, and finished by conquering the other in England.

*Anne Boleyn—Schism*, 1534.—The cause of the aristocratic and royal Reformation of England was trifling; it seemed to arise from the ephemeral passion of Henry VIII. for Anne Boleyn, maid of honour to the queen, Catharine of Aragon, aunt of Charles V. At the expiration of twenty years after marriage, he remembered that the queen had for some months been the wife of his brother. It was at the moment when the victory of Pavia, breaking the equilibrium of the West, had alarmed Henry VIII. at the success of the emperor, his ally; he went over to Francis, and solicited his divorce from Clement VII. The pope, threatened by Charles V., sought every means to gain time; and after having committed the judgment to the legates, he had the cause tried at Rome. The English were no longer pleased at the prospect of the divorce; besides the interest which Catharine inspired, they feared that a rupture with Spain would arrest the commerce of the Netherlands. They refused to resort to the markets of France, by which they might have replaced those of Flanders. In the mean time, some more daring counsellors, who had succeeded the cardinal legate, Wolsey, Cromwell, the Minister of State, and Cranmer, doctor of Oxford, whom Henry had made Archbishop of Canterbury, destroyed his scruples, by purchasing for him the approbation of the principal universities of Europe. The king triumphed at last, and the clergy of the kingdom were accused for having acknowledged as legate the disgraced minister. The deputies of the clergy only obtained their pardon by a present to the king of 100,000 livres, and by acknowledging him as the protector and supreme head of the Church of England. On the 30th of March, 1534, that declaration having passed both chambers in a bill, was sanctioned by the king, and any appeal to Rome was prohibited. On the 23d of the same month, Clement VII. pronounced sentence against the divorce, after the almost unanimous advice of his cardinals: thus England was separated from the Holy See.

*Prodigality of the King—Pilgrimage of Grace.*— This change, which seemed to terminate the revolution, was only the commencement of it. At first the king declared all ecclesiastical power suspended; the bishops, at the expiration of a month, must present a petition to resume the exercise of their authority. The monasteries were suppressed, and their property, equivalent to 7,000,000 of francs, was united to the crown. But the king soon dissipated all. It is said that he gave a landed estate to one of his cooks who presented him with some delicate dish. The valuable furniture of the convents, with their maps and their libraries, were seized and scattered in all directions. The pious monks were indignant; the poor no longer found their sustenance at the gates of the monasteries. The nobility and landholders imagined that if the convents ceased to exist, their property would not fall again to the crown, but would return to the representatives of the donors. The inhabitants of five counties of the north armed themselves, and marched towards London, to accomplish what they called the *Pilgrimage of Grace;* the other party negotiated with them, and promised much, but when they had dispersed, they hung them by hundreds.

*Bill of the Six Articles.*—The Protestants, who at that time abounded in England, thought that they would be able to establish themselves there, aided by this revolution. Henry VIII. taught them how much they had deceived themselves. Nothing in the world would induce him to renounce his title of *Defender of the Faith,* which his book against Luther had procured. He maintained the ancient faith by his bill of the *Six Articles,* and persecuted both parties with impartial intolerance. In 1540, Protestants and Catholics were drawn on the same hurdle from the Tower to Smithfield; the Protestants were burned as heretics, the Catholics hanged as traitors, for having denied the *supremacy.*

*Lambert.*—The king having in every point replaced the pope, solemnly established his religious and political infallibility. He forced the Parliament to make a decree that his proclamation should have the same power as bills passed in both chambers. But, what was more terrible, he believed in his own infallibility, and regarded as sacred every caprice of his passions. Of six wives which he had, two were driven away, two beheaded under the pretext of adultery: the last with difficulty escaped the same fate for having supported the opinions of the Protestants He exercised a cruel and meddling despotism in his family, and treated all the nation as if they were of his household. He had a translation made of the Bible, and prohibited all others ; those of good condition alone were permitted to read it, and any other individual was liable to one month's imprisonment for every time he opened the Bible. He wrote or revised two books himself for the religious instruction of the people (the Institution and Erudition of the Christian). He disputed in person against the innovators. A schoolmaster named Lambert, prosecuted for having denied the real presence, was called by the archbishop to the head of the Church ; the king argued with him, and after a five hours' dispute, asked him if he would yield or die ; Lambert chose death, and was burned. A yet stranger scene was the sentence of St. Thomas of Canterbury, who had died in 1170. He was cited to Westminster, as if alive, accused of treason, and at the expiration of the usual delay of thirty days, he was condemned for non-appearance. His relics were burned, and his wealth, (that is), the shrine and the offerings which decorated it, were confiscated for the benefit of the king.

*Scotland.*—Henry VIII. would have extended his religious tyranny over Scotland, but the French party which governed there was attached to the

Catholic religion, and all the nation abhorred the English yoke. In speaking of the King of England, Sir George Douglas wrote, "There is not a child who would not throw stones at him; the women would break their distaffs on him; the people would sooner die than attempt to prevent them; the greater part of the nobility, and all the clergy, are against him."

The young Queen of Scotland (Mary) remained under the care of James Hamilton, count of Arran, son of him of whom we have already spoken; he was named governor by the Lords, although the will of the deceased king designed the Cardinal Beaton for regent; and Scotland was comprised in the treaty concluded between England and France in 1546 (see chapter viii.). The King of England died one year after.

*Servility of the English Parliament.*—During the last year of his reign, Henry having expended the prodigious sums which he had drawn from the suppression of the monasteries, sought new resources in the servility of his parliament. He had disciplined it at an early hour, and at the least resistance he reprimanded the *varlets of the mob.* Since 1543, he demanded an enormous subsidy. He had forced out new sums under every form—duties, free gifts, loans, alteration of coin. Finally, the Parliament, sanctioning the bankruptcy, left to him all that he had borrowed since the thirty-first year of his reign. They maintained that before the twenty-sixth, the receipts of the Exchequer had surpassed the sums of all the taxes imposed by his predecessors, and that before his death this sum was more than doubled.

*Wales and Ireland.*—It was under Henry VIII. that Wales was subjected to the regular forms of the English administration, and that Ireland knew some civil order. The innovations of Henry VIII. were not well received in this island, neither by the English colonists, nor by the native population. The government of the country was commonly intrusted to the Irish, to Kildare or Ossory (Osmond), chiefs of the rival families of Fitzgerald and Butler. The young son of Kildare, believing his father to have been killed at London, presented himself to the council, and in his name declared war against Henry VIII., king of England. The wise counsels of the Archbishop of Armagh could not prevail over the chanting of an Irish bard, who, in the national tongue, excited the hero to avenge the blood of his father. His valour could do nothing against the English discipline : he stipulated for a full pardon for himself and his friends, and was beheaded at London. Thus tranquillity re-established itself. The Irish chiefs solicited for themselves the dignity of the peerage : O'Neal, the most celebrated of them all, will reappear later under the name of the Count of Tyrone.

## § II. DENMARK, SWEDEN, AND NORWAY, 1513–60.

Christian II. turns the Danish Nobility, Sweden, 1520, and the Hansa, 1517, against himself.—Gustavus Vasa.—Insurrection of Dalecarlia.—Christian II. replaced in Sweden by Gustavus Vasa, 1523; in Denmark and Norway by Frederic of Holstein, 1525.—Independence of the Danish Church, 1527; of the Swedish Church, 1529.—Death of Frederic I.; Civil War, 1533.—Christian III. abolishes the Catholic Worship, 1536, and incorporates Norway with Denmark, 1537.

WHILE Protestant Germany sought in political liberty a guarantee for her religious independence, Denmark and Sweden confirmed their revolution by the adoption of the Reformation.

*Christian II.*—Christian II. had equally irritated the Danish nobility, against whom he protected the peasants; Sweden, which he inundated with blood (1520); and the Hanseatic cities, to which he had closed the ports of Denmark by prohibitions (1517). He soon found himself punished both for the evil and the good which he had done. Governed by the German priest Slagheck, who was once a barber, and by the daughter of a Dutch tavern-keeper, he followed with little dexterity the path which led the princes of the South of Europe to absolute power. He wished to ruin the nobility of Denmark and conquer Sweden. He kept troops in pay in Germany, Poland, and Scotland; he had obtained 4000 men from Francis I. One battle rendered him master of Sweden, which was already rent asunder by the quarrels of the young Stenon Sture, *administrator*, and the Archbishop of Upsal, Gustave Troll. He had all those bishops and senators tried by an ecclesiastical court who had voted for the deposition of Troll, and on the same day they were beheaded and burned at Stockholm, in the midst of a mourning people. In all the provinces of Sweden through which Christian passed, gallows and scaffolds were erected. He abused the conquered, declared himself hereditary king, and proclaimed that he made no knights among the Swedes, because he owed Sweden to his own sword.

*Gustavus Vasa.*—In the mean time, the young Gustavus Vasa, the nephew of the former king, Charles Canutson, succeeded in escaping from the prison in which Christian retained him. The Lubeckians, who saw in the latter the brother-in law of Charles V., sovereign of the Dutch, their enemies, and who knew that he had demanded their city of the emperor, obliged Gustavus Vasa to go to Sweden: discovered by the Danes, Gustavus escaped from retreat to retreat, and was one day wounded by the lances of those who sought him in a load of straw. They still show at Falhun, at Ornay, the retreats of their liberator. He at last arrived at Dalecarlia, among that hardened and intrepid race of peasants by whom the revolutions of Sweden have always been commenced. He mingled with the Dalecarlians of Copparberg (country of copper mines), adopted their costume, and offered his services to one among them. At Christmas, 1521, seizing the opportunity of an assembly celebrating the feast, he addressed them on the great plain of Mora. They remarked, with joy, that the north wind had not ceased to blow while he spoke: two hundred of them followed him; their example drew all the people after them; and, at the expiration of a few months, the Danes possessed in Sweden only Abo, Calmar, and Stockholm.

*Frederic of Holstein.*—Christian had chosen precisely this critical moment to attempt a revolution in Denmark, which was sufficient to shake the strongest throne. He published two codes, which armed against him the two most powerful orders in the kingdom—the clergy and the nobility. He suppressed the temporal jurisdiction of the bishops, prohibited the plundering of shipwrecked effects, took from the lords the right to sell their peasants, and permitted the ill-treated peasant to quit the domain of his lord. The protection of the peasants, which had caused the popularity of the Stures in Sweden, ruined the King of Denmark. The nobles and bishops called his uncle Frederic, duke of Holstein, to the throne. Thus Denmark and Sweden escaped from him at the same time.

*The Swedish Church.*—After having conquered Sweden from strangers, Gustavus freed it from the Swedish bishops. He took from the clergy their titles and jurisdiction; encouraged the nobles to recover the ecclesiastical lands upon which they could have some claim; finally, he took from the bishops the castles and strongholds which they had in their hands, and by the suppression of the appeals to Rome, the Swedish Church found herself independent, without abandoning the hierarchy and the greater part of the Catholic ceremonies (1529). They increased the number of farms to 13,000, of which the king was master. Having thus humbled the head of the aristocracy in the episcopal power, he had easier work with the nobility, and taxed unmolested the feudal lands, and declared the crown to be hereditary in the house of Vasa.

*States of Odensee*, 1527.—The bishops of Denmark, although they had contributed to the revolution, were not happier than those of Sweden. It only benefited the nobles, who demanded from Frederic I. a right over the life and death of their peasants. The preaching of the Lutheran doctrine was ordered; the States of Odensee

(1527) decreed liberty of conscience, abolished the celibacy of ecclesiastics, and broke all ties between the Danish clergy and the Holy See.

*Captivity of Christian.*—The most distant countries of the North, who were less accessible to the new opinions, did not yield to this religious revolution without resistance. The Dalecarlians were armed by the clergy against the king whom they had themselves chosen. The Norwegians and Islanders only saw in the introduction of the Protestant Creed a new tyranny of the Danes. Christian II., who had fled to the Netherlands, thought to profit by this disposition. This man, who had once chased a fugitive bishop with bulldogs, now joined his cause to that of the Catholic religion. With the aid of several princes of Germany, of Charles V., and some Dutch merchants, he equipped a fleet, landed in Norway, and penetrated from thence into Sweden. The Hanseatics armed themselves against the Dutch, who led on Christian. Beat, and obliged to shut himself up in Opslo, he gave himself up to the Danes, who promised him liberty, and kept him twenty-nine years in the dungeon at Scanderbourg, with no companion but a dwarf.

*Lubeck — Christophe of Oldenburg.* — At the death of Frederic I. (1534), the bishops made an effort to prevent their impending ruin. They endeavoured to place on the throne the youngest son of this prince, aged eight years, who was not yet in favour of Lutheran doctrines, as was his oldest (Christian III.); they were much influenced by the circumstance that this child was born in Denmark, and had *spoken the language of the country from his infancy*, while his brother was considered as a German. This attack of the bishops against the nobility, of the Catholic faith against the new doctrines, of Danish patriotism against foreign influence, encouraged the ambition of Lubeck. This republic had gained little by the ruin of Christian II. Frederic had formed companies. Gustavus favoured the English. The democratic administration, which had replaced at Lubeck the ancient oligarchy, was animated more by the spirit of conquest than by that of commerce. The new men who conducted it, the burgomaster Wullenwever, and the commandant Meyer, a locksmith, entertained the project to renew in a kingdom the democratic revolution which they had made in a city, in order to conquer and divide Denmark. They intrusted the command of the revolutionary war to an illustrious adventurer, the Count Christophe of Oldenburg, who had signalized himself in the war against the Turks; he had only his name and his sword, but he consoled himself for his poverty, it is said, by reading Homer in the original. He entered Denmark, stirring up the inferior c.asses in the name of Christian II. : a magical name, which always rallied the Catholics and peasants. All was deception in this wicked war: the Democrats of Lubeck named Christian II. to the people, but thought only of themselves; their general Christophe worked neither for Christian nor for Lubeck, but for his own interests. The calamities of this war were such, that the *War of the Count* has remained a proverbial expression in Denmark. The general consternation turned all minds to Christian III. The Senate retired to Jutland, which alone remained to them, and summoned him from Holstein, to which he had withdrawn. Gustavus aided him. The young king himself besieged Lubeck, and forced it to call back its troops. The peasants, beaten everywhere, lost all hope of liberty. Christian III. entered Copenhagen after a long siege. The Senate had the bishops arrested, deprived them of their property, and substituted for them superintendents, charged to preach the *Evangelic Religion.* Thus arose the absolute power of the nobility by the defeat of the clergy and peasants. Christian III. acknowledged the throne elective, and promised to consult the grand-master of the kingdom, the chancellor, and the marshal, who were to receive complaints against the king. The Danish nobility decided that Norway should be only a province of the kingdom. Protestantism was established there. The powerful archbishopric of Drontheim became a simple bishopric; the ancient spirit of resistance ceased to manifest itself, if we except the troubles at Bergen, excited by the tyranny of the Hanseatic factors, and the revolt of the peasants, who were forced to work in mines under the order of German miners.

*Iceland.*—Poor Iceland, between its snows and volcanoes, endeavoured also to repulse the new faith which they wished to impose on it. The Icelanders had the same repugnance to a Danish government as the Danes had to German influence. The bishops Augmont and Arneson resisted, at the head of their people, until the Danes had cut off the head of Arneson. Arneson was not esteemed for the regularity of his conduct, but he was deplored as the man of the people and as a national poet: it was Arneson who, about 1528, introduced printing in this distant isle.

Thus was the religious and political revolution of Denmark everywhere confirmed, notwithstanding a new attempt of Charles V. in favour of the elector palatine, husband of his niece, daughter of Christian II. Finally, the alliance of Christian III. with the Protestants of Germany and Francis I., decided the emperor to acknowledge him. He obtained for his subjects of the Netherlands the liberty to navigate the Baltic Sea: this privilege was the last blow aimed at the Hanseatic League, and one from which it did not recover.

---

## CHAPTER IX.

### CALVIN — REFORMATION IN FRANCE, ENGLAND, SCOTLAND, THE NETHERLANDS, TO ST. BARTHOLOMEW, 1555–1572.*

Calvin at Geneva, 1535.—Calvinism passes into France, the Netherlands, England, and Scotland.—Opposition of Philip II.—His Marriage with Mary, Queen of England, 1555.—Peace between the King of Spain and the King of France.—Henry II., 1559.—Institution of the Inquisition, 1561. — Marriage of Mary Stuart with Francis II., 1560. — Struggle between England and Scotland, 1559-1567.—Accession of Charles IX., 1561. — Massacre of Vassi; Civil War, 1562.—Peace of Amboise, 1563; of Longjumeau, 1568.—Battles of Jarnac and Montcontour, 1569.—Prosecutions in the Netherlands.—Council of Troubles, 1567.—Revolt of the Moors of Spain, 1571.—St. Bartholomew, 1572.

PHILIP II., son and successor of Charles V., did not, like his father, unite the Empire with the crown of Spain; but he became in good measure the sovereign of England by his marriage with Mary

* To separate, in the 2d part of the sixteenth century, the history of Spain, the Netherlands, France, England, and Scotland, would be condemning ourselves to continual repetition; yet, to facilitate the instruction, we will look back to chapter xii. of the *Chronological Tables* (part i., p. 515–520), which contains the programme of these different histories. We shall find there many facts or dates which could not enter into a general view of this period.

(1554), daughter of Henry VIII. The King of France had to encounter in him the master of Spain and the Netherlands, the ruler of Italy and England, and the possessor of the mines in America. He made his attack, however, on the first. The Guises, a junior branch of the house of Lorraine, claimed, as heirs of Réné of Anjou, the kingdom of both Sicilies; they found means to conduct an army to Italy. The track seemed to be beaten; Brissac, master of Piedmont, had made a descent upon Milan; the Gascon Montluc defended the city of Sienna obstinately. But no one in Italy believed in the lasting success of the French; no Italian power declared itself for Guise. The Duke of Alba, who waited for him in the Abruzzo, exhausted the ardour of the French. Guise himself demanded his recall, and went to repair the defeat of St. Quentin (1557) by the taking of Calais. France, encouraged by this last victory, thought to find in him a saviour. The Constable of Montmorency, then prisoner of the Spaniards, negotiated the peace of Cateau-Cambresis (1559). Of all his conquests, Henry II. only retained Calais (for eight years), the three bishoprics, and some places of Savoy. This went to destroy the hope of foreign conquests; but the kingdom found itself closed against foreign invasions; this treaty had secured to it the three gates of England, Germany, and Italy.

The reconciliation of the kings of France and Spain was but a league against the Reformation, which daily took a more alarming character. At its first outbreak it had done little more than destroy; in its second stage it endeavoured to lay the foundation of a system. At its appearance it had leagued itself with the civil power; the Lutheran Reformation had been in several respects the work of princes, to whom it subjected the Church. The people waited for a reformation which should inure to them. It was given by John Calvin, a French Protestant exiled at Geneva. The first reformation had conquered Germany in the north, the second subdued the Netherlands, England, and Scotland. Everywhere it encountered an obstinate adversary in the Spanish power, which it everywhere conquered.

*Calvin*, 1535.—When Calvin passed from Nerak to Geneva (1535), he found this city liberated from its bishop and from the dukes of Savoy, but kept in the greatest fermentation by the plots of the servile classes, and the continual indignities offered by the gentry. Calvin became the apostle and legislator of it (1541–64), making himself judge between the *paganism of Zwingle and the popery of Luther*. The Church was a democracy, and the State was absorbed in it. Calvinism, like the Catholic religion, had a territory independent of all temporal power. The union of Berne and Fribourg permitted the reformer to preach behind the lances of the Swiss. Placed between Italy, Switzerland, and France, Calvin shook all the West. He had neither the impetuosity, the simplicity, nor the facetiousness of Luther. His style was sad and stern, but powerful, concise, penetrating. More consistent in his writings than in his conduct, he began by asking toleration from Francis I.,* and finished by causing Servitus to be burned.

*Progress of his Doctrines.*—At once the Vaudois, and all the restless and ingenious population of the south of France, who had been the first to rebel against the yoke of the Middle Ages, rallied around the new doctrine. From Geneva and Navarre, it had spread to the commercial city of Rochelle, and from thence to the then literary cities of the interior, Poictiers, Bruges, Orleans; it penetrated into the Netherlands, and associated itself with the bands of *Rederikers*, who overran the country, preaching against abuses. From thence, passing over the sea, it came to disturb the victory of Henry VIII. over the pope, and seated itself on the throne of England with Edward VI. (1547). From England it was carried by Knox

* *Præfatio ad Christianissimum regem quâ hic ei liber pro confessione fidei offertur.* This eloquent morsel opens his book of *Christian Education*, published in 1536, which he has translated himself.

into uncivilized Scotland, and only stopped at the entrance of the mountains, where the *Highlanders* preserved the faith of their ancestors with their hatred of the *Saxon* heretics.

*Assemblies of Paris*, 1550.—At first the assemblies were secret: the first which met in France were held at Paris in the street of St. Jacques (towards 1550); they soon multiplied. Fires to burn heretics were useless. It was so delightful for the people to hear the Word of God in their own language. Many were attracted by curiosity, others by compassion; some were tempted by the danger even. In 1550 there was but one Reformed church in France; in 1561 it had more than two thousand. Sometimes they assembled in the open fields to the number of eight or ten thousand persons; the preacher mounted a cart or a pile of trees; the people placed themselves before the wind, to gather the words with more ease, and finally all united, men, women, and children, in singing psalms. Those who had arms watched around. Then came the colporteurs, who unpacked catechisms, small books and prints against the bishops and the pope.*

* There was, for example, the Cardinal of Lorraine holding the young Francis II. in a bag, who endeavoured to force out his head to breathe from time to time. In the Netherlands they sold the Cardinal Granvelle, prime minister of Philip, hatching eggs, from which bishops crept forth, while the devil touched the head of each, blessed him, and said,

They did not hold these assemblies a long time. Not less intolerant than their persecutors, they wished to exterminate what they called *Idolatry*. They commenced by overthrowing the altars, burning the paintings, and demolishing the churches. In 1561 they called on the King of France to break down the images of Jesus Christ and the saints.

*Philip II.*, 1556.—Such were the adversaries that Philip II. undertook to combat and annihilate; he everywhere met them in his path; in England, to prevent him from marrying Elizabeth (1558); in France, to balance the power of the Guises, his allies (1561); in the Netherlands, supporting by their fanaticism the cause of public liberty.*

The cosmopolitan character of Charles V. had been succeeded by a prince all Castilian, who disdained all other language, who abhorred any creed foreign to his own, who wished everywhere to establish the regular forms of Spanish administration, legislation, and religion. First he constrained himself to marry Mary, queen of England (1553), but he did not deceive the English. The glass of beer which he solemnly drank at his landing, the sermons of his confessor on toleration, gave him no popularity. They believed rather in

*Behold my much-beloved son.*—Mem. of Condé, i., 656; and Schiller, *Hist. of the Revolt of the Netherlands*, b. iii., chap

* Everywhere since 1563

the burning piles erected by his wife. After the death of Mary (1558) he no longer dissembled; he introduced Spanish troops into the Netherlands, maintained there the Inquisition, and at his departure, in a measure declared war against the defenders of the liberties of the country in the person of the Prince of Orange.* Finally, he united himself with Henry II. against domestic enemies, who threatened them both alike, by espousing his daughter, Elizabeth of France (peace of Cateau-Cambresis, 1559). Mournful circumstances saddened the festivities of this ominous peace. A tournament was given near the Bastile, where the Protestant Anne Dubourg awaited death. The king was wounded, and the marriage took place in the night at St. Paul's. Philip II. returned to his States never again to leave them, and in memory of his victory of St. Quentin he built the monastery of the Escurial, and consecrated with it fifty millions of piasters. This gloomy edifice, all built of granite, is visible at the distance of seven leagues. No sculpture embellishes the walls; the boldness of the arches constitutes the sole beauty. The buildings are arranged in the form of a gridiron.†

* The king, on embarking, said to the Prince of Orange, who cast the blame on the representatives, *No, nolos etados, ma vos, vos, vos.—Van der Vyncht.*

† Instrument of martyrdom of St. Laurence; the battle of St. Quentin was gained by the Spaniards on the day of his feast.

*Jesuits.*—At this period the minds of the people in Spain had reached the last degree of religious exaltation. The rapid progress of the heretics in all Europe, the victory which they had attained over Charles V. by the treaty of Augsburg, their violence against the images, their outrages on the holy host, which the priests related to the frightened Spaniards, had produced a redoubled fervour. Ignatius of Loyola, who was entirely devoted to the Holy See, founded the order of the Jesuits (1434–40). St. Theresa de Jesus reformed the Carmelites, and inflamed all their souls with the fire of a mystic love. The monks of the same name, of the mendicant order, soon followed in this reformation. The constitution of the Inquisition was fixed in 1561. If we except the Moors, Spain was united as a single man in violent horror against the infidels and the heretics. Closely united to Portugal, which the Jesuits governed, disposing of the ancient bands of Charles V., and of the treasures of the two worlds, she undertook to subject Europe to her empire and to her faith.

*Elizabeth*, 1559.—The dispersed Protestants rallied themselves in the name of Queen Elizabeth, who offered them an asylum and protection. Everywhere she encouraged their resistance against Philip II. and the Catholics. Absolute in their kingdoms, these two monarchs conducted with the violence of two party chiefs. The scrupulous devotion of Philip, and the chivalrous spirit of the court of Elizabeth, blended themselves with a system of intrigue and corruption; but victory awaited Elizabeth; the times were on her side. She ennobled despotism by the enthusiasm with which she inspired the nation. Those even whom she persecuted were for her, in spite of everything. A Puritan, condemned to lose one hand, had it hardly cut off, when he took his hat with the other, and waving it in the air, cried *Long live the queen!*

It was thirty years before the two adversaries met in battle. The combat had taken place previously in Scotland, France, and the Low Countries.

*Mary Stuart.*—It did not continue long in Scotland (1559–1567). The rival of Elizabeth, the fascinating Mary Stuart (widow of Francis II. at 18 years), saw herself a stranger in the midst of her subjects, who detested in her the Guises, her uncles, who were chiefs of the Catholic party in France. Her nobles, sustained by England, joined with Darnley, her husband, and stabbed an Italian musician, Rizzio, her favourite, before her eyes. Soon after, the house which Darnley inhabited, near Holyrood, blew up; he was buried under its ruins, and Mary, carried away by the principal author of the crime, was married to him of choice or through constraint. The queen and the party of the lords accused each other. But the queen was weakest. She found no refuge but in the states of her deadly enemy, who retained her a prisoner, gave the guardianship of her young son to whom she pleased, reigned in her name in Scotland, and was enabled in future to wrestle with less disadvantage against Philip II.

*William of Orange.*—But it was principally in France and the Netherlands that Elizabeth and Philip carried on a secret war. The soul of the Protestant party in these two countries was the Prince of Orange, William the Taciturn, and his father-in-law, the Admiral Coligni, unfortunate generals, but profound politicians, of melancholy temperament, and in spite of the blood of Nassau and of Montmorency, animated by the democratic instinct of Calvinism. A colonel of the infantry under Henry II., Coligni collected around him all the lesser nobility; he gave to La Rochelle a Republican organization, while the Prince of Orange encouraged the confederation of the *Gueux*, and laid the foundation of a more durable republic.

*Francis of Guise.*—The great Guise and his brother, the Cardinal of Lorraine,* governed France

* See, in the Memoirs of Gaspar de Tavennes, the comparison of the advantages which the rival houses of Guise and Montmorency had obtained from Henry II., part xxiii., page 410.

under Francis II., husband of their niece, Mary Stuart (1560). Guise had been the idol of the people since he took Calais in eight days from the English. But he had found France ruined. He found it necessary to recover the alienated domains, and to suppress the *levy of* 50,000 *men*, that is to say, to disarm government at the moment in which the revolution burst forth. Thousands of petitioners besieged Fontainebleau ; and the Cardinal of Lorraine, not knowing what to answer them, had a notice posted, that every one who did not leave the city within 24 hours should be hung.

*Conspiracy of Amboise*, 1560. — The Bourbons (Antoine, king of Navarre, and Louis, prince of Condé), who saw with regret the public affairs in the hands of the two youngest of the house of Lorraine, profited by the general discontent. They associated themselves with the Calvinists, with Coligni, with the English, who came at night to negotiate with them at St. Denis. The Protestants marched in arms towards Amboise to seize the person of the king ; but they were betrayed to the Guises, and slain on their way. Some of the Protestants, who had been kept to be executed before the king and all the court, bathed their hands in the blood of their beheaded brethren, and raised them to Heaven against those who had betrayed them. This horrible scene seemed to bring misfortune on all who had witnessed it — Francis II., Mary Stuart, the great Guise, and the Chancellor Olivier, Protestant at heart, who had condemned them, and who died from remorse on that account.

*Charles IX.—Hôpital.*—At the accession of the young Charles (the ninth of his name, 1560), the power belonged to his mother, Catharine of Medicis, if she had known how to keep it; she caused it to be taken from the Guises, the chiefs of the Catholics, and the government stood isolated between the two parties. She was not an Italian with the ancient politics of the Borgia, who could hold the balance between energetic men who despised her: she was not worthy of this period of deep convictions, and the period itself was not worthy of the Chancellor Hôpital,* a noble picture of calm wisdom, which is powerless in the midst of passion. Guise seized again, as chief of the party, the power which he had lost. The court furnished him with a pretext by softening the edicts against the Reformers, by those of St. Germain and of January, and by admitting their doctors to a solemn discussion in the conference of Poissi. At the same time that the Calvinists took up arms at Nismes, the Duke of Guise pass-

* The Chancellor Hôpital, who had the lilies in his heart.—*L'Etoile*, xlv., 57.

ing through Vassi to Champagne, his men quarrelled with some Huguenots who were listening to preaching, and killed them (1562). The civil war commenced. *Cæsar*, said the Prince of Condé, *has passed the Rubicon.*

*First Civil War*, 1562–1563.—At the approach of so terrible a conflict, both parties scrupled not to apply for the aid of foreigners. The old political barriers which separated the people fell before religious interest. The Protestants demanded aid from their brethren in Germany; they gave up Havre to the English, while the Guises entered upon a vast plan, formed, they say, by the King of Spain, to crush Geneva and Navarre, the two seats of heresy; to exterminate the Calvinists of France; and, finally, to vanquish the Lutherans in the Empire. The parties assembled on all sides with a wild enthusiasm. In these first armies there was no gambling, no profane language, nor dissipation; prayers were held in common morning and evening. But under this exterior of sanctity their hearts were not the less cruel. Montluc, the governor of Guienne, went through his province with hangmen. *One could know*, said he himself, *where he had passed, for on the trees by the roadside they would find the signs.* In Dauphiny there was a Protestant, the Baron of Adrets, who precipitated his prisoners from the top of a tower on the point of pikes

*Death of Francis of Guise*, 1563.—Guise was first conqueror at Dreux; he took Condé, the general of the Protestants, prisoner, divided his bed with him, and slept profoundly at the side of his mortal enemy. Orleans, the principal place of the Protestants, was only saved by the assassination of the Duke of Guise, whom a Protestant wounded from behind by the discharge of a pistol (1563). Whatever his ambition and connexions with Philip II. may have been, posterity will pardon a man who said to his assassin, "Now I will show you how much sweeter that religion which I follow is than the one you profess: yours has counselled you to kill without hearing me, having received no offence from me; and mine commands that I forgive you, fully convinced, as I am, that you wished to kill me without cause."

*Treaty of Amboise*, 1563—*of Longjumeau*, 1568—*of St. Germain*, 1570.—The queen-mother, relieved of a master, made a treaty with the Protestants (at Amboise, 1563), and found herself obliged, by the indignation of the Catholics, to violate all the articles of the treaty by degrees. Condé and Coligni tried in vain to seize the young king; defeated at St. Denis, but always formidable, they imposed on the court the peace of Longjumeau (1568), *surnamed* "Boiteuse et malassise," which confirmed that of Amboise. An attempt of the court to seize the two chiefs led to a third war. All moderation left the councils of the king with the Chancellor Hôpital. The Protestants took La Rochelle, instead of Orleans, for a place of arms ; they assessed themselves, in order to pay their German auxiliaries, whom the Duke of Deux-Ponts and the Prince of Orange led with them through all France. Notwithstanding their defeat at Zarnac and Moncontour (1569), notwithstanding the death of Condé and the wounds of Coligni, the court was obliged to grant them a third peace (St. Germain, 1570). Their worship was to be free in two cities of a province ; they left to them for places of security, La Rochelle, Montauban, Cognac, and La Charité. The young King of Navarre was to marry the sister of Charles IX. (Margaret of Valois). They even led Coligni to hope that he should command the aid, which, they said, the king wished to send to the Protestants of the Netherlands. The Catholics shuddered at a treaty so humiliating after four victories ; the Protestants themselves, hardly realizing it, only acquiesced on account of their weakness,* and the wisest among them expected from this hostile peace some dreadful calamity.

*Persecution in Flanders.*—The situation of the

* The admiral says that he would wish rather to die than fall back into these confusions, and see so many evils happen before his eyes. —*Lanoue*, vol. xxxiv., p. 290.

Netherlands was not less frightful. Philip II. comprehended neither the liberty or spirit of the North, nor the interests of commerce; all his subjects, Belgians and Dutch, turned against him; also the Calvinists, persecuted by the Inquisition; and the nobles, from henceforth without hope of re-establishing their fortunes, ruined in the service of Charles V.; the monks, who feared the reform ordered by the Council of Trent, as well as the establisbment of new bishoprics, to be endowed at their expense; finally, the good citizens, who beheld the introduction of Spanish troops, and the overthrow of the ancient liberties of the country, with indignation. At first the opposition of the Flemings obliged the king to recall his old minister, the Cardinal Granvella (1563); the greatest lords formed the confederation of the *Gueux*, and hung wooden porrengers around their necks, associating themselves thus with the lower classes (1566). The Calvinists raise their heads on all sides; print more than five thousand works against the ancient worship; and in the provinces of Brabant and Flanders alone they plunder and profane four hundred churches.

This last excess filled up the measure of crime. The savage soul of Philip II. already conceived the most fatal plans; he resolved to pursue and exterminate his terrible enemies, whom he met everywhere, even in his family. He included in the same hatred as well the legal opposition of the noble Flemings as the image-breaking fury of the Calvinists, and the obstinate attachment of the poor Moors to the religion, language, and customs of their fathers. But he would not act without the sanction of the Church; he obtained from the Inquisition a secret condemnation of his rebels in the Netherlands; he questioned even the most celebrated doctors, among others, Oradug, professor of theology at the University of Alcala, upon the measures which he ought to take with regard to the Moors; Oradug replied by the proverb, "*Des ennemies toujours le moins.*" The king, confirmed in his plans of vengeance, swore to give an example in the persons of his enemies *in a manner that should make the ears of Christendom tingle, though it placed all his estates in danger.*

He began by following, without distinction of person, and with an atrocious inflexibility, the bloody councils which he had caused to be given to the court of France by the Duke of Alba. His son, Don Carlos, spoke of going to place himself at the head of the rebels of the Netherlands; Philip caused his death to be hastened by physicians (1568). He organized the Inquisition in America (1570); he disarmed all the Moors of Valencia in one day; forbade the Moors of Grenada to wear the Arabian dress, or to speak their own language; he prohibited the use of the baths, of the *Zembras*, the *Leilas*, and even the green branches, with which these unfortunate beings covered their graves; their children of more than five years must go to school to learn the Castilian religion and language (1563–68). In the mean time, the bloody Duke of Alba, at the head of an army fanatical as Spain, and profligate as Italy,* marched from Italy to Flanders. At the report of his coming, the Swiss armed themselves to cover Geneva. One hundred thousand persons, imitating the Prince of Orange, fled from the Netherlands.† The Duke of Alba established, at his arrival, the *Council of Troubles*, the *Council of Blood*, as the Belgians called it, and which he composed partly of Spaniards (1567). All those who refused to abjure heresy—all who had been present at sermons, were they even Catholics—all who had tolerated heretics, were equally put to death. The *Gueux* are prosecuted; those even who had only solicited the recall of Granvella, were sought after and punished; the Count Egmont, whose victories at St. Quentin and Gravelines had conferred honour on the commencement of the reign of Philip II., the idol of the people, and one of the most loyal servants of the king, perished on the scaffold. The efforts of the Prot-

* See the details in Meteren, book iii., page 52.

† Nothing has been done since they permitted the *Taciturn* to escape, said Granvella.

estants of Germany and France, who raised an army for Louis, son of the Prince of Orange, were baffled by the Duke of Alba; and, as a greater insult to his victims, he had a statue of bronze erected in the citadel of Antwerp, which trampled slaves under its feet, and threatened the city.

There was the same barbarity, the same success in Spain; Philip seized with joy the opportunity of the revolt of the Moors to overwhelm those unfortunate people. At the moment that he turned his arms abroad, he would leave no resistance behind him; the weight of the oppression gave some courage to the Moors; a manufacturer of Carmine, of the family of Abencerrages, had secret communication with some others; clouds of smoke arose from mountain to mountain; the red colours were raised again; the women even armed themselves with long packing needles, to pierce the bellies of the horses; the priests were killed everywhere. But soon the veteran regiments of Spain arrived. The Moors received some feeble succour from Algiers; in vain they implored the aid of the Sultan Selim. Old men, children, suppliant women, were massacred without mercy. The king ordered that all over ten years who remained should become slaves (1571).

*St. Bartholomew*, 1572.—The feeble and despicable government of France was unwilling to be left behind. The exasperation of the Catholics had become extreme since they saw at the nuptials of the King of Navarre and Margaret of Valois, in Paris, those gloomy and severe men whom they had so often encountered on the field of battle, and whose presence they regarded as an insult. They counted their own number, and began to cast dark looks on their enemies. Without giving credit to the queen-mother or to her sons for a dissimulation so long continued, and a plan so well devised, we can imagine that the possibility of such an event had strengthened the inducements to the peace of St. Germain. Yet so daring a crime would not have been resolved on had they not feared for a moment the power of Coligni over the young Charles IX. His mother and brother, the Duke of Anjou, whom he began to threaten, recovered their influence over this feeble and capricious being, through fear, which soon turned to rage, and which caused him to resolve upon the massacre of the Protestants as readily as he would before have ordered that of the principal Catholics. On the 24th of August, 1672, about two or three o'clock in the morning, the bell of St. Germain l'Auxerrois sounded, and the young Henry of Guise, thinking to avenge the death of his father, commenced the massacre by cutting the throat of Coligni. There was heard nothing but the cry, "*Kill! kill!*" The greater part of the Protestants were surprised in their beds. A wounded gentleman was pursued, the halbert in his back, even to the chamber and bedside of the Queen of Navarre. A Catholic boasted that he bought from the murderers more than 30 Huguenots, to torture them at pleasure. Charles IX. had his brother-in-law and the Prince of Condé brought before him, and said to them, the *Mass* or *Death!* It is said that he fired from the window of the Louvre on the Protestants, who fled from the other side of the river. The next morning a hawthorn having reblossomed in the churchyard of the Innocents, fanaticism was reanimated by this pretended miracle, and the massacre recommenced. The king, the queen-mother, and all the court went to Montfaucon to see *what remained of the body of the admiral.* We must add Hôpital to the victims of St. Bartholomew; when he heard the odious news, he wished the gates of his house to be opened to the *murderers* who might come; he survived it only six months, always repeating, "*Excidat illa dies ævo!*"

A circumstance as horrible as St. Bartholomew itself was the joy which it excited. They struck medals of it at Rome, and Philip II. congratulated the court of France. He thought Protestantism subdued. He associated St. Bartholomew, and the massacres ordered by the Duke of Alba, with the glorious event of the battle of Lepanto, in which the fleets of Spain, the pope, and Venice, commanded by John of Austria, natural son of Charles V., had destroyed the Ottoman navy in the preceding year. The Turks conquered by sea, the Moors reduced, the heretics exterminated in France and in the Netherlands, seemed to prepare the way for the King of Spain towards that universal monarchy to which his father had vainly aspired.

---

## CHAPTER X.

### FARTHER EVENTS TO THE DEATH OF HENRY IV., 1572–1610 — GLANCE AT THE SITUATION OF THE BELLIGERANT POWERS AFTER THE RELIGIOUS WARS.

Death of Charles IX., 1574.—Insurrection of the Netherlands, 1572.—Union of Utrecht, 1579.—Formation of the League in France, 1577.—Power of the Guises.—Battle of Contres, 1587.—Barricades, States of Blois, 1588.—Murder of Henry III., 1589.—Accession of Henry IV.—Death of Mary Stuart, 1587.—Armament of Philip II., 1588.—Grandeur of Elizabeth.

*Death of Charles IX.*—King Charles, hearing on the evening of the same day, and all the next day the accounts of the murders and slaughters of old men, women, and children, drew aside Mr. Ambroise Paré, his first surgeon, to whom he was much attached, although he was of the Protestant religion, and said to him, "Ambroise, I know not what has come over me these two or three days, but I find my mind and body in disorder: I see everything as if I had a fever; every moment, as well waking as sleeping, the hideous and bloody faces of the killed appear before me; I wish the weak and innocent had not been included." From that time he lingered on, and eighteen months after a bloody flux carried him off (1574.)

*Henry III.*—The crime had been useless. In several cities the governors refused to consummate it. The Calvinists throwing themselves into La Rochelle, Sancerre, and other places of the South, defended themselves there most desperately. The horror inspired by St. Bartholomew gave them auxiliaries, by creating among the Catholics a moderate party, which they called the *Politicians.* The new king, Henry III., who returned from Poland to succeed his brother, was known as one of the authors of the massacre. His own brother, the Duke of Alençon, fled from the court with the young King of Navarre, and thus united the Politicians and Calvinists.

*Philip loses half of the Netherlands.*—The tyranny of the Duke of Alba was not more successful in the Netherlands. As long as he contented himself with erecting scaffolds the people remained quiet; they saw, without revolting, the most illustrious heads of the nobility fall. There was but one way to render the discontent common to Catholics and Protestants, to nobles and citizens, to Belgians and Dutchmen: it was to establish oppressive duties, and let the badly-paid soldiers plunder the inhabitants: the Duke of Alba did both. The duty of the tenth, levied upon provisions, made the agents of the Spanish revenue interpose in the smallest sales in the markets and shops. The innumerable forfeits, the continued vexations, irritated all the population. While the shops were closed, and the Duke of Alba had the merchants who were guilty of having closed them hung, the *gueux marins* (it is thus that they called the fugitives, who lived by piracy), driven from the ports of England on the demand of Philip II., seized the fort of Brielle, in Holland (1572), and commenced the war in this country, intersected by so many branches of the sea, rivers, and canals. A number of cities drove away the Spaniards. Perhaps there yet remained some means of pacification, but the Duke of Alba taught the first cities which gave themselves up that they had neither clemency nor good faith to hope for. At Rotterdam, Malines, Zutphen, Naarden, the capitulations were violated, the inhabitants killed. Harlem, knowing what she had to expect, broke the dams, and sent ten Spanish heads as payment of her tenth. After a memorable resistance, she obtained pardon, and the Duke of Alba confounded in a general massacre the sick and wounded. The Spanish soldiers felt themselves some remorse at this want of faith, and in atonement they consecrated a part of the booty to build a house for the Jesuits in Brussels.

Under the successors of the Duke of Alba, the licentiousness of the Spanish troops, who plundered Antwerp, forced the Walloon provinces to unite in the revolt with those of the North (1567); but this alliance could not last. The revolution was consolidated by being concentrated at the North in the union of Utrecht, the commencement of the Republic of the United Provinces (1579). The intolerance of the Protestants restored the southern provinces to the yoke of the King of Spain. *The Dutch population, all Protestant, all* German in character and language, entirely composed of citizens, and given to maritime trade, drew that which was analogous to itself from the southern provinces. The Spaniards could reconquer in Belgium the walls and the territory, but the most industrious part of the population escaped them.

The insurgents had offered successively to submit themselves to the German branch of the house of Austria, to France, and to England. The Archduke Mathias offered them no succour. Don Juan, brother and general of Philip II., the Duke of Anjou, brother of Henry III., Leicester, favourite of Elizabeth, who wished successively to become sovereigns of the Netherlands, showed themselves equally treacherous (1577, 1582, 1587). Holland, regarded, by all to whom she addressed herself, as prey, decided finally, for want of a sovereign, to remain a republic. The genius of this rising state was the Prince of Orange, who, abandoning the southern provinces to the invincible Duke of Parma, contended against him by policy, until a fanatic, armed by Spain, had assassinated him (1584).

*The League,* 1577.—While Philip lost half of the Netherlands, he gained the kingdom of Portugal. The king, Don Sebastian, had thrown himself on the coast of Africa with ten thousand men, in the vain hope of conquering it and penetrating to India. This hero, as he would have been in the time of the Crusades, was in the sixteenth century but an adventurer. His uncle, the Cardinal D. Henri, who succeeded him, having died soon after, Philip II. seized Portugal in spite of France, and of the Portuguese themselves (1580).

*Battle of Coutras,* 1587.—In France all was propitious to Philip. The fickleness of Henry III., that of the Duke of Alençon, who placed himself at the head of the French Protestants, and afterward of those of the Netherlands, had decided the Catholic party to seek a chief out of the royal family. By the treaty of 1576, the king had granted the liberty of worship to the Calvinists throughout all the kingdom, excepting Paris: he gave them a divided chamber, whose members were one half Roman Catholics, and the other half Protestants, in every parliament; and several cities for security (Angoulême, Niort, La Charité, Bourges, Saumur, and Mezières), where they might hold armed garrisons, paid by the king. This treaty determined the formation of the League (1577). The associates swore to defend the religion; *to bring the provinces back to the same laws, exemptions, and liberties which they had at the time of Clovis*; to proceed against those who should injure the union, *without respect of person; finally, to render prompt obedience and faithful services to the chief who should be named.* The king thought to become master of the association by declaring himself its chief. He began to have a glimpse at the designs of the Duke of Guise; they had found in the papers of a lawyer who had died at Lyon, returning from Rome, a piece in which he said that the descendants of Hugh Capet had hitherto reigned illegally, and by a usurpation, cursed of God; that the throne belonged to the princes of

Lorraine, the true posterity of Charlemagne. The death of the brother of the king encouraged these pretensions (1584.) Henry having no children, and the majority of the Catholics repudiating the heretic prince, to whom the crown would devolve, the Duke of Guise, and the King of Spain, brother-in-law of Henry III., united themselves to dethrone the king, leaving the spoils to be quarrelled for afterward. They had but too many means to make him odious. In the reverses of his army there seemed as much of treachery as of misfortune; the feeble prince was at the same time beaten by the Protestants and accused by the Catholics. The victory of Coutras, where the King of Navarre made himself illustrious by his valour and his clemency towards the conquered (1587), exasperated the irritation of the Catholics to the highest degree. While the League organized itself in the capital, Henry III., divided between the claims of a monkish devotion and the excesses of a disgusting debauchery, gave to all Paris the spectacle of his scandalous prodigality and puerile tastes. He spent 1,200,000 francs at the marriage of Joyeuse, his favourite, and had nothing to pay a messenger to carry a letter, on which depended the safety of the kingdom, to the Duke of Guise. He passed his time in arranging the collars of the queen and in curling his own hair. He had himself made prior of a fraternity of *white penitents.* "At the beginning of November, the king made known through the churches of Paris, which were the oratories, otherwise called Paradises, that he daily went to, in order to bestow his alms and pray in great devotion, leaving off his ruffled shirts, of which he had formerly been so careful, to adopt the Italian fashion of wearing the collar turned over. He generally rode in his coach with the queen, his wife, through the streets and squares of Paris, carried small lapdogs, had grammar read to him, and learned to decline."*

Thus the crisis became imminent in France and all the West (1585–1588); it seemed necessarily favourable to Spain; the taking of Antwerp by the Prince of Parma, the most memorable achievement of arms in the sixteenth century, completed the reduction of Belgium (1585). The King of France had been obliged to place himself at the discretion of the Guises (the same year), and the League took for its home an immense city, where religious fanaticism was re-enforced by democratic fanaticism (1588). But the King of Navarre resisted the reunited forces of the Catholics, even against all probability of success (1586–87). Elizabeth gave an army to the United Provinces (1585), money to the King of Navarre (1585); she frustrated all

* L'Étoile, part xlv., p. 123.

the conspiracies (1584–5–6), and struck Spain and the Guises in the person of Mary Stuart.

*Death of Mary Stuart.*—For a long time Elizabeth had replied to the solicitation of her counsellors, *Can I kill the bird which sought refuge in my bosom?* She had accepted embroidery and Parisian robes which her captive offered her. But the increasing provocations of the great European contest, the fear which it constantly caused Elizabeth for her own life, and the mysterious power of the Jesuits, who from the Continent constantly disturbed England, brought the queen to the last extremity.

Notwithstanding the mediation of the Kings of France and Scotland, Mary was condemned to death by a commission, as guilty of having conspired with foreigners for the invasion of England and the death of Elizabeth. A saloon was hung with black in the castle of Fotheringay; the Queen of Scotland appeared there in her richest garments; she consoled her weeping domestics, protested her innocence, and pardoned her enemies. Elizabeth aggravated the horrors of this cruel decision by affected regrets and hypocritical denials (1587).

*Barricades*, 1588.—The death of Mary Stuart was nowhere more resented than in France. But who should avenge it? Her brother-in-law, Henry III., fell from the throne; her cousin, Henry of

Guise, thought to ascend it. *France was mad after this man, for to say in love with him would be too little.* Since his success over the Germans, the allies of the King of Navarre, the people called him by no other name than the *New Gideon*, the *New Macabee;* the nobles called him *Our Great;* he had only to go to Paris to be master of it. The king forbids him; he arrives, and all the city runs before him, crying, "*Vive le Duc de Guise! Hosanna filio David!*" He braves the king in the Louvre, at the head of 400 gentlemen. From that time the Lorraine party believed they had gained their cause: the king was to be thrown into a convent; the Duchess of Montpensier, sister of the Duke of Guise, shows the scissors of gold with which she was to shear the *Valois.* The people everywhere raised barricades, disarmed the Swiss, whom the king had just called into Paris, and had them all massacred without the sanction of the Duke of Guise. A moment of irresolution caused the latter to loose all; while he delayed attacking the Louvre, the aged Catharine de Medicis amused him with proposals, and the king, in the mean time, escaped to Chartres. Guise tried in vain to reunite himself to the Parliament. "'Tis a great pity," said to him the president Achille, of Harlay, "when the valet chases the master; as for the rest, my soul is for God, my heart for the king, my body in the hands of the wicked."

*States of Blois.*—The king, liberated, but abandoned by all, was obliged to yield; he approved of all that had been done, gave up a great number of cities to the duke, named him chief-general of the armies of the kingdom, and called the States-General to Blois. But the duke wished a higher title. He overwhelmed the king with so many outrages, that he wrung from the most timid of men a bold resolution—that of assassinating him.

Thursday, December 22, 1588, the Duke of Guise found a billet under his napkin, in which was written, "Take care! they are about to play you a foul game." Having read it, he wrote below, "*They will not dare,*" and threw it under the table. "This is," said he, "the ninth warning today." Notwithstanding these warnings, he persisted in going to the council, and as he crossed the chamber *where the forty-five members had assembled,* he was killed.

*Destruction of the Armada.*—During this tragedy, which favoured more than it thwarted the designs of Spain, Philip II. undertook the conquest of England, and the avenging of the death of Mary Stuart. On the 3d of June, 1588, the most formidable armament which ever appalled the Christian world left the mouth of the Tagus: one hundred and thirty-five vessels, of a size till then unheard of, eight thousand sailors, nineteen thousand soldiers, the flower of the Spanish nobility, and Lope de Vega with the fleet, to chant the victory. The Spaniards, intoxicated at the spectacle, honoured the fleet with the name of the *Invincible Armada*. She was to join the Prince of Parma at the Netherlands, and to guard the passage of thirty-two thousand veteran soldiers. The forest of Waes, in Flanders, was converted into transport ships. The alarm was extreme in England; they showed at the church doors the instruments of torture which the inquisitors brought over in the Spanish fleet. The queen appeared on horseback before the army assembled at Tewksbury, and promised to die for her people. But the strength of England was in her navy. The greatest seamen of the age, Drake, Hawkins, Frobisher, served under Admiral Howard. The small English vessels harassed the Spanish fleet, already partly disabled by the elements; they beset her with their fire-ships; the Prince of Parma could not leave the ports of Flanders, and the rest of this formidable fleet, driven by the tempest even to the coasts of Scotland and Ireland, went to conceal itself in the ports of Spain.

The remainder of the life of Elizabeth was but one triumph; she baffled the attempt of Philip II on Ireland, and prosecuted her victory over all the seas. The enthusiasm of Europe, roused by such success, assumed a form the most flattering to woman, that of ingenious flattery. The age of Elizabeth was forgotten (55 years). Henry IV. declared to the ambassador of England that he thought her handsomer than his Gabriele. Shakspeare pronounced her *the fair Vestal, seated upon the throne of the West;* but no homage touched her more than that of the witty Sir Walter Raleigh, and the young and brilliant Earl of Essex; the former had commenced his fortune by throwing his cloak under the feet of the queen, who was crossing a muddy place; Essex had charmed her by his heroism. He fled from court in spite of her orders, to take part in the expedition of Cadiz; he there jumped on shore the first one, and if they had confided in him, Cadiz might, perhaps, have remained in the hands of the English. His ingratitude and tragical end saddened the last days of Elizabeth.

## § II. TO THE DEATH OF HENRY IV.—GLANCE AT THE SITUATION OF THE BELLIGERANT POWERS.

**Mayenne.—Combat of Argues.—Battle of Jori, 1590.—State of Paris, 1593.—Abjuration and Absolution of Henry IV., 1593-1595.—Edict of Nantes.—Peace of Vervins, 1598.—Weakness of Spain; Expulsion of the Moors from Valencia, 1609.—Administration of Henry IV.—Affluence of France.—Assassination of Henry IV., 1610.**

Philip II., repulsed from Holland and England,

turned all his forces against France; the Duke of Mayenne, brother of Guise, not less able, but less popular, could not counterbalance the gold and the intrigues of Spain.

*Assassination of Henry III.*, 1589. — As soon as the news of the death of Guise had arrived in Paris, the people dressed themselves in mourning; the preachers thundered; they hung the churches in black; they placed wax images of the king on the altar, and pierced them with needles. Mayenne was created chief of the League; the States named forty persons to govern. Bussi Le Clerc, who from a master-at-arms and an attorney had become governor of the Bastile, sent half of the Parliament there. Henry III. had no resource but to throw himself into the arms of the King of Navarre; both came to besiege Paris. They encamped at St. Cloud, when a young monk named Clement assassinated Henry III. by stabbing him in the lower part of his stomach. The Duchess of Montpensier, sister of the Duke of Guise, who awaited the news on the road, received it first, almost frantic with joy. They offered in the churches the image of Clement for the adoration of the people; his mother, a poor country woman of Burgundy, having gone to Paris, the people came before her, crying, "*Happy the womb that has borne thee, and the paps which thou hast sucked!*" (1589).

*Henry IV.—Arques—Ivri.*—Henry IV., abandoned by the greater part of the Catholics, was soon closely pressed by Mayenne, who confidently expected to lead him, bound hand and foot, to the Parisians. Already they let out the windows to see him pass. But Mayenne had to deal with an adversary who slept not, and *who wore out,* as the Prince of Parma said, *more boots than slippers.* He waited for Mayenne near Arques, in Normandy, and fought with three thousand men against thirty thousand. Henry, supported by a crowd of gentlemen, now took his turn to attack Paris and pillage the Faubourg St. Germain.

The following year (1590) there was another victory at Ivri on the Eure, where he beat Mayenne and the Spaniards. We have the words which he addressed to his troops before the battle: "*If you will run the hazard for me, my companions, I will also for you. I will conquer and die with you . . . guard well your ranks, I beg of you, and if you lose your colours or standard, lose not sight of my white feather; you will always find it in the path of honour and victory.*" From Ivri he came to blockade the capital; this unfortunate city, a prey to the fury of the *Seize** and the tyranny of the Spanish soldiers, was reduced to the last extremity

* A fanatical league formed at Paris, called *the League of the Sixteen.*

of hunger: they made bread even of the bones of the dead; mothers devoured their children. The Parisians, oppressed by their defenders, only found pity from the prince who besieged them. He allowed a great number of useless mouths to pass out. *Shall I, whose duty it is to feed them, be their destroyer? Paris must not be a graveyard; I will not reign over the dead.* And again he said, *I resemble the true mother of Solomon; I would rather not have Paris than to have it torn in pieces.* Paris was delivered only by the arrival of the Duke of Parma, who, by his skilful manœuvres, forced Henry to raise the siege, and afterward returned to the Netherlands.

*Abjuration of Henry IV.*, 1594.—In the mean time the party of the League was daily growing weaker. The bond of their party was hatred towards the king. It had prepared its own dissolution by assassinating Henry III. A war at the time divided the principal factions: that of the Guises, upheld especially by the nobility and Parliament; and that of Spain, sustained by obscure demagogues. The second concentrated in the large cities, and, without military spirit, distinguished itself by the persecution of the magistrates (1589–91). Mayenne repressed it (1591), but only at the expense to the League of its democratic energy. In the mean time, the Guises, twice beaten, twice blockaded in Paris, could not sustain themselves without the support of those same Spaniards whose agents they had proscribed. Divisions broke out in the States of Paris (1593); Mayenne caused the pretensions of Philip II. to miscarry, but without gain to himself. The League, which was in effect dissolved from that moment, lost every pretext for its continuance, by the abjuration, and, above all, by the absolution of Henry IV. (1593–95), and it lost its principal point of support by the entrance of the king into the capital (1594). He pardoned every one, and the very evening of his entrance visited Madame de Montpensier. From that time the League was nothing but a burlesque, and the Satire Ménippée gave it the finishing stroke. Henry gained his kingdom, piece by piece, from the hands of the nobles, who had divided it among themselves.

*Peace of Vervins*, 1598.—In 1595 the civil war made room for a foreign war. The king turned the military ardour of the nation against the Spaniards. In the memorable year 1588 Philip II. at last yielded; all his projects had failed, his treasures were exhausted, his navy nearly ruined. He renounced his pretensions to France (May 2), and transferred the Netherlands to his daughter (May 6). Elizabeth and the United Provinces were alarmed at the peace of Vervins, and made a closer alliance with each other; Henry IV. had seen that nothing more was to be feared from Philip II. (who died September 13). The King of France terminated its internal troubles at the same time with the foreign war, by yielding religious toleration and political guarantees to the Protestants (Edict of Nantes, April).

*Weakness of Spain.*—The situation of the belligerant powers, after these long wars, presented a striking contrast. It is the master of both Indies who is ruined. The weakness of Spain only increased under the reign of Cardinal Lerma and the Duke of Olivarez, favourite of Philip III. and of Philip IV. Spain, not producing enough to buy the metals of America, they cease to enrich her. Of all that is imported in America, a twentieth or more is manufactured in Spain. At Seville, the sixteen hundred looms which worked on wool and silk in 1536, were reduced to four hundred towards 1621. In one year alone (1509) Spain drove out a million of industrious subjects (the Moors of Valencia), and was forced to grant a truce of twelve years to the United Provinces.

On the contrary, France, England, and the United Provinces made rapid improvement in population, wealth, and greatness.

*Prosperity of England, the Netherlands, and France.*—Since 1595, Philip II., by closing the port of Lisbon against the Dutch, had forced them to seek the commodities of the East in the Indies, and there to found an empire on the ruins of that of the Portuguese. The Republic was troubled within by the quarrels of the Stadtholder and the Syndic (Maurice of Orange and Barneveldt), by the contest between the military power and civil liberty, between the war party and the peace party (Gomarus and Arminius), but the want of national defence assured the victory to the former of these two parties. It cost the life of the venerable Barneveldt, who was beheaded at seventy years of age (1619).

At the expiration of the twelve years' truce there was no more civil war, but a regular war, a scientific war, a school for all the soldiers of Europe. The military skill of the general of the Spaniards, the celebrated Spinola, was balanced by that of Prince Frederic Henry, brother and successor of Maurice.

In the mean time, France, under Henry IV., had emerged from her ruins. Notwithstanding the weak points of this great king, and the faults which an attentive examination may discover in his reign, he merited not the less the title to which he aspired, that of restorer of France. All his cares were bent upon regulating and making the kingdom which he had conquered flourish: useless troops were discharged; order in the finances succeeded to the most shameful peculations and robbery; he paid, by degrees, all the debts of the crown, without pressing the people. The peasants even now repeat that he wished them *to have a fowl in their pots every Sunday:* a trifling expression, but a paternal sentiment. It was an astonishing circumstance, that, notwithstanding the exhausted state of the kingdom, and the practice of peculation, he had, in less than fifteen years, diminished the burden of taxes four millions; that all other duties were reduced to one half; that he paid one hundred millions of debts. He purchased domains to the amount of more than fifty millions; all the public places were repaired, the magazines and the arsenals filled, the great roads maintained. Eternal praise is due for all this to Sully and to the king, who dared to choose a soldier to re-establish the finances of the State, and who earnestly cooperated with his minister.

*Administration.* — Justice was reformed, and, what was much more difficult, both religions lived in peace, at least to appearance. Agriculture was encouraged. "*Tillage and pasturage,*" said Sully, "*are the two breasts which have nourished France, the true mines and treasures of Peru.*" Commerce and the arts, less patronised by Sully, were still held in honour. Fabrics of gold and silver enriched Lyons and France. Henry established factories of tapestry, both of wool, and of silk worked with gold. They began to make small glass mirrors, after the fashion of Venice. To him, too, we owe silkworms, and the plantations of mulberry-trees, in spite of the opposition of Sully. Henry had the canal of Briare cut, by which the Seine was joined to the Loire. Paris was enlarged and embellished; he built the Place Royal; he restored all the bridges. The Faubourg St. Germain belonged not to the city; it was not paved; the king charged himself with all. He had that beautiful bridge built on which the people still behold with emotion his statue. St. Germain, Mouceaux, Fontainebleau, and especially the Louvre, were enlarged, and almost entirely rebuilt. He gave lodgings in the Louvre, under that long gallery which is his work, to all kinds of artists, whom he often encouraged by kind attentions, as well as by rewards. He was, finally, the true founder of the Royal Library. When Don Pedro, of Toledo, was sent as ambassador by Philip III. to Henry, he no more recognised a city, which he had once seen so unfortunate and languishing. "*It is because then the father of the family was not here,*" said Henry to him; "*now that he takes care of his children, they prosper.*"—*Voltaire.*

*Projects of the King.*—France had become the

arbiter of Europe. Owing to her powerful mediation, the pope and Venice had been reconciled (1607); Spain and the United Provinces had at last ended their long conflict (1609–1621); Henry IV. went to humble the house of Austria; if we believe his minister, he designed to establish a perpetual peace, and to substitute law in place of that state of nature which still obtained among the members of the great European family. All was ready: a numerous army, provisions of all kinds, the most formidable artillery of the world, and forty-two millions in the vaults of the Bastile. A blow from a dagger saved Austria. The people suspected the emperor, the King of Spain, the Queen of France, the Duke of Epernon, the Jesuits. All profited by the crime, but the fanaticism which pursued during all his reign a prince who was always suspected of being a Protestant at heart, and who wished to make his religion triumph in Europe, is sufficient to explain it. The blow had been attempted seventeen times before Ravaillac.

*His Death* (1610).—"Friday, the 14th of May, 1610, a solemn and fatal day for France, the king, at 6 o'clock A.M., heard mass at the Feuillants; on returning he retired to his cabinet, where the Duke of Vendôme, his natural son, whom he loved much, came to tell him that La Brosse, who professed astrology, had said to him that the constellation under which his majesty had been born threatened him with great danger this very day; therefore he advised him to take care of himself. To this the king replied, laughing, to M. de Vendôme, 'La Brosse is an old rogue, who desires to have your money, and you are a young fool to believe him. Our days are numbered by God.' The duke then told the queen of the same prediction, who begged the king not to leave the Louvre for the rest of the day; to her he made the same reply. After dinner the king laid down on his bed to sleep, but not being able to do so, he arose sad, disquieted, and thoughtful, and, after walking in his chamber for some time, he threw himself again on the bed. But still not being able to sleep, he arose and asked one of his life-guards what time it was. He replied that it was four o'clock, and said, 'Sir, I see your majesty sad and pensive; it would be better to take a little air; this would revive you.' 'That's well said: have my carriage prepared; I will go to the arsenal, to the Duke of Sully, who is indisposed, and who takes a bath to-day.'

"The carriage being ready, he left the Louvre, accompanied by the Duke of Montbazon, the Duke of Epernon, the Marshal of Lavardin, Roquelaure, La Force, Mirabeau, and Liancourt, who was the first equerry. At the same time he charged M. de Vitry, captain of his guards, to go to the palace and hasten the preparations for the entrance of the queen, and he ordered his guards to remain at the Louvre. Thus the king was only followed by a small number of gentlemen on horseback and some footmen. The carriage was, unluckily, open on all sides, as it was fine weather, and the king wished to see the preparations which were making in the city. His carriage passing from the street St. Honoré into that of Ferronnerie, found on the one side a cart laden with wine, on the other a wagon with hay, which caused a confusion; he was obliged to stop. The street is very narrow, caused by the shops which are built against the wall of the graveyard of St. Innocents'.

"In this embarrassment, the greater number of the footmen went into the graveyard, to run more at their ease, and to go before the carriage of the king at the head of the street. Of the only two valets who had followed the carriage, one advanced to remove this obstacle, and the other stooped to tie his garter, when a wretch, a demon from the infernal regions, named Francis Ravaillac, a native of Angoulême, who had time, during the embarrassment, to see on which side the king was seated, stepped on the wheel of the carriage, and, with a knife sharpened on both edges, struck him a blow between the second and third ribs, a little below the heart, which made the king exclaim, 'I am wounded!' But the wretch, without being frightened, repeated the blow, and struck him a second time in the heart with such force that the king could only heave a heavy sigh, and die. This second blow was followed by a third, so much was the parricide exasperated towards his king; but it only touched the sleeve of the Duke of Montbazon.

"Amazing thing! none of the gentlemen who were in the carriage saw the king struck; and if this monster of the infernal regions had thrown away his sword, no one would have known from whence the blow came; but he remained there, as if to show himself, and to glory in being the greatest of assassins."*

---

## CHAPTER XI.

### REVOLUTION OF ENGLAND, 1603–1649.†

James I., 1603. — Charles I., 1625. — War against France, 1627. — The King tries to govern without a Parliament, 1630–1638.—Trial of Hampden, 1636.—Covenant of Scotland, 1638.—*Long Parliament*, 1640.—Commencement of the Civil War, 1642. — Covenant of England and Scotland, 1643. — Success of the Parliament. — The Power passes to the Independents. — Cromwell. — The King gives himself up to the Scots, who betray him, 1645. — Revolution and Predominance of the Army. — Trial and Execution of Charles I. — Overthrow of the Monarchy, 1649.

*James I.*, 1603. — When James I. succeeded

* L'Etoile, part xlviii., p. 447–450.

† If this chapter presents any interest, we are indebted for it to the

Elizabeth, the long reign of this princess had somewhat wearied the enthusiasm and submissive spirit of the nation. The character of the new prince was not calculated to change this disposition. England beheld with evil eye a Scottish king, surrounded by Scotchmen, belonging, on the side of his mother, to the house of Guise, more versed in theology than in politics,* and who turned pale at the sight of a sword. He displeased the English in everything, as well by his imprudent proclamations in favour of the Divine right of kings, as by his project to unite England and Scotland, and his toleration towards the Catholics, who conspired against him (Gunpowder Plot, 1605). On the other hand, the Scotch saw with no greater satisfaction his attempts to subject them to the English Church. James, entirely devoted to his favourites, made himself, by his prodigality, dependant on the Parliament, at the same time that he irritated it by the contrast between his pretensions and his weakness.

It had been the glory of Elizabeth to elevate the nation in its own eyes; the misfortune of the Stuarts was to humble it. James abandoned the title

works of Messrs. Guizot and Villemain, from which we have made extracts, and have often copied. We have also drawn some precious information from the works of M. Mazure, although the object of his work is generally foreign to that of this chapter.—*History of the Revolution*, 1688.

* Henry IV. called him Maître Jacques.

of adversary of Spain and chief of the Protestants in Europe. He did not declare war against Spain till 1625, and then in spite of himself. He had his son married to a Catholic princess (Henrietta of France).

*Charles I.*, 1625.—At the accession of Charles I. (1625), the king and people knew not themselves to what degree they were already estranged from each other. While the monarchical power triumphed on the Continent, the English Commons had acquired an importance inconsistent with the ancient system of government. Under the Tudors, the humiliation of the aristocracy, the division of estates, the sale of the ecclesiastical property, had both enriched the people and given them confidence in their own strength. They sought political guarantees. The institutions which might have afforded these guarantees existed already; they had been respected by the Tudors, who made an instrument of them. But a motive as powerful as religious interest was necessary to give life to those institutions. The Presbyterian reformation, an enemy to the Anglical reformation, found the throne standing between herself and episcopacy. The throne was attacked.

*Petition of Right.*—The first Parliament sought to obtain, by the delay of subsidies, the redress of public grievances (1625). The second accused the Duke of Buckingham (the favourite of the king) as their author (1626). During these two assemblies, the unfortunate wars of Spain and France took from the government what popularity it yet possessed. The second war had been undertaken to aid the Protestants, and to deliver La Rochelle (the misfortune of Buckingham at the Isle of Rhé, 1627). The third Parliament, waiving all minor contests, demanded, in the *Petition of Right*, an explicit sanction of those public liberties which were to be acknowledged sixty years after in the *Declaration* or *Bill of Rights*. Charles, seeing all his demands rejected, made peace with France and Spain, and tried to govern without calling the Parliament (1630–1638).

*Strafford and Laud.*—He anticipated no farther resistance. His only difficulty was to reconcile both parties who disputed for the ascendency, the queen and the ministers, the court and the council. The Earl of Strafford and Archbishop Laud, who wished to govern, at least in the general interest of the king, were precipitated into very many violent and vexatious measures. The monopoly of the greater part of provisions was sold, illegal duties were sustained by servile judges, and by tribunals of exception. Unheard-of fines were the punishment of most offences. The government, badly supported by the proud aristocracy, had recourse to the English clergy, who usurped, by degrees, the civil power. The Nonconformists were persecuted. A great number of men, who could no longer support so odious a government, went to America. At the moment when an order of the council forbade the emigrations, eight vessels, ready to depart, lay at anchor in the Thames; in one of them Pym, Hampden, and Cromwell were already embarked.

*Trial of Hampden—Long Parliament* (1640).—The public indignation burst forth on the occasion of the trial of Hampden. This gentleman preferred being imprisoned to paying an illegal tax of twenty shillings. One month after his condemnation, the Bishop of Edinburgh having tried to introduce the new English liturgy, a frightful tumult broke out in the Cathedral; the bishop was insulted, and the magistrates were chased by the populace. The Scotch engaged by oath in a *covenant*, by which they bound themselves to defend the sovereign, the religion, the laws, and the liberties of the country against all danger. Messengers, who repaired from village to village, carried it to the most remote parts of the country, as the *fiery cross* was carried into the mountains, to call to war the vassals of a lord. The Covenanters received arms and money from the Cardinal Richelieu, and the English army having refused to fight against their *brothers*, the king was obliged to place himself at the discretion of a fifth Parliament (Long Parliament, 1640).

*Civil War* (1642).—This new assembly, having so much to revenge, implacably prosecuted all those who were styled *delinquents*, Strafford especially, who had irritated the nation, less by actual crimes, than by the violence of an imperious temper. Strafford himself entreated the king to sign the bill of his condemnation, and Charles had the deplorable weakness to consent. The Parliament took possession of the government, directed the employment of the subsidies, reformed the decisions of the tribunals, and disarmed the royal authority by proclaiming itself indissoluble. The dreadful massacre of the Protestants of Ireland gave to Parliament an opportunity to seize the military power; the Irish Catholics had risen against the English who were established among them, and everywhere attacked their tyrants, mocking the queen, and displaying a false commission of the king. Charles, driven to extremity by a threatening remonstrance, went in person to the House to arrest five of the members. He failed in this great stroke of policy, and left London to commence the civil war (January 11th, 1642).

The Parliament party had the advantage of enthusiasm and of numbers: it had the capital, the great cities, the ports, the fleet. The king had the majority of the nobility, more skilled in arms than the Parliamentary troops. In the counties of the north and west the Royalists ruled, the Parliament in those of the east, in the middle and southeast, the most populous and richest. These latter counties, joining each other, formed a circle around London.

*Edge Hill—Newbury*, 1643.—*Marston Moor.*—The king soon marched towards the capital, but the indecisive battle of Edge Hill saved the adherents of the Parliament. They had time to organize themselves. Colonel Cromwell formed in the counties of the east volunteer squadrons, who opposed religious enthusiasm to the sentiments of honour which animated the cavaliers. The Parliament was again successful at Newbury, and united itself with Scotland by a solemn *covenant* (1643). The good understanding of the king with the Highlanders of the north and the Irish Catholics accelerated this unexpected union of two people who, until then, were enemies. It is said that a great number of Irish *papists*, called by the king, were mixed with the troops from their island; and that even women, armed with long knives, and in a savage dress, had been seen within their ranks. This Parliament would not receive the letters of that which the king had convoked at Oxford, and pushed on the war with new vigour. Enthusiasm had carried some families so far as to deprive themselves of one repast a week, to offer its value to the Parliament; an ordinance converted this offering into an obligatory tax for all the inhabitants of London and the adjacent parts. The nephew of the king, Prince Rupert, was defeated at Marston Moor, after a bloody battle, by the invincible stubbornness of the *saints* of the Parliamentary army, the cavaliers of Cromwell, who received on the field of battle the surname of *Ironsides*. They would have been able to send to the Parliament more than one hundred standards of the enemy, if, in their enthusiasm, they had not torn them in pieces to ornament their caps and their arms with them. The king lost York and all the north. The queen saved herself in France (1664).

*Second Battle of Newbury.*—This disaster seemed, for an instant, repaired. The king had obliged the Earl of Essex, general of the Parliament, to capitulate in the county of Cornwall. The Irish bands had landed in Scotland, and Montrose, one of the bravest *cavaliers*, having appeared suddenly in their camp in the dress of a Highlander, had gained two battles, raised the clans of the north, and spread terror even to the gates of Edinburgh. Already the king marched towards London; the people closed their shops, fasted and prayed, when they heard that he had been defeated at Newbury (for the second time). The Parliamentary troops had performed wonders ; at sight of the cannons, which they had but lately lost in the county of Cornwall, they threw themselves upon the royal batteries, seized their own pieces, and carried them away, embracing them with joy.

*Act of Renunciation.*—At this time a misunderstanding broke out among the conquerors. The power escaped from the Presbyterians to pass to the Independents. This latter party was a mixture of enthusiasts, philosophers, and libertines; but it drew its unity from one principle, the right to freedom of conscience. Notwithstanding their crimes and their reveries, this principle ought to have given them victory over adversaries less energetic and less consistent. While the Presbyterians believed that they were preparing peace by vain negotiations with the king, the Independents placed themselves at the head of the war. Cromwell declares that those in power prolonged it designedly, and the Parliament, through disinterested motives, or through fear of losing its popularity, decided* that every one should *renounce his own advancement*, and that the members of the Parliament should no more hold any civil or military office.

*Naseby—The King given up to the English.*—

* By what was called the *Self-denying Ordinance*.

Cromwell found means, by new success, to exempt himself from the common rule, and the Independents overthrew the royal army at Naseby, near Northampton. The papers of the king, found after the victory, and publicly read at London, proved that, notwithstanding his protestations, repeated a thousand times, he had called for the aid of foreigners, especially of the Irish Catholics. In the mean time, Montrose, abandoned by the Highlanders, who went to hide their booty at home, had been surprised and defeated. Prince Rupert, known until then by his impetuous courage, had given up Bristol at the first summons. The king wandered for a long time from city to city, from castle to castle, constantly changing his disguise; he stopped at Harrow-on-the-Hill, hesitating to enter the capital, which he saw at a distance. Finally, he retired, from fatigue more than choice, to the camp of the Scotch, where the resident minister of France had given him hope of finding an asylum, and where he soon perceived that he was a prisoner. His hosts spared not their outrages towards him. A Scotch clergyman, preaching before him at Newcastle, gave out to the congregation the 52d Psalm, which commences, "Why boastest thou thyself, thou tyrant, that thou canst do mischief?" The king, suddenly rising, sung, "Be merciful unto me, O God, for man goeth about to devour me ; he is daily fighting and troubling me. Mine enemies are daily on hand to swallow me up; for they be many that fight against me ;" and, from a sudden transport, the whole congregation joined him. But the Scotch, despairing of making him accept the covenant, gave him up to the English, who offered to pay the expenses of the war.

The unfortunate prince was but an instrument for which the Independents and Presbyterians disputed until they destroyed it. The misunderstanding was at its height between the army and Parliament. They took the king from the place where the commissioners of the latter guarded him, and, without receiving the orders of the chief general, Fairfax, Cromwell had him led to the army.

*Cromwell.*—In the mean time a reaction in favour of the king took place. Bands of citizens and apprentices, half-pay officers, and marines forced the gates of Westminster, and constrained the chamber to vote for the return of the king. But sixty members fled to the army, which marched towards London. Its entrance into the capital was the triumph of the Independents. Cromwell, seeing the Presbyterians eclipsed, fearing for his own party, hesitated for a moment if he should not work for the re-establishment of the king. But knowing well that he could not in any way se cure this prince's confidence, he began to aim higher, and thought of withdrawing the king from the army, as he had taken him from the Parliament. Charles, alarmed by menacing intelligence, escaped, and went to the Isle of Wight, where he found himself in the power of Cromwell.

*The Levellers.*—The ruin of the king was the seal of reconciliation between Cromwell and the Republicans. He had been obliged to repress the anarchical faction of the *Levellers* in the army; he had seized one of them in the midst of a regiment, and had him condemned and executed on the spot, in the presence of the army; but he was careful not to be always at variance with a party so energetic.

*Condemnation of the King*, 1649.—He regained them by beating the Scotch, whose army came to second the reaction in favour of the king. The Parliament of England, alarmed by a victory so prompt, which must turn to the profit of the Independents, hastened to negotiate anew with the king. While Charles was disputing with the deputies of Parliament, and repulsing with probity the means of escape which his servants prepared for him, the army removed him from the Isle of Wight, and *purged* the Parliament. Colonel Pride, with the list of the proscribed members in his hand, occupied the gate of the Commons at the head of two regiments, and repulsed with violence and insult those who persisted in claiming their rights. From the time that the party of the Independents had gained the ascendency the enthusiasm of the fanatics was at its height. The king was put on trial before a commission over which John Bradshaw, a cousin of Milton, presided. Notwithstanding the opposition of most of the members, and, among the rest, of the young and virtuous Sidney; notwithstanding the challenge of Charles, who maintained that the Commons could not exercise a parliamentary authority without the concurrence of the king and lords; notwithstanding the mediation of the Scotch commissioners, and the ambassadors of the States-General of the Netherlands, the king was condemned to death. At the moment when the judge pronounced the name of *Charles Stuart, brought to answer a charge of treason, and other great crimes presented against him in the name of the people of England* . . . . . "*Not by one half of the people,*" cried a voice. "*Where are the people? where is its consent? Oliver Cromwell is a traitor!*"

The whole assembly quickly rose, all eyes turned towards the gallery: "*Down with the women!*" cried Colonel Axtel: "*Soldiers, fire upon them!*" They recognised Lady Fairfax.

After the sentence, they refused to hear the

king. They dragged him out amid the insults of the soldiers, and cries of "*Justice! Execution!*" When it was necessary to sign the order for his death, they had great trouble to assemble the commissioners. Cromwell, almost the only one gay, bustling, bold, gave way to the most violent fits of his accustomed buffoonery; after having signed as the third, he daubed the ink in the face of Henry Martyn, who was seated near him, and who instantly returned it. Colonel Ingoldsby, his cousin, whose name was among the judges, but who had not set in the court during the trial, by accident entered the hall. "This time," cried Cromwell, "he will not escape us;" and seizing Ingoldsby with loud bursts of laughter, aided by some members who were there, he placed the pen between his fingers, and, guiding his hand, forced him to sign. Finally, they collected fifty-nine signatures, several names scratched in such a manner, either designedly, or from agitation of mind, that it was hardly possible to decipher them.*

*Execution of Charles I.*, 1648. — The scaffold was erected against a window of Whitehall. The king, after having blessed his children, went there, his head raised, with firm step, walking before his soldiers, who escorted him. Many people soaked their handkerchiefs in his blood. Cromwell wished

* Guizot.

to see the body, already placed in the coffin; he looked at it attentively, and raising its head with his hands, as if to assure himself that it was well severed from the body, said, "There was a body well built, and that promised a long life."

The House of Lords was abolished the year after. A great seal was engraved, with this motto: *The first year of liberty restored by the blessing of God*, 1648.*

---

## CHAPTER XII.

### THE THIRTY YEARS' WAR, 1618–48.

Maximilian II., 1564–1576.—Rodolph II., 1576–1612.—Mathias Emperor, 1612–1619.—Insurrection of Bohemia.—Commencement of the Thirty Years' War. — *Palatine Period*, 1619–1623: Ferdinand II. — War against the Protestants, Bohemia, the Palatinate.—Triumph of Ferdinand. — *Danish Period*, 1625–1629: League of the States of Lower Saxony.—Success of Tilly and Waldstein.—Intercession of Denmark and Sweden. — *Swedish Period*, 1630–1635.: Gustavus Adolphus invades the Empire.—Battle of Leipzig, 1631. — Invasion of Bavaria. — Battle of Lutzen; Death of Gustavus Adolphus, 1632. — Assassination of Waldstein, 1634. — Peace of Prague, 1635. — *French Period*, 1635–1648: Ministry of Richelieu, &c., &c.—Battle of the Dunes, 1640. —Battle of Leipzig, 1642; of Friburg, Norlingen, Sens, 1644, 1645, 1648, &c., &c.—Treaty of Westphalia, 1648.

The Thirty Years' War is the last conflict sustained by the Reformation. This war, indeterminate in its march and its object, is composed of

* Old style. This date corresponds to February 9, 1649.

four distinct wars, wherein the Elector of Palatine, Denmark, Sweden, and France, successively play the principal part. It becomes more and more complicated, until it embraces all Europe. Several causes prolong it indefinitely: first, the close union of both branches of the house of Austria and the Catholic party; the opposite party is not homogeneous; second, the inaction of England, the tardy mediation of France, the weakness of Denmark and Sweden.

The armies which carried on the Thirty Years' War were no longer feudal militia; they were standing armies, but armies which the sovereigns could not maintain (see, above, the armies of Charles V., in the wars of Italy). They lived at the expense of the country, and ruined it. The ruined peasant became a soldier, and sold himself to the first comer. The war prolonging itself, thus formed armies without a country, an immense military force, which floats in Germany, and encourages the most gigantic projects of princes, and of private individuals even.

Germany again becomes the centre of European politics. The first contest of the Reformation with the house of Austria was renewed, after sixty years' interruption; all the powers took part in it.

*Results.*—Europe seems as if it must be overthrown, and yet we perceive but one important change ; France had succeeded to the supremacy of the house of Austria. The influence of the Reformation will no longer be sensible, and the treaty of Westphalia commences a new world.

*Maximilian II.—Rudolph II.*—Whether from fear of the Turks, or from the personal moderation of the princes, the German branch of the house of Austria, in the second part of the sixteenth century, followed a policy entirely opposite to that of Philip II. The tolerant policy of Ferdinand I. and Maximilian II. favoured the progress of Protestantism in Austria, Bohemia, and Hungary; they even suspected Maximilian to be Protestant at heart (1555–1576). The feeble Rudolph II., who succeeded him, had neither his moderation nor his ability. While he shut himself up with Tycho Brahe, to study astrology and alchymy, the Protestants of Hungary, Bohemia, and Austria made one common cause. The Archduke Mathias, brother of Rudolph, favoured them, and forced the emperor to yield Austria and Hungary to him (1607–1609).

*Succession of Juliers.*—The Empire was not less agitated than the hereditary states of the house of Austria. Aix-la-Chapelle and Donawerth, where the Protestants had made themselves masters, were put under the ban of the Empire. The archbishop, Elector of Cologne, who wished to secularize his states, was deposed. The reopening of the succession of Cleves and Juliers again complicated the situation of Germany. Protestant and Catholic princes, the Elector of Brandenburgh, the Duke of Deux-Ponts, and others, claimed it equally. The Empire divided itself into two leagues. Henry IV., who favoured the Protestants, intended to enter Germany, and to avail himself of this state of things to humble the house of Austria, when he was assassinated (1610). Instead of being deferred, the Thirty Years' War only became more terrible.

*Mathias, Emperor—Battle of Prague,* 1621. —Mathias, after having forced Rudolph to yield Bohemia to him, succeeded him in the Empire (1612–19), and also in all the embarrassments of his position. The Spaniards and Dutch invaded the dukedoms of Cleves and Juliers. The Bohemians, conducted by the Count of Turn, rose for the defence of their religion. Turn, at the head of a part of the States, repaired to the council-room, and precipitated the four *gouverneurs* into the ditches of the castle of Prague (1618). The Bohemians pretended it to be an *ancient custom of their country* to throw double-dealing ministers out of the window. They levied troops, and, not wishing to acknowledge as successor to Mathias a pupil of the Jesuits, Ferdinand II., they gave the crown to Frederic V., elector of Palatine, son-in-law of the King of England, and nephew of the Stadtholder of Holland.

*Palatine Period of the Thirty Years' War*, 1619–23.—At the same time, the Hungarians elected the Waiwode of Transylvania, Betlem Gabor, for king. Ferdinand, who was besieged for a short time by the Bohemians in Vienna, was supported by the Duke of Bavaria, by the Catholic league of Germany, and by the Spaniards. Frederic, who was a Calvinist, was abandoned by the Lutheran *union*. James I., his father-in-law, was satisfied with negotiating for him. Attacked in the capital of Bohemia itself, he lost the battle of Prague by his negligence or his cowardice. He dined tranquilly at the castle, while his subjects died for him in the field (1621). Notwithstanding the valour of Mansfield, and other partisans who ravaged Germany in his name, still he was driven from the Palatinate ; the Protestant union was dissolved, and the electoral dignity transferred to the Duke of Bavaria.

*Waldstein—Danish Period*, 1625–1629.—The States of Lower Saxony, threatened by an approaching restitution of ecclesiastical property, called the princes of the North, who were united to them by community of religious interest, to the aid of Germany. The young King of Sweden,

Gustavus Adolphus, was at that time occupied in a glorious war against Poland, the ally of Austria. The King of Denmark, Christian IV., undertook their defence. At the approach of this new war, Ferdinand would not depend on the Catholic league, of which the Duke of Bavaria was the chief, and of which the celebrated Tilly commanded the troops. The Count of Waldstein,* officer of the emperor, offered to form him an army, provided he was permitted to enrol fifty thousand men. He kept his word. All the adventurers who wished to live by pillage surrounded him, and he made laws equally for the friends and the enemies of the emperor. Christian IV. was defeated at Lutter. Waldstein reduced Pomerania, and received from the emperor the estates of the two Dukes of Mecklenburg, and the title of *General of the Baltic.* But for the succour which the Swedes threw into the place, he would have taken the powerful city of Stralsund (1628). All the North trembled. The emperor, in order to divide his enemies, granted to Denmark a humiliating peace (1629). He ordered a restitution to the Protestants of all the property secularized since 1555. Then the army of Waldstein fell back upon Germany, and overran it at pleasure; several states were exhausted by enormous contributions. So great was the distress of

* He signed himself *Waldstein*, not *Wallenstein*.

the inhabitants, that some of them dug up corpses to satisfy their hunger, and the dead were found with their mouths still filled with raw herbs.

*Gustavus Adolphus,* 1630—*Battle of Leipzig,* 1631 — *Swedish Period,* 1630–1636. — Deliverance came from Sweden and France. Cardinal Richelieu disengaged the Swedes by procuring for them a truce with Poland. He disarmed the emperor by persuading him that he could not have his son elected king of the Romans unless he sacrificed Waldstein to the resentment of Germany, and, while he thus deprived himself of his best general, Gustavus Adolphus entered the Empire (1630). Ferdinand was but little alarmed at first; he said that this *king of snow* would melt away on approaching the South. They knew not yet what these men of iron were; this army, heroic and pious in comparison with the mercenary troops of Germany. A short time after the arrival of Gustavus Adolphus, Torquato Conti, general of the emperor, demanded a truce, in consequence of the severe cold; Gustavus replied that the Swedes *knew not winter.* The genius of the conqueror disconcerted the German routine by an impetuous tactics, which sacrificed everything to the rapidity of its movements, and which lavished men to shorten the war. To make himself master of the strongholds by following the course of the rivers, to secure Sweden by closing the Baltic against the Imperials, to deprive them of all their allies, to hem in Austria before attacking it, such was the plan of Gustavus. If he had marched straight to Vienna, he would only have appeared in Germany as a foreign conqueror; by driving off the Imperials from the Northern and Western States, which they were destroying, he presented himself as the champion of the Empire against the emperor. Tilly, who had first opposed him, arrested not the torrent; he only drew the hatred of Europe on the Imperial troops by the destruction of Magdebourg. Saxony and Brandenburgh, which wished to remain neutral, were drawn into an alliance with Gustavus by the rapidity of his success. He defeated Tilly in the bloody battle of Leipzig (1631). While the Saxons prepared themselves to attack Bohemia, he beat the Duke of Lorraine, penetrated into Alsace, and subjected the Electorates of Treves, Mayence, and the Rhine, to which Richelieu would have extended the rights of neutrality; but Gustavus wanted either friends or enemies. Finally, Bavaria is invaded at the same time as Bohemia, Tilly dies in defending the Lech, and Austria is opened on all sides.

It was now absolutely necessary that Ferdinand should have recourse to that proud Waldstein whom he had driven away. For a long time he saw the emperor and the Catholics, as it were, at his feet; he was, he said, too happy in his retreat. They could only conquer this philosophical moderation by giving him in the Empire a power nearly equal to that of the emperor.

*Lutzen*, 1632.—At this price he saved Bohemia, and marched on Nuremberg, to arrest the arms of Gustavus. There was great astonishment in Europe when they saw the two invincible men for three months encamped face to face without taking advantage of an opportunity so long expected. Waldstein at last put himself in motion, and was met by the King of Sweden near Lutzen. Gustavus made an attack, wishing to defend the Elector of Saxony. After several charges, the king, deceived by the darkness of a fog, threw himself before the enemy's ranks, and fell, struck by two bullets. The Duke of Saxe Lauenburg, who afterward went over to the Imperial party, was behind him at the fatal moment, and was accused of his death. They sent the buff-skin coat which the Swedish hero wore to Vienna (1632). All Europe mourned Gustavus. But why? He may have died most opportunely for his glory. He had saved Germany, and had not had time to oppress it. He had not restored the Palatinate to the dispossessed elector; he had destined Mayence for his Chancellor Oxenstiern; he had showed his disposition to reside at Augsburg, which would have become the seat of a new empire.

*Assassination of Waldstein.* — While the able Oxenstiern continued the war, and had himself declared chief, at Heilbron, of the League of the Circles of Franconia, Swabia, and Rhine, Waldstein remained in Bohemia in a state of formidable inaction. It was for him that Gustavus seemed to have laboured in destroying throughout all Germany the Imperial party. He had served him both by his victories and by his death. "*Germany,*" said Waldstein, "*cannot contain two men like us.*" After the death of Gustavus he was alone. Shut up in his palace at Prague, with a royal train of attendants, and surrounded by a crowd of adventurers who had attached themselves to his fortune, he there watched for the proper opportunity. This terrible man, who was seldom seen, who never laughed, and who only spoke to his soldiers to make their fortune or to pronounce their death, was the hope of Europe. The King of France called him *his cousin*, and Richelieu offered his interest to make him King of Bohemia. It was time that the emperor made a decision; he took the decision of Henry III. in respect to the Duke of Guise. Waldstein was assassinated at Egra; and Ferdinand, remembering the services he had formerly rendered to him, had 3000 masses said for the peace of his soul (1634).

In the mean time, the Elector of Saxony had made his peace with the emperor. The Swedes were not strong enough to remain alone in Germany. It was necessary that France, in her turn, should descend to the field of battle.

*Richelieu*, 1635—*French Period*, 1635–1648.—Richelieu, who then governed France, found it given up to Spanish influence, and harassed by the prinçes and the nobles, by the mother of the king, and by the Protestants (government of Mary of Medicis, 1610–17, and of the favourite De Luynes, 1617–21). This great minister, employed against the last the system of Henry IV., with this advantage, that he was not obliged by any former engagement, or by any motives of gratitude, to have that respect for them which might be inimical to his own interests. He had taken La Rochelle from them by constructing a dam of 800 toises in the sea (as Alexander formerly did at the siege of Tyre); had conquered, disarmed, and by a magnanimous policy appeased them (1627–28). He turned himself against the grandees, had the mother and brother of the king driven from France, and caused a Marillac and a Montmorency to perish on the scaffold (1630–32). He had prisons in his house at Ruel; he had his enemies condemned there, that he might safely deride or defy the judges. Nothing remained for him but to give some dignity to these odious victories over his internal enemies by conquests abroad (1635).

*Bernard of Weimar.*—First, he bought over Bernard of Weimar (the best disciple of Gustavus Adolphus), with his army. He united himself with the Dutch to divide the Spanish Netherlands, while at the other end of France he retook Roussillon; the alliance with the Duke of Savoy secured to him the passages of Italy. Having commenced from the side of the Netherlands, France gained in Italy more glory than real advantage. But the Dutch, her allies, destroyed the Spanish navy in the battle of the Dunes (1639). Bernard of Weimar took the four forest towns,* and also Friburg and Brisach, under the walls of which he obtained four victories. He forgot that France had already purchased his conquests from him. He was going to make himself independent, when he died, as opportunely for Richelieu as the death of Waldstein was for Ferdinand.

*Success of the French.*—Everything became favourable to the French from the moment that the rebellion of Catalonia and of Portugal forced Spain into a defensive war (1640). The house of Bra-

* Rhinfeld, Valdshut, Sechingen, Lauffenburg, called forest towns, because near the Black Forest.

ganza ascended the throne of Portugal with the applause of Europe. The French victors in Italy took, in the Low Countries, Arras and Thionville. The great Condé gained the battle of Rocroi five days after the accession of Louis XIV.: a happy omen for this great reign, which encouraged France after the death of Richelieu and Louis XIII.

*Battle of Leipzig*, 1642.—The war had now changed its character for the second time. To the fanaticism of Tilly, and of his master Ferdinand II., to the revolutionary genius of the Waldsteins and the Weimars, had succeeded able tacticians, a Piccolomini, a Merci, generals of the emperor, Banner, Torstenson, and Wrangel, pupils of Gustavus. War being a profitable trade for so many people, peace became more and more difficult. France, entirely occupied with protecting her conquests of Lorraine and Alsace, refused to join the Swedes to overthrow the house of Austria. Torstenson thought for a moment that he could conquer without the aid of the French. This paralytic general, who astonished Europe by the rapidity of his manœuvres, had renewed the glory of Gustavus Adolphus at Leipzig (1642). He had given a blow to the Danes, the secret friends of the emperor; the alliance with Transylvania permitted him, finally, to penetrate Austria (1645). The defection of Transylvania, and the death of Torstenson, saved the emperor.

*Ferdinand III.*, 1637—*Condé—Treaty of Westphalia,* 1648.—In the mean time, negotiations had been opened since 1636; the accession of Ferdinand III. to the Empire seemed necessarily to favour them (1637). Although the mediation of the pope, of Venice, and of the kings of Denmark, Poland, and England, had been rejected, the preliminaries of peace were signed in 1642. The death of Richelieu revived the hopes of the house of Austria, and retarded the peace. The victories of Condé at Friburg, at Nordlingen, and at Sens (1644–45–48), that of Turenne and the Swedes at Sommershausen, and, finally, the taking of Little Prague by Wrangel (1648), were necessary to decide the emperor to sign the treaty of Westphalia. The war continued only between Spain, France, and Portugal. Principal articles: 1st. The peace of Augsburg (1555) is confirmed and extended to the Calvinists. 2d. The sovereignty of the different States of Germany within their own territory is sanctioned, also their right to the general diets of the Empire; those rights are warranted *internally*, by the position of the Imperial Chamber and Aulic Council, to which an equal number of Protestants and Catholics were hereafter to be admitted; *externally*, by the mediation of France and Sweden. 3d. Indemnities awarded to several states, and, to secure them, a great amount of ecclesiastical property is secularized. *France* obtains Alsace, the three bishoprics, Philipsburg, and Pignerol, the keys of Germany and Piedmont: *Sweden*, a part of Pomerania, Bremen, Verden, Wismar, &c., three votes at the diets of the Empire, and five millions of German dollars: *The Elector of Brandenburg*, Magdebourg, Halberstadt, &c., &c.: *Saxony, Mecklenburg*, and *Hesse Cassel*, are also indemnified. 4th. The son of Frederic V. recovers the Lower Palatinate of the Rhine (the Upper Palatinate remains in the hands of Bavaria); an eighth electoral dignity is created in his favour. 5th. The United Provinces are acknowledged as independent of Spain; the United Provinces and Swiss Cantons, independent of the German Empire.

---

## CHAPTER XIII.

### THE EAST AND NORTH IN THE FIFTEENTH CENTURY.

### § I. TURKEY, HUNGARY, 1566–1648.

*Solyman the Magnificent.*—The reign of Solyman the Magnificent had been the summit of Ottoman grandeur. Under him the Turks were equally formidable by land and by sea; they were admitted into the system of Europe by their alliance with France against the house of Austria. Solyman endeavoured to give fixed laws to his people, collected the maxims and ordinances of his predecessors, supplied those which were lost, and settled the civil hierarchy. He embellished Constantinople by rebuilding the ancient aqueduct, of which the water is divided among eight hundred fountains; he founded the Mosque Souleimanieh, to which four colleges are attached, a house of refuge for the poor, an hospital for the sick, and a library of two thousand manuscripts. The Turkish language ennobles itself by a mixture of Arabian and Persian; Solyman himself made verses in these languages. In his old age the sultan was entirely governed by Rouschen (Roxalana), whom he had married, and who caused him to put his children by a former marriage to death. The empire, exhausted by so many wars, seemed to grow old with him under the influence of the government of a seraglio. Solyman prepared its ruin by taking the command of the armies from the members of the imperial family.

*Lepanto*, 1571.—Under his indolent successor, Selim II. (1566–1574), the Turks took Cyprus from the Venitians, who received but little assistance from Spain; but they were defeated in the Gulf of Lepanto by the combined fleets of Philip II., Venice, and the pope, under the orders of Don Juan of Austria. Since this check, the Turks allow that

God, who has given them the empire of the land, has left the dominion of the sea to infidels.

Under Amurat III., Mohammed III., and Achmet I. (1574–1617), the Turks sustained, with various success, long wars against the Persians and the Hungarians. The janizaries, who by their revolts had troubled the reigns of these princes, put to death their successors, Mustapha and Othman (1617–1623). The Empire rose under Amurat IV., the Intrepid, who employed the turbulent spirit of the janizaries abroad, took Bagdad, and interposed in the troubles of India. Under the imbecile Ibrahim (1645–49), the Turks, always following the impulse given to them by Amurat, took Candia from the Venitians.

*Hungary.*—This kingdom had been divided between the house of Austria and the Turks since 1562. From this division rose a continual war. The jurisdiction of Transylvania was another cause of war between Austria and the Porte. In the interior, Hungary was not more tranquil. The Austrian princes, hoping to increase their power by leading Hungary back to religious uniformity, persecuted the Protestants and violated the privileges of the nation. The Hungarians rose under Rudolph II., Ferdinand II., and Ferdinand III.; the princes of Transylvania, Etienne Botschkaï, Betlem Gabor, George Regotzi, placed themselves successively at the head of the malecontents. By the pacifications of Vienna (1622) and of Lintz (1645); by the decrees of the diets of Oldenburg (1622) and Presburg (1647), the kings of Hungary were forced to consent to the public exercise of the Protestant religion, and to respect the national privileges.

## § II. POLAND, PRUSSIA, RUSSIA, 1505–1648.

Poland triumphed over the Teutonic Order, a German power, which, though feebly sustained by the Empire, had pushed itself beyond Germany into the heart of the Sclavonic States. In recompense for this, however, she neglected to protect the Bohemians and Hungarians in their revolts against Austria.

The two great nations of Sclavonic origin had frequent communication with each other, but little intercourse with the Scandinavian States, till the revolutions of Livonia engaged them in a common war, towards the middle of the 16th century. Livonia then became for the North of Europe what Milan had been for the South.

*Prussia,* 1525—*State of Poland and Prussia in the first half of the* 16*th Century—Accession of Wasili IV.* (*Iwanowitch*), 1505, *and of Sigismond I.*, 1506.—The feeble Wasili had the imprudence to break with the Tartars of the Crimea, whose services had been so useful to Iwan III.; he completed the subjection of Plescof, took Smolensk from the Lithuanians, but was defeated by them in the same year (1514). He united himself to the Teutonic Order against the Poles, but was not able to save Prussia from submitting to Poland. The grand-master, Albert of Brandenburg, embraced Lutheranism (1525), secularized Teutonic Prussia, and received it in fief from Sigismond I.

*Iwan IV.*, 1533–1584. 1533, *Accession of Iwan IV.* (*Wasiliewitch*) *in Russia;* 1548, *of Sigismond II., called Augustus, in Poland.*—During the minority of Iwan IV., the power passed from the hands of the Regent Helene to several princes, who supplanted each other. 1547, under the influence of the Empress Anastasia, Iwan IV. restrained at first the violence of his character. He completed the humbling of the Tartars by the definitive reunion of Kasan, and by the conquest of Astrakan (1552–1554).

*Livonia*, 1558–83 — *War of Livonia.* — The order of the knights of Porte-Glaive, conqueror of the Russians (1502), had been independent of the Teutonic Order since 1521. But towards this epoch all the powers of the North preferred their claims on Livonia. Iwan IV. having invaded it in 1558, the grand-master, Gotthar Kettler, preferred to reunite it to Poland by the treaty of Wilna

(1561), creating himself Duke of Courland. The King of Denmark, Frederic II., master of the island of Œsel, and of certain districts, and the King of Sweden, Eric XIV., having been called to aid the city of Revel, and the nobility of Esthonia, took part in the war, which was prosecuted by land and by sea.

The Czar encountered two obstacles in his plans of conquest: the jealousy of the Russians against the strangers, whom he preferred before them, and the fear which his cruelty had impressed upon the Livonians. He crushed all his subjects who were able to resist him, whether in the trading class or among the nobility (1570), and finally invaded Livonia in the name of a brother of the King of Denmark (1575). But Poland and Sweden united themselves against the Czar, who made peace with Poland by giving up Livonia to her, and concluded a truce with Sweden, which remained in possession of Carelia (1582–83). He died in 1584.

[*Code of Iwan IV.*, 1550, presenting a systematized view of all the ancient laws—Gratuitous justice—All landholders subjected to military service—Establishment of a regular pay of the soldiers—Institution of the permanent militia of the guards—Commerce with Tartary, Turkey, and Lithuania. The wars of Livonia and Lithuania closing the Baltic to the Russians, they had no longer communications with the rest of Europe, except by winding round Sweden through the seas of the North. 1555, the Englishman, Chanceller, sent by Queen Mary to find a northern passage to the Indies, landed at the place where, afterward, Archangel was founded; there was regular commerce between Russia and England until the civil wars of Russia (1605). —1577–81, discovery of Siberia.]

*Successions of Poland*, 1572; *of Russia*, 1593.— The dynasty of the Jagellons was extinguished in 1572, by the death of Sigismond Augustus; that of Rurick in 1598, by the death of Czar *Fedor I.*, son and successor of Iwan IV. From these two events resulted directly, or indirectly, two long and bloody wars, which again set up as prizes all the northern dominions; one war had the succession of Sweden for its object, the other the succession of Russia. The first war, which lasted sixty-seven years (1593–1660), was twice interrupted: first by the second war (1609–1619), and afterward by the Thirty Years' War (1629–1655).

*False Demetrius.*— The throne of Poland became purely elective 1573–1575. *Henry of Valois* appeared in this kingdom only to sign the first *Pacta Conventa*, 1570–1587. The accession of *Ethienne Batthon*, prince of Transylvania, delayed the moment when Poland was to lose her preponderance. He limited the power of his subjects

(Dantzic, Riga, 1578–1586); he humbled Russia and Denmark (1582–85). 1587, *Sigismond III.*, son of John III., king of Sweden, elected King of Poland, found himself, at his accession to the throne of his father, in a difficult position. Sweden was Protestant; Poland Catholic; they both claimed Livonia. The uncle of Sigismond (Charles IX.), chief of the Lutheran party in Sweden, prevailed over him, both by policy (1593) and by arms (1598). Thence a war between the two nations, which was interrupted only at the moment that they took Russia for a field of battle. The usurpation of Borris-Godunow, and the impostures of several false Demetrii, who called themselves heirs of the throne of Moscow, made the Poles and Swedes hope either to dismember Russia, or to give her one of their princes as master. Their hopes were defeated. A Russian (1613–1645), *Michael Fedrowitch,* founded the house of Romanow. 1616–1618, Russia gave up to Sweden Ingria and Russian Carelia; to Poland the territories of Smolensko, Tschernigow, and Nowgorod-Serverskoi, and she lost all communication with the Baltic. 1620–1629, the war recommenced between Poland and Sweden, and was continued to the period in which Gustavus Adolphus engaged in the Thirty Years' War (1629. Treaty of six years, renewed in 1635 for twenty-six).

Sigismond III. and his successor, Wladislas VII. (1632–1648), sustained long wars against the Turks, the Russians, and the Cossacks of the Ukraine.

Poland yielded to Sweden the part of predominant power in the North, but she retained her superiority over Russia, whose development had been retarded by her civil wars.

*Prussia*, 1563.— Joachim II., elector of Brandenburg, obtained from the King of Poland the investiture of the fief of Prussia. 1618, at the death of the Duke Albert-Frederic (son of Albert of Brandenburg), the Elector John Sigismond, his son-in-law, succeeded him. 1614–1666, the electoral branch also received a part of the succession of Juliers, in virtue of the claims of Anne, daughter of the Duke of Prussia, Albert-Frederic, and wife of the Elector of Brandenburg, John Sigismond. The son of the latter, Frederic William, founded the grandeur of Prussia.

## § III. DENMARK AND SWEDEN.

In the 16th century these two states were the prey of internal troubles, and sustained long wars. The resources of the two nations, however, were developed, and they became prepared for the Thirty Years' War. The conduct of Sweden at that time was a prelude to the heroic part which she was to play throughout all the 18th century.

*Peace of Stettin*, 1570.—The weakness of Denmark and the internal troubles of Sweden terminated (by the peace of Stettin, 1570) a long quarrel, which had existed between these kingdoms since the rupture of the Union of Calmar. Denmark was from that time tranquil, under the long reigns of Frederic II. (1559–1588) and of Christiern IV., down to the period when the latter, rather an able minister than a great general, compromised the repose of Denmark by attacking Gustavus Adolphus (1611–1613), and by taking part in the Thirty Years' War (1625).

The unworthy son of Gustavus Vasa, Eric XIV. (1560–1568), had been dispossessed by his brother, John III. (1568–1592), who undertook to re-establish the Catholic religion in Sweden. The son of John Sigismond, king of Sweden and Poland, was supplanted by his uncle, Charles IX. (1604), father of Gustavus Adolphus. See, above, the article *Poland*.

## CHAPTER XIV.

DISCOVERIES AND COLONIES OF THE MODERNS—DISCOVERIES AND ESTABLISHMENTS OF THE PORTUGUESE IN BOTH INDIES, 1412–1582.

### § I. DISCOVERIES AND COLONIES OF THE MODERNS.

*Principal Motives which have determined the Moderns to seek new Countries, and to establish themselves there.*—1st. Martial and adventurous spirit, desire to gain by conquest and pillage. 2d. Commercial spirit, desire to acquire by the legitimate method of exchange. 3d. Religious spirit, desire either to convert the idolatrous nations to the Christian faith, or to escape themselves religious persecution.

*We owe the foundation of the principal modern colonies* to the five most western nations who have held, successively, the empire of the seas: to the Portuguese and Spaniards (15th and 16th centuries); to the Dutch and French (17th century); finally, to the English (17th and 18th centuries). The Spanish colonies had, at first, the exploring of the mines for their principal object; the aim of the Portuguese was commerce, and the raising of tributes imposed upon the conquered. The Dutch colonies were essentially commercial; those of the English were both commercial and agricultural

The principal difference between the ancient and modern colonies is, that the ancient only remained united to their mother-country by a sort of filial bond. The moderns are regarded as the property of their parent country, which interdicts to them all commerce with strangers.

*Direct Results of the Discoveries and Establishments of the Moderns.*—Commerce changed both its form and route. For land commerce, maritime was generally substituted; the commerce of the world passed from the countries situated on the Mediterranean to the Western countries. *The indirect results* are innumerable; the one most remarkable is the development of the maritime powers.

*Principal Routes of the Commerce of the East during the Middle Ages.*—In the first half of the Middle Ages, the Greeks carried on the commerce with India through Egypt, then through the Black and Caspian Seas; in the second, the Italians carried it on through Syria and the Gulf of Persia; finally, through Egypt. *Crusades. Voyages* of Rubruquis, Marco Paolo, and John Mandeville, from the 11th to the 14th century. At the commencement of the 14th century the Spaniards discovered the Canaries.

## § II. DISCOVERIES AND ESTABLISHMENTS OF THE PORTUGUESE.

*The Infant Don Henry.*—It belonged to the most

western nation of Europe to commence a train of discoveries, which have spread European civilization over all the world. The Portuguese, restrained by the power of Spain, and always at war with the Moors, from whom they had conquered their country, had to turn their ambition towards the coast of Africa. After a crusade of several centuries, the ideas of the conquerors were enlarged; they conceived the project of seeking new infidel nations, in order to subject and convert them. A thousand old narratives excited their curiosity, their valour, and their avarice; they wished to see those mysterious countries where nature had created monsters, or where she had strewed gold on the surface of the ground. The Infant Don Henry, third son of John I., seconded the ardour of the nation. He spent his life at Segres, near the Cape of St. Vincent; there, with his eyes fixed on the seas of the South, he gave instructions to the pilots who first visited those unknown climes. Cape Non, the fatal limit of ancient navigators, had already been passed; they had discovered Madeira (1412–13); they passed even Cape Boyador and Cape Verde; they discovered the Azores (1448); they had gone, too, beyond that formidable line where they believed that the air burned like fire. When they had pushed beyond Senegal, they saw, with astonishment, that the men, who were of a lead colour north of this river, were entirely black at the south. On arriving at Congo, they saw a new heaven and new stars (1484). But what encouraged the spirit of discovery more powerfully, was the gold which they had found in Guinea.

*Cape of Good Hope*, 1486.—They now began to pay more respect to the reports of the ancient Phœnicians, who pretended to have made the circuit of Africa, and they hoped that, by following the same route, they would be able to reach the East Indies. While the king, John II., sent two gentlemen by land to the Indies (Covillam and Payva), Barthelemy Diaz touched at the promontory which terminates Africa in the South, and named it Cape of Tempest; but the king, who from that time was sure of finding the route to the Indies, called it the *Cape of Good Hope* (1486).

It was then that the discovery of the New World astonished the Portuguese, and redoubled their emulation. Two nations, however, were ready to dispute the empire of the sea; they had recourse to the pope; Alexander VI. divided the two new worlds: all which was east of the Azores was to belong to Portugal; all west was given to Spain. They traced a line on the globe, which marked the limits of these reciprocal rights, and which they called the *line of demarcation*. New discoveries soon disturbed this line.

*Vasco de Gama*, 1497–1498.—At last the King of Portugal, Emmanuel the Fortunate, gave the command of a fleet to the famous Vasco de Gama (1497–1498). He received from the king the journal of the voyage of Covillam; he took out ten men condemned to death, whose lives he might risk if needful, and who by their courage might merit pardon. He spent one night in prayers in the Chapel of the Virgin, and received the sacrament on the eve of his departure. The people, in tears, conducted him to the shore. A magnificent convent has been founded on the spot from which Gama departed.

The fleet approached the *terrible cape*, when the crew, terrified by this stormy sea, and dreading a famine, rose against Gama. Nothing could stop him; he put the ringleader in irons, and taking the helm himself, he doubled the extremity of Africa. Greater dangers awaited him on the eastern coast, which, as yet, no European vessel had visited. The Moors, who traded with Africa and India, laid snares for these new-comers, who appeared to share the treasures with them. But the artillery terrified them, and Gama, traversing the gulf of seven hundred leagues which separated Africa from India, landed at Calicut, thirteen months after his departure from Lisbon.

Upon landing on this unknown shore, Vasco

forbade his men to follow him, or to come to his help, if they heard that he was in danger; and notwithstanding the plots of the Moors, he caused Zamorin to accept the alliance of Portugal.

*Alvarès Cabral.* — A new expedition soon followed the first, under the orders of Alvarès Cabral; the admiral received from the hands of the king a hat blessed by the pope. After having passed the Cape Verde Islands, he took to the wide sea, moved far towards the west, where he saw a new country, rich and fertile, where everlasting spring reigned: this was Brazil, the country, of all the American Continent, nearest to Africa. There are but thirty degrees of longitude from this country to Mount Atlas: this was the land which they ought to have discovered first (1500).

*Albuquerque*, 1505–1515.—The address of Cabral, Gama, and Almeida, first viceroy of the Indies, frustrated the efforts of the Moors, divided the natives of the country, and armed Cochin against Calicut and Cananor. Quiloa and Sofala, in Africa, received the laws of Europe. But the principal founder of the Empire of the Portuguese in the Indies was the valiant Albuquerque; he took, at the entrance of the Gulf of Persia, Ormus, the most brilliant and polished city of Asia (1507). The King of Persia, to whom she had belonged, demanded a tribute from the Portuguese;

Albuquerque showed to the ambassador his cannons and balls: "There," said he, "is the coin with which the King of Portugal pays tribute."

*The Venitians.*—In the mean time, Venice saw the sources of her riches drained; the route from Alexandria began to be neglected. The Sultan of Egypt perceived that there were no more duties upon provisions from the East; the Venitians leagued with him, and sent to Alexandria frames of wood, which were transported to Suez, and of which they made ships (1508). She had at first the advantage over the Portuguese, but she was afterward defeated, as were also the other armaments which continued to descend the Red Sea. To prevent new attacks, Albuquerque proposed to the King of Abyssinia to alter the course of the Nile, which would have changed Egypt into a desert.

He made Goa the chief of the Portuguese establishments in India (1510). The occupation of Malacca and Ceylon rendered the Portuguese masters of the vast sea which terminates the Gulf of Bengal at the north (1511–1518). The conqueror died at Goa, poor and disgraced, and with him departed all the justice and all the humanity of the conquerors. Long after his death, the Indians went to the grave of the great Albuquerque to demand justice from him for the grievances caused by his successors.

*Empire of the Portuguese.* — The Portuguese having introduced themselves to China and Japan (1517–42), possessed for some time all the maritime commerce of Asia. Their sway extended over the coasts of Guinea, of Melinde, of Mozambique, and of Sofala; over those of both Indies, over the Malaccas, Ceylon, and the Sonda Islands. But they had little more in this vast extent of country than a chain of factories and forts. The decay of their colonies was accelerated by several causes: first, the distance of their conquests; second, the feeble population of Portugal little calculated to extend their establishments; their national pride prevented an amalgamation of the conquerors with the conquered; third, the love of plunder, which was soon substituted for the spirit of commerce; fourth, the disorder of the administration; fifth, the monopoly of the crown; sixth, and finally, the Portuguese, who were satisfied with transporting the merchandise to Lisbon, and did not distribute it in Europe, must sooner or later be supplanted by more industrious rivals.

*John of Castro.*—The downfall of their Empire was retarded by two heroes, John of Castro (1543–48) and Ataïde (1568–72). John of Castro had to fight the Indians and the Turks united. The King of Camboja had received from the great Solyman engineers, founders, and all the implements for a European war. Castro, nevertheless, delivered the citadel of Diu, and triumphed at Goa, after the manner of the generals of antiquity. He wanted funds to repair the fortifications of Diu; he made a loan in his own name from the inhabitants of Goa, giving them his whiskers for security. He expired in the arms of St. Francis Xavier, in 1548. Only three reals were found in the house of this man, who had the management of the treasury of the Indies.

*Ataïde.*—The government of Ataïde was the epoch of a universal rising of the Indies against the Portuguese; he faced every opponent, beat the army of the King of Camboja, composed of a hundred thousand men, defeated Zamorin, and made him swear to have no more vessels of war. Even when he was again pressed in Goa, he refused to give up the most remote possessions, and made vessels depart for Lisbon with the yearly tribute of the Indies.

After his death everything rapidly declined. The division of India into three governments again weakened the Portuguese power. At the death of Sebastian, and his successor, the Cardinal Henri (1581), Portuguese India followed the fate of Portugal, and passed into the unskilful hands of the Spaniards (1582), until the period that the Dutch came to divest them of this vast empire.

## CHAPTER XV.

DISCOVERY OF AMERICA—CONQUESTS AND ESTABLISHMENTS OF THE SPANIARDS IN THE 15TH AND 16TH CENTURIES.

"One of the most wonderful facts in regard to our globe was, that one half of its inhabitants had always been ignorant of the other half; all which had before appeared grand sinks into insignificance when compared with this species of new creation.

"*Christopher Columbus.*—Columbus, struck with the enterprises of the Portuguese, conceived that one might do something even greater, and from only attentively observing a map of the globe, he judged that there must be another world, and that he would find it by steering continually towards the west. His courage was equal to the force of his genius, and only the greater, that he had had to combat the prejudices of all the princes. Genoa, his native city, treated him as a visionary, and thus lost the only opportunity which could be offered for its aggrandizement. Henry VII., king of England, more eager for money than capable of hazarding it in so noble an enterprise, would not listen to the brother of Columbus ; he was himself refused by John II., of Portugal, whose views were entirely turned towards the coast of Africa. He could not address himself to France, where the navy was always neglected, and where affairs were more than ever in confusion, under the minority of Charles VIII. The Emperor Maximilian had neither ports for a fleet, nor money to equip it. Venice might have undertaken it, but, whether the aversion of the Genoese for the Venitians did not permit Columbus to address the rival of his country, or that Venice could imagine no grandeur beyond her commerce with Alexandria and the Levant, Columbus had no hope left but in the court of Spain. It was, however, only after eight years of solicitation that the court of Isabella accepted the advantages which the citizen of Genoa desired to bring her. The court of Spain was poor ; the Prior Perez, and two merchants, named Pinzone, advanced 17,000 ducats for the expenses of the fleet. Columbus had a patent from the court, and finally departed from the port of Palos, in Andalusia, with three small vessels, and the empty title of admiral.

" *Discovery of America,* 1492—*Second Voyage,* 1493.—Thirty-three days from the Canary Islands, where he took in water, he discovered the first island of America (October 12th, 1492), and during this short passage he suffered more from the mur-

murs of his crew than he had endured from the rebuffs of the princes of Europe. This island, situated about a thousand leagues from the Canaries, was named St. Salvador. He soon after discovered the other Bahama Islands, Cuba, and Hispaniola, which latter is now called St. Domingo. Great was the surprise of Ferdinand and Isabella when they beheld Columbus, at the end of seven months, returning with Americans of Hispaniola, with curiosities of the country, and, above all, with gold, which he presented to them. The king and queen made him sit down, wearing his hat, as a grandee of Spain, and they conferred on him the title of the First Admiral and Viceroy of the New World. He was everywhere regarded as a peculiar being, sent from heaven. It was the same with all who had embarked under his orders. He again departed with a fleet of seventeen vessels (1493), and discovered the Antilles and Jamaica. The doubts and fears which his enterprise had excited were changed into admiration after the success of his first voyage, but that admiration became an envious jealousy in the course of his second.

"He was an admiral and a viceroy, and he might also add to these titles that of benefactor of Ferdinand and Isabella; and yet, judges sent in his own vessels to watch over his conduct, brought him back a prisoner to Spain; the people, who heard that Columbus had arrived, ran to meet him, as the tutelary genius of their country. They led Columbus from the vessel—he appeared before them—but it was with irons on his hands and on his feet.

" *Third Voyage*, 1498.—This cruel treatment was inflicted by order of Fonseca, bishop of Burgos, and superintendent of the armament. The ingratitude was as great as the services were memorable. Isabella was scandalized at it: she repaired this insult as well as she was able; but they retained Columbus four years, either from fear that he might appropriate to himself that which he had discovered, or that they only wished to obtain time to inform themselves of his conduct. Finally, they sent him back to the New World (1498). It was on this third voyage that he perceived the continent at ten degrees from the equator, and that he saw the coast where they have since built Carthagena.

" *Americo Vespucci.*—The ashes of Columbus are no longer interested in the fame which he enjoyed during his life, of having doubled the works of creation. Yet men love to render justice to the dead, whether it is that they flatter themselves with the hope that thereby it will be the better rendered to the living, or that they naturally love the truth.

Americo Vespucci, a merchant of Florence, has enjoyed the glory of giving his name to the new half of the globe, in which he did not possess an inch of ground; he pretended to have first discovered America. Were it true that he had made that discovery, the glory of it would not be his; it appertains incontestably to him who had the genius and the courage to undertake the first voyage."—*Voltaire.*

*The Spaniards at the Antilles — Las Casas.*— While daring navigators pursued the work of Columbus, and the Portuguese and English discover North America, and while Balboa perceives from the heights of Panama the Southern Ocean (1513), the blind cupidity of the Spanish colonists depopulate the Antilles. These first conquerors of the New World were the refuse of the Old. Adventurers, impatient to return to their own country, could not await the slow returns from agriculture or from industry. They knew no other riches than gold. This error cost America ten millions of men. The feeble and effeminate race which inhabited the country soon succumbed under their excessive and unhealthy labours. The population of Hispaniola was reduced, in 1507, from a million of people to sixty thousand. Notwithstanding the benevolent orders of Isabella, notwithstanding the efforts of Ximenes, and the pathetic remonstrances of the Dominican monks, the depopulation spread itself between the tropics. No voice was raised in favour of the Americans more courageously, nor with more firmness, than the voice of the celebrated Bartholomew de Las Casas, bishop of Chiapa, the protector of the Indians. Twice he went to Europe to plead their cause solemnly before Charles V. It is heart-breaking to read in his *Destruccion de las Indias* of the barbarous treatment which those unfortunate beings suffered.

*Ferdinand Cortez.*—We hardly know whether to admire the bravery of the conquerors of America or to detest their ferocity. They had in four expeditions discovered the coasts of Florida, Yucatan, and Mexico, when Ferdinand Cortez left the island of Cuba for new expeditions on the Continent (1519). "This simple lieutenant of the governor of a newly-discovered island, followed by less than six hundred persons, having only eighteen horses and a few pieces of cannon, went to subjugate the most powerful nation of America. At first he was happy enough to find a Spaniard who had been for nine years prisoner at Yucatan, on the road to Mexico; he served him as interpreter. Cortez advanced along the Gulf of Mexico, sometimes caressing the natives of the country, sometimes making war upon them. He found cultivated cities where the arts were honoured.

The powerful republic of Tlascala, which flourished under an aristocratic government, opposed his passage ; but the sight of the horses, and the sound of a single cannon, put these badly-armed multitudes to flight. He made a peace as advantageous as he desired ; six thousand of his new allies of Tlascala accompanied him on his way to Mexico. He entered that empire without resistance, in spite of the fortifications of its sovereign ; this sovereign commanded thirty vassals, each of whom could appear at the head of one hundred thousand men, armed with arrows and sharp stones, which served them instead of iron.

" *Mexico.*—The city of Mexico, built in the middle of a great lake, was the finest monument of American industry ; immense causeways crossed the lake, and it was covered with little barges, made from the trunks of trees. In the city were spacious and commodious houses, constructed of stone ; markets ; shops which shone with works of gold and silver, engraved and carved ; varnished earthenware ; stuffs of cotton and feathers, which formed designs, made brilliant by the most vivid colours. Near the great market was a palace, where summary justice was administered to the tradesmen. Several palaces of the emperor, Montezuma, increased the magnificence of the city ; one of them was surrounded by gardens, where they cultivated only medical plants; superintendents distributed them gratuitously to the sick; they gave an account to the king of the success attending their use, and the physicians kept a register thereof, in their manner, without knowing how to write. The other species of magnificence only indicated the progress of the arts; this last shows the progress of morals. If human nature did not unite good and evil, one would not be able to comprehend how this morality could be reconciled with human sacrifices, the blood of which flowed before the idol Visiliputsli, who was regarded as the god of the armies. The ambassadors of Montezuma said to Cortez (if we may believe the latter) that their master had sacrificed in his wars near twenty thousand enemies each year in the great temple of Mexico. This is, perhaps, an exaggeration; the reporter may have wished to excuse in this way the cruel injustice of the conqueror of Montezuma; but afterward, when the Spaniards entered the temple, they found among its ornaments human sculls suspended as trophies. Their police, in every other respect, was humane and wise: the education of youth formed one of the great objects of the government. There were public schools established for both sexes. We still admire the ancient Egyptians for having known the year to contain about three hundred and sixty-five days. The

Mexicans had carried their astronomy as far. War was among them reduced to an art; it was this which had given them such superiority over their neighbours. Great order in their finances maintained the grandeur of an empire, which was regarded by its neighbours with fear and envy.

"*Reception of the Spaniards.*—But those warlike animals on which the principal Spaniards were mounted, that artificial thunder which was formed in their hands, those wooden castles which had brought them over the ocean, the iron with which they were covered, and their marches, reckoned by their victories, all were so many subjects for admiration, and added to that weakness of human nature which is so attracted by novelty, they caused Cortez to be received in the city of Mexico by Montezuma as his master, and by the inhabitants as their god. They threw themselves on their knees in the street when a Spanish servant passed. It is related that a cacique of the district through which a Spanish captain passed offered him slaves and game. 'If thou art God,' says he, 'there are men, eat them; if thou art man, there are provisions, which these slaves shall prepare for thee.'

"*Montezuma.*—By degrees, the court of Montezuma, growing familiar with their guests, ventured to treat them as men. A part of the Spaniards were at Vera Cruz, on their road to Mexico; a general of the emperor, who had secret orders, attacked them, and although his troops were conquered there were three or four Spaniards among the kill ed; the head of one of them was even carried tc Montezuma. Cortez then performed the most da ring, as well as the most guilty act of his life: he went to the palace, followed by fifty Spaniards, led the emperor prisoner to the Spanish quarters, forced him to give up those who had attacked his men at Vera Cruz, and had irons placed on the hands and feet of the emperor himself, as a general would punish a common soldier; finally, he compelled him publicly to acknowledge himself vassal of Charles V. Montezuma and the principal men of his empire gave, as a tribute incident to this homage, six hundred thousand marks of pure gold, with an incredible quantity of jewels and works of gold, and of whatever was most rare in the fabrics of several centuries. Cortez destined one fifth for his master, took one fifth for himself, and distributed the rest among his soldiers.

"We may count it among the greatest of prodigies, that while the conquerors of this New World were at war among themselves, their conquests did not suffer. Never was truth less like truth; while Cortez was on the point of subjecting the Empire of Mexico with 500 men who remained to him, the

Governor of Cuba, Velasquez, more offended at the glory of Cortez, his lieutenant, than at his disobedience, sent nearly all his troops, which consisted of eight hundred foot-soldiers, eighty horsemen, well mounted, and two small pieces of cannon, to reduce Cortez, to take him prisoner, and to follow out the course of his victories. Cortez, having on the one side to fight a thousand Spaniards, and on the other to hold the Continent in submission, left eighty men to be responsible to him for all Mexico, and marched, followed by the rest, against his compatriots; he defeated a part of them, and gained over the rest. In short, this army, which came to destroy him, ranged itself under his banner, and he returned to Mexico with it.

" The emperor was constantly in prison in his capital, guarded by eighty soldiers; he who commanded them, on a true or false report that the Mexicans were conspiring to deliver their master, had seized the opportunity of a feast, when two thousand of the first lords were completely intoxicated by their strong liquors; he fell on them with fifty soldiers, killed them and their suite without resistance, and robbed them of all the gold ornaments and jewels with which they had decorated themselves for this feast. This enormity, which all the people attributed, with reason, to the fury of avarice, exasperated these men, heretofore too patient;

and when Cortez arrived, he found 200,000 Americans in arms against eighty Spaniards, who were occupied with defending themselves and guarding the king. They besieged Cortez, to deliver their king; they precipitated themselves in crowds on the cannons and muskets. The Spaniards were fatigued with firing on them, and the Americans followed each other in crowds, without being discouraged. Cortez was obliged to leave the city, where he would have been starved; but the Mexicans had broken all the causeways; the Spaniards made bridges with the bodies of their enemies; in their bloody retreat, they lost all the treasures which they had seized for Charles V. and themselves; victorious in the bloody battle of Otumba, Cortez undertook to lay siege to that immense city. He caused more vessels to be built by his soldiers and by the Tlascalians, whom he had with him, that he might re-enter Mexico by the lake itself, which seemed to forbid his entrance. The Mexicans feared not a naval battle; four or five thousand canoes, each one laden with two men, covered the lake, and came to attack the nine vessels of Cortez, on which he had about 300 men. These nine brigantines, which had cannons, soon overthrew the fleet of the enemy. Cortez, with the rest of his troops, fought on the causeways. Seven or eight captured Spaniards were sacrificed in the temple of

Mexico. But, finally, after new combats, they took the new emperor. It was Gatimozin, so famous for the words which he pronounced when a receiver of the treasures of the King of Spain had him placed on burning charcoal, to know in what part of the lake he had thrown his riches; his grand priest, condemned to the same punishment, uttered cries: Gatimozin said to him, 'And I, am I on a bed of roses?'

" *Taking of Mexico,* 1521.—Cortez was absolute master of the city of Mexico (1521), with which all the rest of the Empire fell under the Spanish dominion, as also Castille d'Or, Darien, and all the neighbouring countries. What was the reward of the wonderful services of Cortez? That of Columbus—he was persecuted. Notwithstanding the titles with which he was decorated in his native country, he was little respected there; he could hardly obtain an audience of Charles V. One day he pushed through the crowd which surrounded the coach of the emperor, and stepped on the step of the door. Charles asked who this man was. 'It is he,' replied Cortez, 'who has given you more kingdoms than your ancestors have left you cities.'

" *Peru.*—In the mean time, the Spaniards sought for new countries to conquer and depopulate. Magelhaens (Magellan) had gone round South America, traversed the Pacific Ocean, and was the first to circumnavigate the globe. But the greatest American nation, next to Mexico, yet remained to be discovered. One day, when the Spaniards weighed some pieces of gold, an Indian, turning the scales upside down, said to them that at six days' journey towards the south they would find a country where gold was so common that they used it for the most common purposes. Two adventurers, Pizarro and Almagro, a foundling and a swineherd, who had become soldiers, undertook the discovery and the conquest of these vast countries, which the Spaniards have distinguished by the name of Peru.

"From the country of Cusco and the neighbourhood of the tropic of Capricorn, to the height of the Isle of Pearls, a simple king stretched his absolute dominion over a space of nearly thirty degrees; he was of a race of conquerors which they called Incas. The first of these Incas, who had subjected the country and imposed laws upon it, passed as the son of the sun. The Peruvians transmitted important facts to posterity by knotted cords. They had obelisks, regular dials to mark the points of equinoxes and solstices. Their year had 365 days. They had raised prodigies of architecture, and cut statues with a surprising skill. This was the best governed and most industrious nation of the New World.

"The Inca Huescar,* father of Atabalipa, the last Inca, under whom this vast empire was destroyed, had increased and embellished it much. This inca, who conquered all the country of Quito, had made, by the hands of his soldiers and conquered people, a grand road of five hundred leagues, from Cusco to Quito, over valleys filled up, precipices and mountains levelled. Relays of men, established every half league, carried the orders of the monarch over all his vast empire. Such was its police; and if one would judge of its magnificence, it is sufficient to say that the king was carried in his journeys on a throne of solid gold, which was found to weigh twenty-five thousand ducats, and that the litter, composed of bars of gold, on which was the throne, was borne by the highest personages of the kingdom.

"*Pizarro*, 1552.—Pizarro attacked this empire with two hundred and fifty foot-soldiers, sixty horsemen, and twelve small cannon. He arrived through the South Sea on the heights of Quito, beyond the equator. Atabalipa, son of Huana, reigned at that time (1532); he was at Quito with about forty thousand soldiers, armed with arrows and pikes of gold and silver. Pizarro, like Cortez, commenced by offering the friendship of Charles V. to the Inca. When the army of the Inca and

* More properly Huana. Huascar was the brother of Atabalipa.—See *Robertson's America*.—*Tr*.

the feeble Castilian troops were in presence of each other, the Spaniards were willing to give the colour of religion to their cause. A monk, named Valverde, advances with an interpreter towards the Inca, a Bible in his hand, and says to him that he must believe *all this book says.* The Inca, approaching it with his ear, and hearing nothing, threw it on the ground, and the combat commenced.

"The cannon, the horses, and arms of iron had the same effect on the Peruvians as on the Mexicans; they took but little pains to kill them; and Atabalipa, dragged from his throne of gold by the conquerors, was loaded with irons. To procure a speedy liberation, he obliged himself to give as much gold as one of the saloons of his palace could contain as high as his hand, which he raised above his head. Each Spanish cavalier had 240 marks in pure gold; each foot-soldier 160. They divided about ten times as much silver in the same proportion. The officers had immense riches; and they sent to Charles V. 30,000 marks of silver, 3000 of unwrought gold, and 20,000 marks of heavy silver, with 2000 of gold coin of the country. The unfortunate Atabalipa was, nevertheless, put to death.

"Diego of Almagro marched to Cusco, making a road through multitudes of human beings. He penetrated into Chili. Everywhere they took possession in the name of Charles V. Soon after, discord embroiled the conquerors of Peru, as it had divided Velasquez and Ferdinand Cortez in Northern America.

"*Civil Wars.*—Almagro and the brothers of Pizarro commenced the civil war in Cusco itself, the capital of the Incas; all the recruits which they had received from Europe divided themselves, and they fought for the chief whom they chose. They had a bloody battle under the walls of Cusco without the Peruvians venturing to profit by the weakness of their common enemy. Finally, Almagro was made prisoner, and his rival had him beheaded; but soon after he himself was killed by the friends of Almagro.

"Already the Spanish government had been organized in all the New World; the great provinces had their governors; tribunals, called *Audiences*, were established; archbishops, bishops, tribunals of inquisition, all the ecclesiastical hierarchy, exercised their duties as at Madrid, when the captains who had conquered Peru for the emperor, Charles V., wished to take it for themselves. A son of Almagro had himself acknowledged governor of Peru; but the other Spaniards, choosing to obey masters who resided in Europe in preference to their companion, who had become a sovereign, had him put to death by the hand of a hangman."—*Voltaire.*

A new civil war was stifled in the same manner. Charles V., finally yielding to the remonstrances of Las Casas, had to guaranty personal liberty to the Indians, by determining the tributes and services to which they should be subjected (1542).

The Spanish colonies took up arms and declared themselves for the chief Gonzalo Pizarro. But the name of the king was so respected that it was sufficient to restore order to send an old man, an inquisitor (Pedro de la Gasca). He gathered round him the greater part of the Spaniards; he gained over some, overthrew the others, and secured to Spain the possession of Peru (1546).

*Spanish Empire in America — Outline of the Spanish Empire in America.*—If we except Mexico and Peru, Spain, in reality, only possessed the coasts. The people of the interior could be subjected only as they were converted by missions, and attached to the soil by civilization.

*Discoveries and Different Establishments*, 1540.—Expedition of Gonzalo Pizarro to discover the land east of the Andes; Orellana traverses South America by a voyage of 2000 leagues. Establishments: 1527, the province of Venezuela; 1535, Buenos Ayres; 1536, province of Grenada; 1540, St. Jago; 1550, Conception; 1555, Carthagena and Porto-Bello; 1567, Caraccas.

*Administration.*—Political government: in Spain, Council of the Indies and Court of Commerce and Justice; in America, two viceroys, audiences, municipalities. Caciques and *protectors* of the Indians. Ecclesiastical government (entirely dependant on the king): archbishops, bishops, curés, or teachers, missionaries, monks; Inquisition established in 1570 by Philip II.

*Commercial Administration—Monopoly.*—Privileged ports in America, Vera Cruz, Carthagena, and Porto-Bello; in Europe, Seville (later, Cadiz); *fleet* and galleons. Agriculture and manufactures are neglected in Spain and in America, for the exploring of the mines; slow increase of the colonies, and ruin of the metropolis before 1600. But in the course of the sixteenth century, the enormous quantity of precious metals which Spain must draw from America contributes to make her the preponderating power of Europe.

---

## CHAPTER XVI.

### LITERATURE — ARTS AND SCIENCES IN THE SIXTEENTH CENTURY—LEO X. AND FRANCIS I.

The fifteenth century had been an age of learning; enthusiasm for antiquity had caused the path so happily opened by Dante, Boccacio, and Petrarch to be abandoned. In the sixteenth century modern genius is brilliant with a new effulgence, never to be extinguished.

The march of mind at this epoch presents two very distinct movements: the first, favoured by the influence of Leo X. and Francis I., belongs to Italy and France; the second is European. The former, characterized by the progress of literature and arts, is arrested in France by civil wars, and retarded in Italy by foreign wars: in Italy the genius of literature is extinguished under the yoke of the Spaniards; but the impulse given to the arts prolongs itself to the middle of the following century. The second movement is the development of a daring spirit of doubt and of examination. In the seventeenth century it was partly arrested by a return to religious creeds, partly turned towards the natural sciences, but it will reappear in the eighteenth.

## § I. LITERATURE AND ARTS.

Independently of the general causes which have produced the regeneration of literature, such as the progress of security and wealth, the discovery of the monuments of antiquity, &c., &c., several particular causes have given it a new energy with the Italians of the sixteenth century: 1st. Books have become plenty, thanks to the progress of printing; 2d. The Italian nation, being no more able to control her destiny, seeks consolation in intellectual and literary enjoyments; a number of princes, and especially the Medici, encourage scholars and artists; illustrious writers profit less by this patronage.

*Italy — Poetry.* — Poetry, which, with the arts, forms the principal glory of Italy in the sixteenth century, unites taste and genius in the first part of this period. The epic muse raises two immortal monuments. Comedy and tragedy present some essays, in truth, not above mediocrity. The most opposite styles of satire and pastoral poetry are cultivated. It is especially in the latter that we remark the rapid decay of taste.

| | | | | | |
|---|---|---|---|---|---|
| Boïardo | died in | 1490 | Trissino | died in | 1550 |
| Machiavel | " | 1529 | Tasso | " | 1596 |
| Ariosto | " | 1533 | Guarini | " | 1619 |

*Prose.*—Eloquence, the slow product of literature, has not time to form itself. But several historians approach the style of antiquity.

| | | | | | |
|---|---|---|---|---|---|
| Machiavel | died in | 1529 | Paul Jove | died in | 1562 |
| Fr. Guicciardini | " | 1540 | Baronius | " | 1607 |
| Bembo | " | 1547 | | | |

*Learning.*—The ancient languages are cultivated much more than in the preceding age, but this glory is eclipsed by many others.

| | | | | | |
|---|---|---|---|---|---|
| Pontanus | died in | 1503 | Sadolet | died in | 1547 |
| Aldus Manucius | " | 1516 | Fracastor | " | 1553 |
| John Second | " | 1523 | J. C. Scaliger | " | 1558 |
| Sannazar | " | 1530 | Vida | " | 1563 |
| A. J. Lascaris | " | 1535 | P. Manutius | " | 1574 |
| Bembo | " | 1547 | Aldus Manutius | " | 1597 |

*Arts.*—Superiority in the arts in Italy is the characteristic trait of the sixteenth century. The ancients remain without rivals in sculpture; but the moderns equal them in architecture, and in painting they perhaps surpass them. The Roman school excels in perfection of design, the Venitian in beauty of colouring.

| | | | | | |
|---|---|---|---|---|---|
| Giorgione | died in | 1511 | Primatice | died in | 1564 |
| Bramante | " | 1514 | Palladio | " | 1568 |
| Leonardo de Vinci | " | 1520 | Titian | " | 1576 |
| Raphael | " | 1518 | Veronese | " | 1588 |
| Corregio | " | 1534 | Tintoret | " | 1594 |
| Parmesair | " | 1534 | Augustin Carrache | " | 1601 |
| Jules Romain | " | 1546 | Caravage | " | 1609 |
| Michael Angelo | " | 1564 | Hannibal Carrache | " | 1609 |
| John Udino | " | 1564 | Louis Carrache | " | 1619 |

*France.*—France followed Italy at a distance The historian Comines died in 1509. Francis I founds the College of France and the royal print ing-press. He encourages the poet Marot (1544), and the brothers Du Bellay (1543, 1560), negotiators and historians. His sister, Margaret of Navarre (1549), cultivates literature herself. Francis I. distinguishes Titian, draws Primatice and Leonardo de Vinci into France. He builds Fontainebleau, St. Germain, Chambord, and commences the Louvre. Under him flourished John Cousin (1589), designer and painter; Germain Pilon, Philibert de l'Orme, John Goujon (1572), sculptors and architects; the scholars, William Budæus (1540), Turnebe (1563), Muret (1585), Henry Stephens (1598), a celebrated printer; finally, the celebrated lawyers Dumoulin (1566) and Cujacius (1590). After the reign of Francis I., the poet Ronsard (1585) enjoyed a brief reputation; but Montaigne (1592), Amyot (1593), and the Satire Menippée, gave a new character to the French language.

*Germany, Spain, &c., &c.*—The other countries are not so rich in eminent talents. Yet Germany boasts her Luther, the shoemaker poet, Hans Sachs, and the painters Albert Durer and Lucas Cranach. Portugal and Spain have their illustrious writers—Camoens, Lope de Vega, and Cervantes; the Netherlands and Scotland their men of letters and their historians—Justus Lipsius (1616) and Buchanan (1582). Among the forty-three universities founded in the sixteenth century, fourteen were established by the kings of Spain alone, ten of them by Charles V.

### § II. PHILOSOPHY AND SCIENCE.

*Philosophy.*—Philosophy, in the preceding century, was cultivated only by the learned. It was limited to attacking the school divinity, and opposing Platonism to it. By degrees, impelled by a more rapid movement, it extends its examination to every subject. But the human mind then sought after knowledge at hazard; there was no method, and too little observation. Many learned men were discouraged, and became the most daring skeptics.

| | | | | | |
|---|---|---|---|---|---|
| Erasmus | died in | 1533 | Montaigne | died in | 1592 |
| Vivès | " | 1540 | G. Bruno | " | 1600 |
| Rabelais | " | 1553 | Charron | " | 1603 |
| Cardan | " | 1576 | Bœhmen | " | 1624 |
| Telesio | " | 1588 | Campanella | " | 1639 |

*Politics.* — The theory of politics began with Machiavel; but at the commencement of the sixteenth century, the Italians had not made progress enough in this science to perceive that it accorded with morality.

| | | | | | |
|---|---|---|---|---|---|
| Machiavel | died in | 1529 | Bodin | died in | 1596 |
| Thomas More | " | 1533 | | | |

*Natural Sciences.*—The natural sciences leave chimerical systems to enter upon the path of observation and experience.

| | | | | | |
|---|---|---|---|---|---|
| Paracelsus | died in | 1541 | Gesner | died in | 1565 |
| Copernicus | " | 1543 | Pare | " | 1592 |
| Fallopius | " | 1562 | Vieta | " | 1603 |
| Vesalius | " | 1564 | Van Helmont | " | 1644 |

---

## CHAPTER XVII.

### TROUBLES AT THE COMMENCEMENT OF THE REIGN OF LOUIS XIII.—RICHELIEU, 1610–1643.

The general characteristic of the seventeenth century is the progress both of royalty and of the *Tiers-Etat.** The progress of royalty was only

* *i. e., Third Estate,* or *Commons.*

suspended twice, *i. e.*, by the minorities of Louis XIII. and Louis XIV. The *Tiers-Etat* is arrested only towards the end of the reign of Louis XIV. At this period, the king, having for a long time had nothing to fear from the nobility, gave up the administration to them. Hitherto all the ministers, Concini, Luynes, Richelieu, Mazarin, Colbert, Louvois, had risen from the plebeians, or, at the most, from the lowest nobility. Some of the admirals and superior officers of the armies of Louis XIV. belonged to the lowest ranks of the people.

In the first part of this century political action was, as it were, negative. It endeavoured to overthrow the great obstacles to monarchical centralization, the nobles and the Protestants. In the second half, there was under Colbert an effort at legislative organization; and, above all, at an administrative one; productive industry was more esteemed. France acts powerfully within and without; she produces, she wages wars. But production keeps not pace with consumption. France exhausts herself to complete her territory, by means of necessary and glorious conquests. The course of her internal prosperity is also retarded by the extent of her wars and conquests, and by an aristocratical reaction. The nobility seize the monarchical power, place themselves everywhere between the king and the people, and communicate to royalty their own decrepitude.

*Louis XIII.—Mary of Medici Regent—Concini.*—Henry IV. found great difficulty in supporting himself between the Protestants and Catholics. This indecision could not continue after his death; one side had to be chosen, and it was the Protestant side. The great war of Germany, which had commenced, offered to the King of France the noble post of chief of the European opposition against the house of Austria; the post which, twenty years later, Gustavus Adolphus took. The king was dead; Louis XIII. an infant, Mary of Medici, the regent, and Concini, her minister, both Italians, could not perpetuate Henry IV. This child, this woman, could not mount on horseback to make war on Austria. Not being able to fight Austria, it was necessary to have her for a friend. As they could not lead the nobles and the Protestants in Germany on a Protestant crusade, they must, if possible, gain over the nobles and weaken the Protestants. This policy of Concini, which has been so much blamed by historians, received its justification from the best judge on this subject, from Richelieu himself, in one of his writings. The nobles, from whom Henry IV. had not been able to take their strongholds, a Condé, an Epernon, a Bouillon, a Longueville, found themselves all armed at his death; they exacted money, and it was necessary, in order to avoid a civil war, to deliver the treasury of Henry IV. to them (twelve millions, and not thirty, according to Richelieu). Then they demanded the States-General (1614). These states doing nothing, did not answer the expectation of the nobles; they showed themselves devoted to the crown; the *Tiers-Etat* claimed a declaration of independence from the crown in regard to the pope. The nobles not being able to draw anything from the States, had recourse to force, and united themselves with the Protestants (1615); a strange alliance of the ancient feudal party with the religious Reformation of the sixteenth century. Concini, tired of a middle course, had the Prince of Condé, chief of the coalition, arrested; this bold proceeding announced the era of new politics; the young Richelieu had appeared (1616).

*De Luynes,* 1617. — An intrigue of the court overthrew Concini for the benefit of the young Luynes, a favourite domestic of the little king, who persuaded him to liberate himself from his minister and from his mother (1617). Concini was assassinated; his widow, Leonora Galigaï, was executed as a sorceress. Their true crimes were robbery and venality. Luynes did little except to continue the ministry of Concini. He had one enemy more, the mother of the king, who twice excited fears of a civil war. The Protestants took daily a more threatening attitude. They demanded, arms in hand, the fulfilment of that dangerous Edict of Nantes, which allowed a republic to exist within the kingdom. Luynes drove them to extremities by reuniting Berne to the crown, and declaring that in that province ecclesiastical property should be made over to the Catholics. This was precisely what the emperor wished to do in Germany, and it was the principal cause of the Thirty Years' War. Richelieu, at a later period, avoided this mistake. He did not trouble the Protestants about their usurped property; he only interested himself about their strongholds. Their assembly of La Rochelle (1621) published a declaration of independence, divided the 700 Reformed Churches of France into eight circles, regulated the raising of money and men, and, in one word, organized the Protestant Republic. They offered to Lesdiguières 100,000 crowns a month if he would place himself at the head of their army and organize it. But the old soldier would not, at the age of eighty, leave his little kingdom of Dauphiny to accept the command of this undisciplined party. Luynes, who had taken the command of the armies and the title of Constable, miscarried disgracefully before Montauban, where he had conducted the king. He died in this campaign (1621).

*Richelieu—War against the Pope and the Protestants—Intrigues of Gaston.*—It was only two years afterward that the queen-mother introduced her creature, Richelieu, into the council (1624). The king had an antipathy for this man, in whom he seemed to foresee a master. The first thought of Richelieu was to neutralize the power of England, the sole ally of the Protestants of France. This was done in two ways: first, he supported Holland; he lent her money to obtain vessels; and, secondly, the marriage of the King of England with the beautiful Henrietta of France, daughter of Henry IV., increased the natural indecision of Charles I., and the distrust of the English towards his government. The cardinal thus began by an alliance with the English and the heretic Dutch, and by a war against the pope; we may judge from this what freedom of mind he brought into politics. The pope, given up to the Spaniards, held for them the small Swiss canton Valteline, thus guarding that entrance of the Alps, by which their Italian possessions communicated with Austria. Richelieu hired some Swiss troops, sent them against those of the pope, and gave Valteline to the Grisons, not without having assured himself by a decision at Sarbonne that he could do it conscientiously. After having defeated the pope, he defeated in the following year the Protestants (1525), who had again taken up arms; he defeated and he managed, but he was not able to destroy them. He was shackled in the execution of his grand projects by the most contemptible intrigues. Women excited the young; the domestics of Gaston, duke of Orleans, spurred his slothful ambition. They wished to give him a support from abroad, by making him marry a foreign princess. Richelieu endeavoured first to gain them over. He gave a marshal's staff to Ornano, governor of Gaston. This imboldened them, and they plotted his death. Richelieu caused, moreover, their principal accomplice, the young Chalais, to join him, but obtained nothing. Then changing his policy, he gave Chalais up to a committee of the Parliament of Bretagne, and had him beheaded (1626). Gaston, while they took off the head of his friend, married, without saying a word, Mademoiselle de Montpensier. D'Ornano was shut up in the Bastile, and died there soon after, doubtless from poison. The favourites of Gaston were condemned to die at the Bastile (Puylaurens, in 1635). Such were the politics of the time; as such, we read them in the Machiavel of the seventeenth century, Gabriel Naudé, librarian of Mazarin. The motto of these politics, as Naudé gives it, is this:

*Salus populi suprema lex esto.* For the rest, they were consistent in the choice of means. It is the same atrocious doctrine which inspired our terrorists of '93. It seems to have left Richelieu neither doubts nor remorse. As he expired, the priest asked him if he pardoned his enemies. "I have never had any," replied he, "other than those of the state." He had uttered at another time these words, which make us tremble: "I dare undertake nothing without having well thought of it; but when I once form my resolution, I proceed straight towards my end: I overthrow all—cut down all; and, finally, I cover all with my red robe."

*Taking of La Rochelle.*—In reality, he marched straight onward with a terrible inflexibility. He suppressed the office of Constable; that of Admiral of France he took for himself, under the title of General Superintendent of the Marine. This title would seem to announce him as destroyer of La Rochelle. Under the pretext of economy, he ordered the reduction of pensions and the demolition of fortresses. The fortress of Protestantism, La Rochelle, was finally attacked. A coxcomb, who governed the King of England, the handsome Buckingham, had solemnly declared himself in love with the great Queen of France; they closed against him all entrance to the kingdom, and he caused war to be declared against France. The English promised succour to La Rochelle; it revolted, and fell under the grasp of Richelieu (1627–28). Buckingham came with several thousand men, to be beaten on the isle of Rhé. Charles I. had afterward many other affairs on hand. With the famous *Petition of Right* (1628) commenced the revolution of England, to which Richelieu was anything but a stranger. In the mean time, La Rochelle, abandoned by the English, saw herself cut off from the sea by a prodigious dam of 1500 toises: we may still distinguish the remains of it at low water. The work took more than a year: the sea carried off the dam more than once. Richelieu did not let go his booty. French Amsterdam, of which Coligny had thought to make himself a second William of Orange, was seized in her waters, and made inland; separated from her proper element, she could but languish. Protestantism was killed by the same blow, at least as a political party. The war still continued in the South. The famous Duke of Rohan put an end to it by an agreement for 100,000 crowns.

*War of Italy*, 1629–30.—After having divided the Protestant party in France, Richelieu beat the Catholic party in Europe; he forced the Spaniards into their Italy, where they had reigned since Charles V. By a short war he cut the knot of difficulty in the succession of Mantua and Montserrat; they were small possessions, but great military posts. The last duke had bequeathed them to a French prince, the Duke of Nevers. The Savoyards, fortified in the Pass of Suza, thought themselves impregnable, and Richelieu himself thought so. The king took this terrible obstacle in person; the Duke of Nevers was confirmed in his authority; France had an advance station in Italy, and the Duke of Savoy knew that the French passed near whenever they wished (1630).

*Day of Dupes.*—During this great war, the mother of the king, the courtiers, the ministers even, made a silent and cowardly attack upon Richelieu. They thought to have dethroned him. He saw Louis again, spoke to him a quarter of an hour, and found himself once more sovereign. This day was called the *Day of the Dupes.* It was a comedy. Richelieu prepared to depart in the morning, and his enemies did the same at night. But the piece had its tragical side. The cardinal had the two Marillacs, the marshal and the superintendent, both creatures of his who had turned against him, arrested. Without speaking of the crime of extortion and peculation, so common at this period, they were guilty of having endeavoured to cause the failure of the war of Italy, by retaining the sums which were appropriated for it. The head of one of them was taken off. What was most odious in this act was, that the criminal was tried by a committee of his personal enemies, in a private house, even in the palace of Richelieu, at Ruel.

*Revolt of Gaston—Montmorency Decapitated.*—The queen-mother, a more embarrassing enemy, had been arrested and intimidated. She had decided to make her escape, with her son Gaston, to Brussels. Gaston, aided by the Duke of Lorraine, whose daughter was his second wife, assembled some undisciplined troops, and entered France. He had been invited by the nobles, by Montmorency among others, to be Governor of Languedoc. The nobles wished this time to play quit or double. To join with Montmorency, it was necessary to traverse the kingdom. The badly-paid soldiers of Gaston recompensed themselves with their own hands on the road. Everywhere the cities closed their gates against these brigands. The junction took place at Castelnaudari, and nevertheless they were beaten (1632). Gaston threw away his arms, and again made peace, delivering up his friends; he took an express oath *to love the ministers of the king, the cardinal in particular*. Montmorency, wounded and taken, was cruelly beheaded at Toulouse. Men deplored this last representative of the chivalrous and feudal world. Already his father, the Duke of Bouteville, father of the celebrated Luxemburg, had been beheaded in 1627 for having fought a duel. When such heads fell, the nobles began to comprehend that they must no more trifle with the government and the law.

*Thirty Years' War.*—The Thirty Years' War was then at its height. Richelieu could not interfere with it directly, as long as he had the nobles upon his hands. The emperor had at that time defeated the Protestant party; the Palatine was ruined (1623); the King of Denmark left the party (1629). The Catholic armies had the greatest generals at their head—the tactician Tilly, and that demon of war, Waldstein. To lift up the Protestants, to rouse unwieldy Germany, required a movement from abroad. Richelieu searched the North, even beyond Denmark, and from Sweden he drew Gustavus Adolphus. He first relieved him from the war with Poland; he gave him money, procured him an alliance with the United Provinces and with the King of England. At the same time, he had the address to determine the emperor to disarm himself. The Swede, a poor prince, who had more to gain than to lose, rushed at once into Germany, fell upon it like a thunderbolt, confounded the famous tacticians, and beat them with ease, while they were studying how to avert his blows. He took from them with one stroke the whole of the Rhine, the whole of the west of Germany. Richelieu had not foreseen that he would proceed so swiftly. Happily, Gustavus perished at Lutzen; happy alike for his enemies, for his allies, and for his own glory. He died honest and unconquered (1632).

*French Period,* 1635–48.—Richelieu continued his aid to the Swedes, closed France on the side of Germany by confiscating Lorraine, and declared war upon the Spaniards (1635). He thought the house of Austria sufficiently checked to enable him to make division of its spoils. He had bought over to his interest the best pupil of Gustavus Adolphus, Bernard of Saxe Weimar. But this war was difficult at first. The Imperialists entered by Burgundy, and the Spaniards by Picardy. They were not more than thirty leagues from Paris. All was confusion; the minister himself seemed to have lost his reason. The Spaniards were driven back (1636). Bernard of Weimar gained his glorious battles of Rhinfeld and Brisach for the benefit of France; Brisach and Friburg, those impregnable places were also taken. The temptation became strong for Bernard; he wished with the money of France to form himself a small sovereignty on the Rhine; his master, the great Gustavus, had not had time; Bernard had as little. He died at thirty-six years, most opportunely for France and Richelieu (1639).

*Catalonia and Portugal*, 1640— *Cinq Mars.*—In the following year (1640) the cardinal found means to simplify the war. It was creating one in Spain among her own subjects, and more than one. The East and West, Catalonia and Portugal, took fire all at once. The Catalonians placed themselves under the protection of France. Spain wished to follow the example of Richelieu, to procure for her benefit an internal war in France. She made a treaty with Gaston, and with the nobles. The Count of Soissons, who moved before he was ordered, was obliged to save himself among the Spaniards, and was killed in fighting for them near Sedan (1641). The faction was not discouraged; a new plot was contrived in concert with Spain. The young Cinq Mars, master of the horse, and favourite of Louis XIII., engaged in it with an imprudence which lost Calais. The prudent De Thou, son of the historian, knew of the affair, but kept it secret. The king himself was not ignorant that they plotted the ruin of the minister. Richelieu, who at that time was very sick, seemed lost beyond help. Yet, having succeeded in procuring a copy of their treaty with the foreigner, he had still time to prosecute his enemies before his death. He caused the head of Cinq Mars and of De Thou to be cut off; the Duke of Bouillon, who had already been denounced, purchased his life by giving up his city of Sedan, the focus of all these intrigues. On the other side of France, Richelieu at the same time took Perpignan from the Spaniards. These two places were a legacy from the cardinal to France, which they covered on the North and South. This great man died in the same year (1642).

# THIRD PERIOD.

## 1648–1789.

# PART I.—164 1715.

## CHAPTER XVIII.

TROUBLES UNDER MAZARIN — COMMENCEMENT OF COLBERT'S ADMINISTRATION—LOUIS XIV., 1643–1661.

*Louis XIV.*, 1643 — *Mazarin.*—The death of Richelieu was a deliverance for all the world. Men breathed freely. The people gave vent to their joy in songs. The king sung them himself, all dying as he was. His widow, Anne of Austria, was regentess in the name of the new King Louis XIV., who was then six years of age. France, after Richelieu and Louis XIII., as after Henry IV., found herself under the feeble sway of a woman who knew not how to resist her enemies or retain her own power. A contemporary writer says, that then there were not more than three little words in the French language—" The queen is so good." The Concini of this new Mary of Medicis was an Italian of much talent, the Cardinal Mazarin. His administration was as deplorable at home as it was glorious abroad; it was disturbed by the ridiculous revolution of the Fronde, and made illustrious by the two treaties of Westphalia and the Pyrenees; the first remained the diplomatic chart of Europe until the French Revolution. The good, the bad, were equally an inheritance from Richelieu; he had taxed to excess every energy of government; it naturally relaxed under Mazarin. Richelieu having daily to engage in some deadly combat, had lived, as it regarded finances, on tyrannical expedients. He had consumed both present and future means by destroying credit. Mazarin, finding affairs in this condition, increased the disorder, letting the people take, and taking himself. He left at his death two hundred millions worth of property. He had always too much sense not to feel the value of order in the finances. On his deathbed he said to Louis XIV., he thought he had acquitted himself of all wrong towards his master by giving him Colbert. A part of this embezzled money was used honourably. He sent Gabriel Naudé all over Europe to purchase valuable books at any price; thus he formed his admirable *Bibliothèque Mazarine,* and he opened it to the public. This was the first public library in Paris. At the same time he gave to Des Cartes, who had retired to Holland, a pension of one thousand crowns, which was regularly paid to him.

*Rocroi*, **1643.**—The new reign was commenced

by victories. The French infantry for the first time took rank in the world by the battle of Rocroi (1643). This event was a very different affair from a battle; it was a great social fact. Cavalry form the aristocratic arm of a nation—infantry the plebeian. The appearance of infantry is the appearance of the people. Whenever a national sentiment springs up, infantry appears. As is the people, so are the infantry. During the century and a half that Spain had been a nation, the Spanish foot-soldier reigned on the field of battle, fearless under its fire; respecting himself, though in rags, and causing everywhere the *Señor Soldade* to be respected; for the rest, gloomy, avaricious, and covetous, badly paid, yet patiently waiting the pillage of some good city in Germany or Flanders. They had in the time of Charles V. sworn "by the sacking of Florence;" they had plundered Rome, then Antwerp, then innumerable cities of the Netherlands. Among the Spaniards there were men of all nations, especially Italians. National character disappeared. Their *esprit de corps*, and the ancient honour of the army, still sustained them when they were carried by land to the battle of Rocroi. The soldier who took their place was the French soldier, the ideal of the soldier, impetuosity disciplined. Though far, as yet, from comprehending the true nature of patriotism, this soldier had still a warm affection for the land of his birth. It was a merry population of the sons of labourers, whose grandfathers had fought in the last religious wars. These wars of partisans, and these skirmishes at pistol-shot distance, made a whole nation of soldiers; there were traditions of honour and bravery in their families. The grandchildren enrolled, and, conducted by a young man of twenty years, the great Condé, forced the Spanish lines at Rocroi, and routed the ancient bands as gayly as their descendants, under the command of another young man, broke the bridges of Arcola and Lodi.

Since the time of Gustavus Adolphus, war had breathed a more liberal spirit. Armies trusted less to *matériel,* more to moral force. Tactics, if I may so speak, had become spiritualized. Since they had felt this inspiration, men could march without counting the enemy. They required a daring spirit at their head; a young man, confident of success. Condé, at Friburg, threw his staff into the ranks of the enemy; all the French ran to bring it back.

*Treaty of Westphalia,* 1648.—Victory engenders victory. The lines of Rocroi forced, the barrier of Spanish and German honour was also forced forever. The following year (1644), the skilful and aged Mercy suffered the lines of Thionville to be carried; Condé took Philipsburg and Mayence, the central position on the Rhine. Mercy was beaten again, and completely routed at Noolingen (1645). In 1646 Condé took Dunkirk, the key of Flanders and of the Straits. Finally, on the 20th of August, 1648, he gained in Artois the battle of Lens. On the 24th of October the peace of Westphalia was signed. Condé had simplified the negotiations.

*Condé.*—These five years of unheard-of success were fatal to the good sense of Condé. He did not think of the people who had gained his victories; he took them to himself, and all the world, it is true, thought with him. This is what made him enjoy in the Fronde the part of bully, and hero of the theatre: soon deceived, disappointed, powerless, and ridiculous, he became angry with himself and with everybody, and joined the enemy; but he failed, for he no longer commanded the French.

*The Fronde.*—The very year of this glorious treaty of Westphalia, which terminated the European war, and gave Alsace to France, the most ridiculous of revolutions broke out. The *Fronde* (this war of children, suitably named after a game of children) was doubtless ridiculous in its issue, but much more in its principle; it was, at bottom, a revolt of the lawyers against the law. The Parliament armed itself against the royal authority from which it was derived. It took to itself the power of the States-General, and pretended to be the delegate of a nation, who knew nothing of it. It was at this time that the Parliament of England, the true Parliament, in the political sense of the term, had decapitated its king (1649). On the other hand, the populace of Naples made for themselves a king of a fisherman (Masaniello, 1648). The Parliament of France, composed of lawyers, who purchased their places, did not make war on the dynasty, nor on royalty, but on royal power alone. From their conduct for two centuries, nothing like this could have been foreseen. In the religious wars, they had shown much timidity and docility. Favourable for the most part to new ideas, they had yet registered the decree of St. Bartholomew. Under Richelieu this same docility continued; the Parliament had furnished him with commissions for his sanguinary courts, and yet had not been the less ill treated, violated, and interdicted (Paris, 1635; Rouen, 1640). They were much humbled. But when they again raised their heads, and felt that those heads were still on their shoulders, and saw their master dead, they thought themselves valiant, and spoke boldly. It was a pleasant escape of scholars from between two severe masters; from Richelieu and Louis XIV., from violence and power.

*Molé — Retz.*—In this tragi-comedy the most amusing actors after the *French Mars*, as they called Condé, were the opposite chiefs of the two parties of Parliament—the immovable President Molé, a simple bar of iron, who yielded to no man, nor to any opinion: and on the other side mobility itself, personified in the coadjutor, the famous Cardinal Retz. This petulant young man had commenced by writing, at the age of seventeen, a history of the conspiracy of Fiesco; then, to join practice with theory, he had entered into a conspiracy against Richelieu. His happiness was to hear himself called the young Catiline. When he entered the Parisian Senate, he let a dagger fall from his pocket. Knowing that Cæsar had debts, he contracted debts. Like Cæsar, he has left commentaries. He only wanted a Pharsalia.

The extreme misery of the people would scarcely admit of new taxes. Mazarin lived upon casual expedients and oppressions. His superintendent of finance, Emeri, another Italian, having in compensation for a heavy tax, withdrawn four years' payment from the Royal Companies, exempted the Parliament. The Parliament would not be exempted alone, and refused to register the edict. It declared its *union* with the Royal Companies, inviting the other Parliaments to accede (May 13, June 15, 1648). Mazarin thought he struck a great blow by having four counsellors arrested while they were carrying the standards taken at the battle of Lens to the Church of Nôtre Dame, and were chanting the *Te Deum*. This was the commencement of the insurrection. Of the four prisoners, the one most dear to the people was an imbecile old counsellor, who pleased them by his simplicity and his fine white hair. His name was Broussel. A mob collected before his door; an old servant harangued them. By degrees the noise increased, and soon the cry of "Liberty and Broussel!" was heard from a hundred thousand lips.

*The Court at St. Germain.*—The princes, the nobles, the Parliament, and the lower classes were all at first against Mazarin. The queen was obliged to leave Paris with her infant son. They slept at St. Germain upon straw. It was a miserable time for kings. The Queen of England, who was a refugee at Paris, remained in bed during the winter for the want of wood. In the mean time the Parliament raised troops, the lawyers mounted their horses, and each carriage-gate furnished one armed footman. The Viscount Turenne, who was of the intriguing house of Bouillon, thought the time had arrived for recovering Sedan, and made himself for a moment general of the Fronde. Turenne was of a cold and grave disposition, yet in joining that party he also made court to Madame de Longueville. Every general, every chief of a party, every true hero of romance or of history, must at that time necessarily have a lady of his thoughts, and be in love.

*Arrest of the Princes*, 1650—*Treaty of the Pyrenees*, 1659.—The Spaniards, who entered France in order to profit by this crisis (1649), reconciled for the moment both parties through fear. Condé, who until then had remained faithful to the court, felt that they could not do without him and became an insupportable necessity. It was then that they created for him and the young men around him the title of *petits maîtres*. He bargained with both parties at the same time; it was necessary to have him arrested (1650). This was a pretext for Turenne, who was about to join the Spaniards, and who declared that he contended for his deliverance. The party of the princes and of the Frondeurs, finding themselves united and supported by Spain, Mazarin had to yield. He retired to let the storm pass by; the following year he returned, gained over Turenne, and vainly endeavoured to bring the king back to Paris (battle of Porte Saint Antoine, 1652). One year more, and, the weakness of the parties having become complete, the Parisians themselves forced the king to return (1653). The Frondeurs crowded the antechambers of Mazarin. Condé and the Spaniards were defeated by the royal army, at that time commanded by Turenne. Mazarin without scruple united himself with the

Republic of England, with Cromwell, and crushed the Spaniards. Turenne gained the battle of the Dunes (1658), which gave Dunkirk to the English, and to France the peace of the Pyrenees (1659). The treaty of Westphalia had guarantied to France her barriers of Artois, Alsace, and Roussillon; that of the Pyrenees gave her Gravelines, Landrecy, Thionville, Montmedy. The young King of France married the Infanta of Spain, with a dowry of 500,000 crowns, which was not paid. The infanta renounced all right of succession to the kingdom of Spain. Mazarin did not dispute this: he foresaw what these renunciations would be worth (1659).

There was at this time the most complete triumph of royalty, and the most perfect harmony between the people and one man, ever known. Richelieu had defeated the nobles and the Protestants; the Fronde had ruined the Parliament by forcing it to acknowledge them. There remained in France but one people and one king. The former lived in the latter; it could no longer be said to live by means of its own vital powers alone. When Louis XIV. said, "The kingdom is mine," it was neither bombast nor boasting, but the simple announcement of a fact.

*Louis XIV.*—The young Louis was the man to act this magnificent part. His cold and solemn figure hovered for fifty years over France with the same majesty. In the first thirty he sat eight hours daily in the councils, connecting business and pleasure—hearing, consulting, but judging for himself. His ministers changed and died, but he was always the same; he went through duties, ceremonies, feasts of royalty, with the regularity of the sun, which he had chosen for his emblem.

*Colbert.*—One of the glories of Louis XIV. was to have retained for twenty-two years as minister one of those men who have done the most for the glory of France: I mean Colbert. He was the grandson of a linendraper of Rheims, of the sign of the *Long-vetû;* his mind was not brilliant, but solid, active, and indefatigable. He reorganized the affairs of the interior, of commerce, of the finances—those even of the navy, which he placed in the hands of his son; he only wanted the offices of minister of war and of justice to be king of France. The war was conducted (since 1666) by Louvois, a violent and fierce administrator, whose influence balanced that of Colbert. Louis XIV. seemed to be placed between them, as between his good and evil genius. Both were at all times necessary; they formed the equilibrium of this great reign.

When Colbert entered upon affairs, in 1661, the

duties were eighty-four millions, and of these the king touched hardly thirty-two. In 1670, in spite of wars, he had raised the revenue to one hundred and sixteen millions. His first financial operation, the reduction of interest, gave a heavy blow to credit. His industrial regulations were singularly vexatious and tyrannical. But he regarded commerce with the most enlightened views. He appointed consulting committees of merchants, established free entrepôts, made public roads, and gave security to commerce at sea by destroying pirates. At the same time he carried a bold hand into political administration. He repressed the exemptions from duties which the ecclesiastics, the nobles, and citizens of the free cities extended to their tenants, by representing them as mere servants. He revoked, in 1664, all the letters of nobility issued since 1630. He declared all the accounting offices to be fortuitous, in order to suppress them by degrees. Colbert is reproached with having encouraged commerce more than agriculture ; yet he forbade seizure, for payment of debts, of the bedding, clothes, horses, oxen, or utensils of husbandmen, and of more than the fifth of their cattle. He kept grain at low prices, by prohibiting its exportation. We must consider, too, that, the greatest part of the country being still in the hands of the princes and nobles, encouragement given to agriculture would have been less profitable to the people than to the aristocracy. On the contrary, commerce was in the hands of the middling class, which began to rise.

This man, who came from a counting-room, had a feeling for the true grandeur of France. He forgot his economy when disbursements would bring glory to his country. "It is necessary," he wrote to Louis XIV., "to save five sous on unnecessary things, and to throw away millions when your glory is in question. A useless repast of three thousand livres gives me incredible pain; but when millions of gold for Poland are required, I would sell all my property, would pawn my wife and my children, and would go on foot all my lifetime to procure it." The principal monuments of Louis XIV., his noblest establishments, the observatory, library, and academies, belong in a great measure to Colbert. He caused pensions to be given to the scientific men and artists of France, and even of foreign countries. "There was not," says a contemporary writer, "a learned man, however distant from France, who did not receive some mark of his respect." "Although the king is not your sovereign," he wrote to the Dutchman, Isaac Vossius, "he wishes, nevertheless, to be your benefactor."

Whatever reproaches may be uttered against

Louis XIV., such letters offer at least some palliation; and to them we must add the Hôtel des Invalides, the city of Dunkirk, the canal between the two seas, and, above all, Versailles. This wonderful monument, to which no other country can furnish a parallel, is the emblem of the greatness of France centralized for the first time in the seventeenth century. Those wonderful masses of verdure, and that hierarchy of bronze, of marble, of fountains, and cascades, rising one above another on the royal mount, from the monsters and tritons which howl below, to those beautiful ancient statues which crown the platform with the serene likeness of the gods; there is through all a glorious picture of the monarchy itself. These waters, which rise and descend with so much grace and majesty, seem to represent the vast social circulation which then for the first time took place: power and wealth ascending from the people to the king, to be returned in the shape of glory, order, and security. The mother of Apollo, the charming Latona, in whom the unity of the garden seems to centre, silences the insolent clamours of the group which surrounds her; from men they become croaking frogs. Is not this the regency triumphing over the Fronde?

# CHAPTER XIX.

## CONTINUATION OF THE REIGN OF LOUIS XIV., 1661–1715.

FRANCE, standing alone and invincible, while the greater part of the states of Europe were prostrate, now claimed, and obtained the supremacy. The pope having permitted the ambassador of France to be insulted in an outrageous manner, and his hotel to be violated, Louis XIV. demanded the most humiliating amends. The pope was obliged to drive his own brother from his dominions, and to erect a pyramid to perpetuate his humiliation (1664). At the same time that he treated the spiritual chief of the Christian world so severely, Louis XIV. defended the interests of Christendom upon the sea and upon land; he freed the sea from the pirates of Barbary (1664). To the Emperor Leopold, engaged in a war against the Turks, he sent troops, who played the most brilliant part at the battle of St. Gothard.

*Spain.*—Against whom will France go to display the power which she has just announced? There are but two nations in the West, England being paralyzed by the return of the Stuarts. There is

Spain and Holland, the conquered and the conqueror. Spain is still that prodigious *vessel, the prow of which was in the Indian seas, and the stern in the Atlantic Ocean;* but the vessel has been dismasted, disabled, and cast ashore in the tempest of Protestantism. A gale of wind has carried away her long-boat—Holland. A second has taken Portugal from her, and laid bare her planks ; a third has detached the East Indies. What remains is vast and imposing, but inert and immovable, yet awaiting ruin with dignity.

*Holland.*—On the other hand was Holland, that hardy, avaricious, and reserved nation, which did so many great things without greatness. First, they lived in spite of the ocean; this was the first miracle : then they salted their herrings and cheese, and changed their infected tuns to tons of gold; next, they made this gold fruitful by means of a bank—their gold pieces *bore young*. In the middle of the seventeenth century they had gathered at pleasure the spoils of Spain, had taken the sea from her, and the Indies besides. The Spanish Netherlands were held in a state of siege by virtue of a treaty. Spain had consented to the closing of the Sheldt and the ruin of Antwerp (1648). The Belgians were prohibited from selling the produce of their soil. Holland was already a vampire couched on Belgium, sucking her life, and growing fat upon her leanness.

*Conquest of Flanders.*—Such was the situation of the West when France attained the summit of her power. The land yet belonged to Spain, the sea to Holland. The office of France in the seventeenth century was the dismembering of the one and the weakening of the other; the first was easier than the last. France had armies, but as yet no vessels. She commenced with Spain. First, France united herself, to appearance, with Holland against Spain and England, who disputed for the dominion of the seas. France promised aid to the Dutch, but she permitted the three powers to dash their vessels against each other, and to destroy their navies in the most obstinate naval battles which as yet had ever been fought. Philip IV. being dead (1667), Louis XIV., quoting the civil law of the Netherlands, pretended that his wife, who was the eldest daughter of the deceased, ought to succeed him in preference to the younger son. It is true she had renounced the succession, but the promised dowry had not been paid. The French army entered Flanders in all the pomp of the new reign. Turenne at the head, then the king, the ministers, the ladies in the golden carriages of the court; then Vauban, who, as they advanced, established himself in the different places and fortified them. Flanders was taken in two months, and has been kept. The same winter, when they thought the war suspended (January, 1668), the troops marched through Champagne to Burgundy, and fell on Franche-Comté. Spain had expected nothing of the kind. The authorities of the country had been purchased beforehand. All was finished in seventeen days. The exasperated court of Spain wrote to the governor, "that the King of France should have sent his lackeys to take possession of the province, instead of coming to it himself."

*Peace of Aix-la-Chapelle*, 1668.—These rapid successes reconciled Spain and Holland. The latter did not care to have the great king for a neighbour. We find the Hollanders interesting themselves for Spain, defending her, and uniting themselves with England and Sweden in her behalf; the Hollanders had the address to make England demand that union. Three Protestant states are thus armed to defend Catholic Spain against Catholic France. This singular event shows how far we already are from the sixteenth century, and from religious wars (triple alliance of the Hague, 1668). Louis XIV. was content with French Flanders, and gave up Franche-Comté.

Holland had protected Spain, and compelled France to draw back. A citizen, a sheriff of Amsterdam, declared to the king, in the midst of all his glory, that he should go no farther. Insolent medals were struck. The sheriff of Amsterdam was represented with a sun and this device: "In conspectu meo stetit sol."

From that time the contest in Europe was between France and Holland. France could not advance one step without meeting Holland. At first the king purchased with ready money the alliance of England and Sweden. Charles II., who had already betrayed England by selling Mardick and Dunkirk to France, once more sold the interests of his country. They promised to the nation some of the Dutch islands; to the king, money for his feasts and his mistresses. The young and seductive Duchess of Orleans, sister-in-law to Louis XIV., sister of Charles II., negotiated, when on a triumphant journey, the shame of her brother. It was she who died so young and so deeply mourned, for whom Corneille and Racine each composed a *Berenice*, and Bossuet the celebrated funeral discourse.

*Creation of a Navy.*—In the mean time, the army of Louis XIV. had been increased to eighty thousand men. It received through Louvois the most formidable organization. For the first time, the bayonet, so terrible a weapon in French hands, was placed on the top of the musket. The indefatigable genius of Colbert created a navy. France, so lately obliged to borrow vessels from Holland, had in 1672 one hundred; five navy arsenals were built—Brest,

Rochefort, Toulon, Dunkirk, Havre. Dunkirk is, unhappily, ruined; but Toulon and Brest, with their vast constructions, their mountains removed to make room for vessels, still attest the Herculean efforts which France then made, and the memorable defiance which she gave to Holland respecting the dominion of the seas

Holland held the sea, and thought to hold all. The party of the sea governed; the De Witts in council, and Ruyter in the fleets; the De Witts were statesmen, geometers, pilots, and sworn enemies of the land party, of the house of Orange, of the stadtholdership. They seemed to forget that Holland belonged to the Continent; they only saw in it an island. The fortresses fell to ruins; Holland had twenty-five thousand bad soldiers, and this, too, when the French frontier had been advanced, and almost touched theirs.

*Conquest of Holland*, 1672.—Suddenly one hundred thousand men moved from Flanders towards Holland (1672). "This was," says Temple, "as a peal of thunder in a clear sky." They left Mastricht behind them, without amusing themselves with taking it; they seized Gueldren, Utrecht, Upper Yssel; they were four leagues from Amsterdam. Nothing could save Holland. Her allies of Spain and Brandenburg, the only ones she had, could not wrest this prize from Louis XIV. It was the conqueror alone who could save her, by his mistakes, and he did it. Condé and Turenne wished to dismantle all the forts; Louvois preferred that garrisons should be stationed there, that is, that they should disperse the army. The king sided with Louvois. They relied on walls; they thought to take Holland by merely placing their hands on the stones, but Holland escaped. At first the amphibious republic wished to throw herself on the water and embark for Batavia with her gold. The war abating, she hoped once more to resist by land: the people threw themselves furiously on the chiefs of the sea party, the De Witts; they were cut in pieces: Ruyter looked for the same fate. All the forces of the Republic were intrusted to the young William of Orange.

*William of Orange.*—This general of twenty-two years, who, as his first trial, undertook, almost without arms, to confront the greatest king of the earth, had in his feeble and almost dying frame the calm and inflexible obstinacy of his grandfather, the *Taciturn*, the adversary of Philip II. He was a man of bronze—a stranger to every feeling of nature and humanity. Raised by the party of De Witt, he was their ruin; a Stuart by the family of his mother, he overthrew the Stuarts; the son-in-law of James II., he dethroned him; and England, which he had taken from his family, he left to those whom he hated, to the princes of the house of Hanover. He had but one passion, but it was atrocious—the hatred of France. It is said that at the peace of Nimeguen, when he endeavoured to surprise Luxemburg, he already had a knowledge of the treaty; but he still thirsted for French blood. It is remarkable that this great and intrepid general almost always waged war while retiring before his foe; but his admirable retreats were worth victories.

*Europe leagued against Louis XIV.*, 1674.—At first, in order to defend Holland, William drowned it: he opened the sluices, while Ruyter made sure of the sea by defeating the French and the English, and came to moor his triumphant fleet in the inundated plain of Amsterdam. Then William armed against France both Spain and Austria. He detached England from Louis XIV.; Charles II. was forced by his Parliament to sign the peace. The Catholic neighbours of Holland, the Bishop of Munster, the Elector of Cologne, then Brandenburg, then Denmark, then the Empire, all Europe, declared themselves against Louis XIV. (1674).

It was now necessary to abandon the towns of Holland, and retreat. The French repaid themselves, as usual, at the expense of Spain. Louis XIV. seized Franche-Comté, which has been retained by France. In the Netherlands, Condé, with an inferior force, gave battle to the prince in that furious contest at Senef. Condé conquered, but it was a victory for the Prince of Orange to have stood his ground before Condé at an equal loss. Upon the Rhine, Turenne, who, like Bonaparte, increased in boldness as he increased in years, kept all the Empire in awe. Twice he saved Alsace, twice he penetrated Germany. It was then that the Palatinate was burned by the order of Louvois. The Palatine was secretly allied with the emperor, and it was proposed to leave only a desert to the Imperials.

*Death of Turenne*, 1675.—Turenne, re-entering Germany, was about to strike a decisive blow, when he was killed at Saltzbach (1675). Condé, being sick, withdrew the same year.

*Duquesne*, 1677.—We see that at this period the destiny of France depended not on one man. The allies, though they believed France disarmed by the retreat of the two great generals, could not break the frontier of the Rhine, and lost in the Netherlands, Condé, Boudrain, Aire, Valenciennes, Cambray, Ghent, Ypres. Duquesne, who was sent to the succour of Messina, which had revolted against Spain, engaged Ruyter in a terrible naval battle in sight of Mount Ætna. The allies alone lost there twelve ships, six galleys, seven thousand men, seven hundred pieces of cannon, and, what was worth more than all, Ruyter. Duquesne destroyed their fleet in a second battle (1677).

*Peace of Nimeguen*, 1678.—The allies now wished peace; France and Holland were equally exhausted. Colbert asked leave to retire from the ministry if the war was continued. Still this peace of Nimeguen was advantageous for France. She retained Franche-Comté and twelve places of the Netherlands; she had Friburg for Philipsburg. Denmark and Brandenburg gave up what they had taken from Sweden, the ally of France. Holland alone lost nothing, and the great European question remained unsettled (1678).

This is the zenith of the reign of Louis XIV. Europe had been armed against him, and he had resisted; he was still increasing in power. He assumed to himself the title of *Great*. The Duke of Feuillade went farther. He kept a burning lamp before his statue, as before an altar. We seem to be reading the history of the Roman emperors.

*Literature*.—The brilliant literature of this epoch is but one hymn to royalty. The voice which rose highest was that of Bossuet; it was as Bossuet himself represented in his "*Discourse on Universal History*;" the kings of Egypt were praised by the priests in the temples, in presence of the gods. The first period of the great reign, that of Des Cartes, of Port Royal, of Pascal, and Corneille, did not present such unanimity: literature at that period was animated by a spirit ruder and more free. At the period at which we have now arrived, Molière had just died (1673), Racine had put forth his Phædra (1677), La Fontaine published the last six books of his Fables (1678), Madame de Sevigné wrote her Letters, Bossuet meditated on the knowledge of God and of himself, and prepared the Discourse on Universal History (1681). The Abbé Fénélon, still young, a simple director of a convent for young ladies, lived under the patronage of Bossuet, who regarded him as his disciple. Bossuet leads the triumphal choir of the great century, in full assurance of the past and of the future, between eclipsed Jansenism and impending Quietism, between the gloomy Pascal and the mystical Fénélon. In the mean time, Cartesianism is pushed to its most formidable consequences. Malebranche makes human intelligence an emanation from God; and in Protestant Holland, struggling with Catholic France, the fathomless gulf of Spinoza is about to open itself, to swallow up at once Catholicism and Protestantism, liberty, morals, God, and the world.

*Chamber of Reunion.*—In the mean time, Louis XIV. reigns in Europe. The sign of royalty is jurisdiction. He wishes the powers of Europe to acknowledge the decision of his Parliaments.

The Chambers of *Reunion* interpret the treaty of Nimeguen, and *reunite the dependances*, which had been yielded to him. One of the dependances was nothing less than Strasbourg (1681). They hesitate to obey; he bombards Luxemburg (1684). He bombards Algiers (1683), Tripoli (1685). He bombards Genoa; he would have crushed it in its marble palaces, had not the doge come to Versailles to ask pardon (1684). He bought Casal, the gate of Italy; he built Huningen, the gate of Switzerland. He interposed in the affairs of the Empire; he wished to make an elector of Cologne (1689). He reclaimed, in the name of his sister-in-law, the Duchess of Orleans, a part of the Palatinate, invoking in this affair, as in that of Flanders, the civil law against the feudal law. The decisions of the law were supported by force, Europe was disarmed, and Louis XIV. remained armed; he increased his navy to 230 vessels; towards the end of his reign his armies amounted to 450,000 men.

*Declaration of the Clergy*, 1682.—At the same time the monarchy attained its greatest degree of centralization. The two chief obstacles were crushed: the pontifical power and the Protestant opposition. Since 1673 an edict had declared all the bishoprics of the kingdom subject to the throne In 1682 an assembly of thirty-five bishops, of which

Bossuet was the soul, decided "that the pope had authority only over spiritual things; that in such things even the general councils were superior to him, and that his decisions were only infallible after the Church had accepted them." The pope from that time refused bulls to all the bishops and abbés whom the king nominated, so that in 1689 there were twenty-nine dioceses in France without bishops. They spoke of making a patriarch. In 1687, the pope, wishing to abolish the right of asylum which the ambassadors enjoyed at Rome for their hotels and quarters, Louis XIV. alone refused. The French ambassador entered Rome at the head of eight hundred men, and maintained his privilege by force of arms.

*Revocation of the Edict of Nantes—Madame de Maintenon.*—That which quieted the religious conscience of Louis XIV. in this affair was, that, while he humbled the pope, he crushed the Protestants. Richelieu had destroyed them as a political party, but he had left them their vote in the Parliaments, their synods, and a part of their interior organization. He vainly flattered himself that he could lead them back by persuasion. Louis XIV. employed money, and seemed greatly to have advanced the work; it was announced to him every morning that a district, a city, were converted; he need only to act with a little vigour, they said, and he would restore the unity of the Church and of France. (Revoking of the Edict of Nantes, 1685.) This was the idea of the greatest men of the time, especially of Bossuet. The employment of violence in a matter of faith, the infliction of a temporal evil to procure an eternal good, was not repugnant, at that time, to the feelings of any person. It is necessary, however, to say that at this period there was great exasperation against the Protestants. France, limited in her success by Holland, felt that she had another Holland in her own bosom which rejoiced at the success of the first. As long as Colbert lived he defended them; excluded from offices, they had turned their activity towards industry and commerce, and they troubled France no more; they enriched it. After Colbert, Louis XIV. was governed by Louvois, the enemy of Colbert, and by Madame de Maintenon, to whom he was secretly married towards 1685. Madame de Maintenon was born a Calvinist, and was granddaughter to the famous Theodore Agrippa d'Aubigné, one of the chiefs of the Protestant opposition against Henry IV. This discreet and judicious person had herself abjured her religion, and would have made all the Protestants do the same; of a cold disposition, the misery of her early years seemed to have petrified her heart, and rendered her more than ever insensible. She was the widow of Scarron, the cripple, the author of the *Æneide Burlesqued,* before she became the wife of *Louis the Great.* She had no children; she knew no maternal affection. It was she who advised the most odious measure of persecution: to take the children from their parents in order to convert them. The cries of the mothers, at this, rose to heaven.

The power of Louis XIV. was limited without by the Protestant opposition of Holland, and within by the Calvinists. Disobeyed for the first time, the government showed a ferocious violence, which was not in the heart of Louis XIV. Vexations of all kinds, confiscations, the galleys, the wheel, gibbets, all were employed. The dragoons, who were placed among the Calvinists, aided the missionaries in their own way. The king did not know one half of the excesses which were committed. In closing the kingdom, confiscating the property of the fugitives, sending those to the galleys who favoured their escape, the state lost two hundred thousand subjects; according to some, five hundred thousand. Multitudes escaped to England, to Holland, and to Germany, but the greater number went to Prussia. They became the most bitter enemies of France. William charged the French more than once at the head of a French regiment. Much of the success of the war of Ireland was due to the old Marshal Schomberg, who preferred his religious faith to his country. The infernal machine, which was made to blow up Saint Malo in 1693, had been invented by a refugee.

*Expulsion of James II.*, 1688.—It was precisely at this time that the majority of the European powers formed the league of Augsburg (1686). Catholics and Protestants, William and Innocent XI., Sweden and Savoy, Denmark and Austria, Bavaria, Saxony, Brandenburg, all, with one accord, were against Louis XIV. They accused him, among other things, of having, by his correspondence with the revolted Hungarians, opened Germany to the Turks, and with having led that terrible invasion, from which Vienna was saved by John Sobieski. Louis XIV. had only the King of England, James II., for him; an unexpected revolution overthrew James, and placed England in the hands of William. The second and definitive catastrophe of the Stuarts, prepared long since by the unworthy government of Charles II., broke out under his brother. James did not imitate the hypocritical evasions of Charles; he was a good man, but of limited faculties, self-willed, and obstinate; he declared himself to be a Catholic and a Jesuit (this is literally correct); he contributed in every way to his own downfall, and he did fall. His son-in-law William, called from Holland, took his place without striking a blow (1688).

Louis XIV. entertained James II. magnificently, and espoused his cause. He threw the gauntlet to Europe, he declared war against England, Holland, the Empire, Spain, and the pope. During the time that the French Calvinists strengthened the armies of the league, multitudes from all nations came to take part in the armies of Louis XIV. He had regiments of Hungarians and Irish. One day, when he was complimented upon the success of the French army, he replied, " Say, rather, the army of France."

This second period of the reign of Louis XIV. is occupied with two wars of succession—the succession of England, and the succession of Spain. The first war terminated honourably for France by the treaty of Ryswick (1698), and yet the result was against her; she acknowledged William. In the second war, terminated by the treaties of Utrecht and Rastadt (1712–1714), France experienced the most humiliating reverses, and yet the result was most favourable to her. Spain was secured to a grandson of Louis XIV., and from henceforth was open to French influence. England and Spain gained by this double revolution. The era of English liberty is the ascension to the throne of William (1688); since that of Philip V. (1701), population, which had been decreasing in Spain, has always increased.

Add to these results the elevation of two secondary states, hereafter indispensable to the preservation of the balance of power in Europe: Prussia and Piedmont, which we may distinguish as the German and Italian resistance. Prussia, both German and Slavonic, unites by degrees the Germany of the North, and counterbalances Austria. The kingdom of Savoy-Piedmont will guard the Alps, and will close them; the Italian Alps against France, the French against Italy.

We must mark in advance these fine and useful results, in order to console ourselves for the many reverses of France which remain to be related.

*Luxembourg.*—France, in 1689, most cruelly defeated Germany. She placed a desert between herself and her enemies. All the Palatinate was burned the second time; Spire, Worms, and more than forty cities and villages, were burned. Two generals made head rapidly in Flanders and the Alps, viz., Luxembourg and Catinat, in whom we see a second Condé and Turenne. Luxembourg was a general of inspiration and of sudden movements, carrying on war as a great lord; often surprised, but never conquered. After his great battles at Fleurus, Steinkerk, and Nerwinden (1690–92–95), from which he brought so many standards, he was called the *upholsterer of Nôtre*

*Dame.* This brilliant general was deformed by nature. William always said, "Can I not beat, then, this little hunchback?"

*Catinat.*—Catinat regarded war as a science. He became an officer by chance; from a family of lawyers, himself a lawyer at first, he was the first example of a plebeian general. There was something of the antique in that man. He made his way slowly by his own merit; it was long before he obtained command, and he was never in favour. He asked for nothing, received little, and often refused offers. The soldiers, who loved his simplicity and good-nature, called him *le Père de la Pensée.* The court received his services with regret. When he had defeated the Duke of Savoy at Staffarde, had taken Saluce, and routed the enemy at Suzes (1690), Louvois wrote to him, "Although you have served the king very badly in this campaign, his majesty yet wishes to preserve for you your ordinary allowance." Catinat was discouraged at nothing; he endured the rudeness of Louvois, and the difficulties of this hard war in the Alps, with the same patience.

*La Hogue,* 1692.—The heaviest blows were struck in Ireland and on the sea. Louis XIV wished to bring England back under French influence. He made James enter Ireland; he sent him supplies after supplies, fleet after fleet. James miscarried. The odious aid of the French and Irish confirmed the English in their hatred of him. Instead of raising Scotland, which waited for him, he remained in Ireland, amused himself with sieges, and was beaten at the Boyne. Louis XIV. was not discouraged; he gave him money to arm and equip thirteen thousand men, and he attempted to send him twenty thousand; Tourville and D'Etrées escorted them with sixty-five vessels. D'Etrées being wind-bound, Tourville found himself with forty-four vessels opposed to eighty. He demanded orders from the court. Louis XIV. bade him force a passage. This terrible battle of La Hogue cost the French only seventeen vessels, but the confidence and pride of their navy was gone. It was reduced in 1707 to thirty-five vessels, and was resuscitated again, but for a moment, under Louis XVI. The battle of La Hogue marks the era of England's dominion over the seas (1692). Louis XIV. caused one of his medals to be struck, bearing a threatening Neptune, with the words of the poet, "Quos ego...." The Dutch struck a medal which bore for its device, "Maturate fugam, regique hæc dicite vestro: Non illi imperium pelagi...."

*Peace of Ryswick*, 1798.—The terrible ravages of our corsairs, of Jean Bart, and Duguay-Trouin, with the bloody battle of Nerwinden gained by

Luxembourg, and that of Catinat at Marseilles (1693), by degrees rendered the allies more tractable. The Duke of Savoy yielded first. Indeed, the war was ended for him, all the strong places being in the hands of the French. They offered him restitution, and for his daughter a prospect of the throne of France; she was to marry the Duke of Bourgoyne, grandson of Louis XIV., heir of the monarchy. The defection of Savoy (1696) decided, by degrees, the others. France retained Roussillon, Artois, Franche-Comté, and Strasburg, but she acknowledged William. This was, in fact, to be conquered (peace of Ryswick, 1698).

*Will of Charles II.*, 1700.—This peace was but a truce accorded to the sufferings of the people. A grand question occupied Europe. This or that province of Spain was not in controversy, but the entire Spanish monarchy, with Naples, the Netherlands, the Indies. As Charles V. had been laid out alive in his coffin, and had assisted at his own funeral, so Charles II., the last of his descendants, assisted at the funeral of the monarchy. This old man of thirty-nine years, governed by his wife, by his mother, by his confessor, and influenced by all the world, made his will and destroyed it. The King of France, the emperor, the electoral prince of Bavaria, and the Duke of Savoy, all born of Spanish princesses, claimed the spoils in advance. At one time they were for the Bavarian, at another for the Austrian; they also spoke of dismembering the kingdom. The poor king saw all this while yet alive; he was exasperated at it. Ignorant and changeable as he was, he still knew that he wished to ensure the unity of the Spanish monarchy. He decided for a prince who was most capable of maintaining this unity; he chose a grandson of Louis XIV.; then opening the tombs of the Escurial, he disinterred his father, mother, and first wife, and kissed their bones. It was not long before he joined them (1700).

Louis XIV. accepted the legacy and the danger. He sent to Spain the second of his grandsons, the Duke of Anjou, who became Philip V., on his departure, he addressed him in those noble words, which from century to century will appear more true and more profound: "There are Pyrenees no longer." The immediate consequence was a European war. Notwithstanding the advice of his council, he also decided to acknowledge the son of James II. as Prince of Wales, and to maintain at once the succession of Spain and of England.

*Declining Vigour of France.*—It was, however, full late to commence such a war. Louis XIV. had reigned fifty-seven years. He had grown old; all had grown old. France seemed to become pale at the age of her king. The glories of his reign were all departing by degrees. Colbert was dead, Louvois was dead (1682, 1691), Arnaud also, and Boileau, and Racine, and La Fontaine, and Madame Sévigné ; soon the great voice of the age, Bossuet, was heard no more (1704). France, in place of Colbert and Louvois, had Chamillart, who increased the number of her ministers ; Chamillart was governed by Madame de Maintenon, Madame de Maintenon by Babbien, her old servant. Strange, too, that another woman should govern England after King William ; I speak of Queen Anne, daughter of James II., and granddaughter, through her mother, of the historian Clarendon, as Madame de Maintenon was granddaughter of Agrippa d'Aubigné.

From being placed in the hands of ennobled citizens (Chamillart, Le Tellier, Pontchartrain, &c., &c.), the government became only more favourable to the nobility, who had been prodigiously increased of late. They were ignorant of commerce and industry, arrogant, and incapable. They had invaded the antechamber, the army, and especially the civil offices. The small nobles were officers or clerks at their option. There were soon as many officers as soldiers, as many clerks as principals. The great lords bought regiments for their young children · they commanded the armies, and allowed themselves to be taken at Cremona and at Hochstadt.

*Marlborough and Eugene.*—There were, at this time, two men at the head of the allied armies capable of profiting by all this: an Englishman and a Frenchman, Marlborough and Eugene. The latter, a younger son of the house of Savoy, but son also of the Count of Soissons and of a niece of Mazarin, may be called French. Marlborough, the *handsome Englishman*, was cold, but acute and judicious; he studied under Turenne, and returned to France her own lessons. Eugene, although Vendome called him a *bad financier*, was a man of extraordinary tact, who troubled himself not much about rules, but who thoroughly understood places, things, persons, knew the strong and the weak, and took advantage of the weak. His most striking and easy successes were over Ottoman barbarism. This man, who always went straight to the point, won victories alternately at the two extremes of Europe, over the great king, and over the Turks, and it seemed as if he had saved both liberty and Christianity.

These two generals had one convenience for prosecuting war, that is, they were practically kings in their respective countries; they fought in the summer, they governed and negotiated in the winter. They had full power, and needed not, on the eve of a battle, to send to Versailles to obtain authority to conquer.

*Villeroi—Vendome.*—In 1701, Catinat gave up the army to the magnificent Villeroi, whom Prince Eugene took in his bed at Cremona. Eugene did not gain by it. Villeroi was replaced by Vendome, grandson of Henry IV., a true soldier, with the manners of a woman. Vendome, like his brother, the great prior, remained in bed until 4 o'clock P.M. He was one of the youngest generals of Louis XIV.; he was only fifty years old. The soldiers adored him even for his bad qualities. There was little order, or foresight, or discipline in this army, but much boldness and gayety; courage made amends for all.

*Villars.*—Catinat commanded on the coast of Germany, and Villars under him. The latter, impatient at the prudence of his chief, gained rashly the battle of Fridlingen (1702); then, piercing into Germany, he gained besides, in spite of the Elector of Bavaria, the ally of Louis XIV., the battle of Hochstadt (1703). Villars excited the enthusiasm of his soldiers by his bravery, his boasting, his handsome military figure. At Fridlingen they proclaimed him Marshal of France on the field of battle.

The road to Austria was open, when it became known that the Duke of Savoy had resolved to take part against France and Spain, against his two sons-in-law (1703). Down to this time the allies had gained no signal advantage over France. She fought, however, along all her frontiers, and within them; at once against the world and against herself. The Calvinists of Cevennes, exasperated by the severity of the intendant Basville, had been in arms since 1702. Among other generals, Villars and Berwick were sent against them. The latter was a Stuart, a natural son of James II., who became one of the first tacticians of the age.

*Defeat of Hochstadt*, 1704—*Of Turin, of Ramillies*, 1705–1706.—Villars was far off in Languedoc, and Catinat had retired when the army of Germany, intrusted to M.M. de Marsin and Tallard, experienced at Hochstadt, on the very theatre of the victory of Villars, one of the most cruel defeats that France had ever suffered. They had thrown themselves blindly into Germany on the road to Vienna, where Marlborough and Eugene cut them off; the plan had been so laid, that, independent of the killed, 14,000 men gave themselves up without having been able to fight (1704). Villars hurries on in time to cover Lorraine, while Vendome gains an advantage over Eugene in the bloody affair of Cassano (1705). In 1706, Vendome was replaced by La Feuillade in Italy. France experiences two great defeats: by that of Turin, Eugene takes from

France the whole of Italy; by that of Ramillies, Marlborough drives her from the Spanish Netherlands.

*Defeat of Oudenarde,* 1708—*Misery of France.* —In 1707, the allies penetrated into France through Provence; in 1708, through Flanders (defeat of Oudenarde); 1709 was a terrible year: first a fearful winter, then a famine. The misery was universal. The footmen of the king begged at the gate of Versailles; Madame de Maintenon ate brown bread. Whole companies of cavalry deserted their unfurled standards to gain a living by contraband trade. The recruiting officers had to chase down men. The taxes assumed every form to reach the people; public documents were taxed; men paid to be born and paid to die. The peasants, pursued into the woods by the officers of the king's revenue, armed themselves, and took the city of Castres by storm. The king could not get a loan at four hundred per cent.; the national debt before the death of Louis XIV. amounted to nearly three thousand millions.

The allies suffered also. England ruined herself in order to ruin France. But Europe was led on by two men who wished for war, and, besides, the humiliation of Louis XIV. was a spectacle too pleasant to be lost. His ambassadors could get no replies except in derision. It was necessary, they said, that he should undo his own work—he must dethrone Philip V. He even condescended to offer money to the allies to keep up the war against his grandson. But no, they wanted that he should drive him away himself; that a French army should fight against a French prince.

*Victory of Malplaquet*, 1709.—The aged king then declared that he would place himself at the head of his nobility, and would go to die on his frontiers. He addressed himself for the first time to his people; he called upon them to judge, and exalted himself even by his humiliation. The manner in which the French fought this year (1709) indicates plainly how much the war had become national. It was on the 9th of September, near the village of Malplaquet; the soldier, who had been in want of provisions all day, came to receive his bread—he threw it away to engage in battle. Villars, seriously wounded, was carried from the field; the army retired in good order, not having lost eight thousand men; the allies left fifteen or twenty thousand on the spot.

*Victory of Denain*, 1712 — *Treaty of Utrecht*, 1712.—In Spain, the throne of Philip V., established by Berwick at Almanza (1707), was confirmed at Villaviciosa by Vendôme (1710); he made the young king sleep on a bed of standards. In the mean time, the elevation of the Archduke

Charles to the Empire (1711) caused Europe to fear the reunion of the Empire with Spain. To humble Louis XIV., in order to elevate a Charles V., was no trouble. England was tired of paying; she saw Marlborough, who had been gained over by the Dutch, carrying on the war for their interest. Finally, the victory by Villars at Denain, gained by a surprise, injured the reputation of Prince Eugene (1712). This terrible war, in which the allies had expected to dismember France, did not take one province from her (treaties of Utrecht and Rastadt, 1712; of La Barriere, 1715).

France only gave up some colonies. She maintained the grandson of Louis XIV. on the throne of Spain. The Spanish monarchy, it is true, lost its possessions in Italy and the Netherlands; she ceded Sicily to the Duke of Savoy; the Spanish Netherlands, Naples, and Milan to Austria; but she gained by concentrating her own estates, and by escaping the embarrassment of those distant possessions, which she could neither defend nor govern; the two Sicilies were soon to return to a branch of the Bourbons of Spain. Holland had several places in the Netherlands to defend with Austria, at their common expense. England secured the recognition of her new dynasty; she gained a footing at Gibraltar and on Minorca, at the entrance of Spain, and in the Mediterranean. She obtained for herself and for Holland a commercial treaty disadvantageous to France. She required the demolition of Dunkirk, and prevented France from furnishing supplies to it by the canal of Mardick. She maintained there, most unworthily, an English commissary, to assure himself, with his own eyes, that France did not rebuild the city of Jean-Bart. "They went to work," says a contemporary, "at the demolition of Dunkirk; they demanded eight hundred thousand livres for demolishing only the third part of it." Even at this day we cannot read without pain and indignation the sorrowful petition addressed by the inhabitants of Dunkirk to the Queen of England.

*Death of Louis XIV.*, 1715.—Such was the end of the great reign. Louis XIV. survived the treaty of Utrecht for a short time (died 1715). He had seen nearly all his children die within a few years, the dauphin, the Duke, the Duchess of Bourgoyne, and one of her sons. In his deserted palace there remained only an old man, almost eighty, and a child of five years. All the great men of the reign had gone; a new age had commenced. In literature, as in society, all energy was relaxed. This epoch of luxury and of ease announced itself at a distance, by the agreeable quietism of Madame Guyon, who reduced religion to love. The able and eloquent Massillon only touched upon doctrine in his discourses, attaching himself chiefly to morals. The political boldness of Fénélon belongs rather to the eighteenth century.

---

## CHAPTER XX.

### LITERATURE, THE SCIENCES, AND ARTS IN THE AGE OF LOUIS XIV.

During the first half of the seventeenth century the genius of literature and of the arts was still brilliant in the states of the South. The genius of philosophy and of the sciences illuminated the nations of the North, more especially in its second half. France, alone stationed between them, shines with a double lustre, spreading over all polished nations the sovereignty of her language, and placing herself from henceforth at the head of European civilization.

### § I. FRANCE.

France, like Italy, has her great literary age, succeeding to long periods of agitation. A monarch, the object of national enthusiasm, animates and encourages genius. The *religious spirit* was at that period the chief inspiration of literature. Religion, between the attacks of the sixteenth and those of the eighteenth century, animates her defenders with a new force. Literature, besides, receives a special impulse from the *social spirit* natural to the French, but which can develop itself only with the progress of ease and security; it is to this character that French literature owes her superiority in dramatic poetry, and in all delineation of manners. A capital and a court are the arbiters of literary merit. They have less originality, but they attain the perfection of taste.

The seventeenth century presents two distinct periods. In France, the first extends to 1661, the epoch at which Louis XIV. begins to reign by himself, and to exercise some influence over literature. The writers who lived, or who formed themselves in this period, still retain something of the style of the sixteenth century. Thoughts are more boldly expressed, and are more profound; still taste is the attribute of some men of genius. To this period belong (besides the painters Poussin and Le Sueur) a great number of writers: Malherbe, Racan, Brébœuf, Rotrou, and the great Corneille; Balzac and Voiture; Sarrasin and Mézerai; Des Cartes and Pascal. Rochefoucault, Cardinal de Retz, and Molière mark the transition from the first period to the second.

France, in the age of Louis XIV., produces no epic; her great poem is written in prose. Brilliant period of dramatic poetry. Tragedy attains nobleness, strength, and sublimity; afterward follow grace and pathos. In comedy, unrivalled by other nations. Three ages of French comedy: profound philosophy, coupled with a naïve gayety; gayety without philosophy; self-interest without gayety. The opera attains the rank of literary works. Satire attacks that which is ridiculous rather than that which is vicious; and, above all, she attacks ridiculous literature. The epilogue becomes a small dramatic poem. Lyric poetry flourishes late, and displays more art than enthusiasm. The pastoral remains feeble, or too spiritual. Light poetry is more graceful than pointed.

DRAMATIC POETS.

| | | | | | |
|---|---|---|---|---|---|
| Rotrou | died in | 1630 | Th. Corneille | died in | 1709 |
| Molière | " | 1673 | Regnard | " | 1709 |
| Pierre Corneille | " | 1684 | Brueys | " | 1723 |
| Quinault | " | 1688 | Campistron | " | 1723 |
| Racine | " | 1699 | Dancourt | " | 1726 |
| Boursault | " | 1708 | Crebillon | " | 1762 |

OTHER POETS.

| | | | | | |
|---|---|---|---|---|---|
| Malherbe | died in | 1628 | Segrais | died in | 1701 |
| Brébœuf | " | 1661 | Boileau | " | 1711 |
| Racan | " | 1670 | La Fare | " | 1713 |
| Benserade | " | 1691 | Chaulieu | " | 1720 |
| Mlle. Deshoulieres | " | 1694 | J. B. Rousseau | " | 1741 |
| La Fontaine | " | 1695 | | | |

The eloquence of the bar did not reach great excellence. (Le Maistre, 1658; Patru, 1681; Pelisson, 1693.) The eloquence of the pulpit surpasses all the models of antiquity. Funeral orations reappear under a form unknown to the ancients.

ORATORS.

| | | | |
|---|---|---|---|
| Cheminais | died in 1689 | Flechier | died in 1710 |
| Mascaron | " 1703 | Fénélon | " 1715 |
| Bourdaloue | " 1704 | Massillon | " 1743 |
| Bossuet | " 1704 | | |

History was loose and coldly elegant. The *Discourse on Universal History* opened a new route for history. Abundant materials are deposited in memoirs and in the correspondence of ministers. A number of other branches are cultivated with success. Novels rival comedy. Woman attains, in the carelessness of an intimate correspondence, the perfection of familiar style. Translation makes some progress, and literary criticism commences.

HISTORIAN .

| | | | |
|---|---|---|---|
| Sarrasin | died in 1654 | Amelot de la Houssai | 1706 |
| Perefixe | " 1670 | Boulainvilliers | " 1722 |
| Cardinal de Retz | " 1679 | Fleuri | " 1723 |
| Mézerai | " 1683 | Rapin de Thoiras | " 1725 |
| P. Maünbourg | " 1686 | Daniel | " 1728 |
| Mme. de Motteville | 1689 | Vertot | " 1735 |
| Saint Real | " 1692 | Dubos | " 1742 |
| Varillas | " 1696 | Saint Simon | " 1755 |
| P. d'Orleans | " 1698 | | |

LEARNED HISTORIANS.

| | | | |
|---|---|---|---|
| Th. Godefroi | died in 1648 | Godefroi | died in 1681 |
| Sirmond | " 1651 | Ducange | " 1688 |
| Pétau | " 1652 | Pagi | " 1695 |
| Labbe | " 1667 | Herbelot | " 1695 |
| Valois | " 1676 | Tillemont | " 1698 |
| Moreri | " 1680 | Cousin | " 1707 |

| | | | |
|---|---|---|---|
| Mabillon | died in 1707 | Basnage | died in 1725 |
| Ruinart | " 1709 | Le Clerc | " 1736 |
| Baluze | " 1718 | Montfaucon | " 1741 |

WRITERS ON DIVERS SUBJECTS.

| | | | |
|---|---|---|---|
| Voiture | died in 1648 | Bouhours | died in 1702 |
| Vaugelas | " 1649 | Perrault | " 1703 |
| Balzac | " 1654 | St. Evremond | " 1703 |
| Du Ryer | " 1656 | Fénélon | " 1715 |
| Scarron | " 1660 | Tourreil | " 1715 |
| D'Ablancourt | " 1664 | Mad. de Maintenon | " 1719 |
| Arnault d'Andilly | " 1674 | Hamilton | " 1720 |
| Le Bossu | " 1680 | Dufresny | " 1724 |
| De Saci | " 1684 | La Motte Houdart | " 1731 |
| Chapelle | " 1686 | Mad. de Lambert | " 1733 |
| Ant. Arnaud | " 1694 | Duclos | " 1742 |
| Lancelot | " 1695 | Mongault | " 1747 |
| Mad. de Sévigné | " 1696 | Le Sage | " 1747 |
| Mlle. de Lafayette | " 1699 | Fontenelle | " 1757 |
| Bachaumont | " 1702 | | |

Metaphysics give a new impulse to the human mind. Moralists accumulate observations without attempting to give to morality a scientific form. They begin to carry the philosophical spirit into natural sciences. Some isolated skeptics in this age form the tie between the sixteenth century and the eighteenth century.

PHILOSOPHERS.

| | | | |
|---|---|---|---|
| Des Cartes | died in 1650 | Bayle | died in 1706 |
| Gassendi | " 1655 | Malebranche | " 1715 |
| Pascal | " 1662 | Huet | " 1721 |
| La Motte le Vayer | " 1672 | Buffier | " 1737 |
| La Rochefoucault | " 1680 | L'Abbé de St. Pierre | 1743 |
| Nicole | " 1695 | Fontenelle | " 1757 |
| La Bruyère | " 1696 | | |

The sciences are not neglected. Rise of mathematics. Beginning of geography. Commencement of scientific voyages

SAVANS AND MATHEMATICIANS.

| | | | |
|---|---|---|---|
| Des Cartes | died in 1650 | L'Hôpital | died in 1704 |
| Fermat | " 1652 | James Bernouilli | " 1705 |
| Pascal | " 1662 | Nicolas Bernouilli | " 1726 |
| Pecquet | " 1674 | John Bernouilli | " 1748 |
| Rohault | " 1675 | | |

TRAVELLERS.

| | | | |
|---|---|---|---|
| Samson | died in 1667 | Tournefort | died in 1708 |
| Bochard | " 1669 | Chardin | " 1713 |
| Bernier | " 1688 | De l'Isle | " 1726 |
| Vaillant | " 1706 | | |

Classical learning is not less cultivated than in the sixteenth century, but is less noticed.

LATIN SCHOLARS AND POETS.

| | | | |
|---|---|---|---|
| Saumaise | died in 1653 | Jouvenci | died in 1716 |
| Lefevre | " 1672 | Madame Dacier | " 1722 |
| Rapin | " 1687 | Dacier | " 1722 |
| Furetière | " 1688 | De la Rue | " 1725 |
| Menage | " 1691 | Da la Monnaie | " 1728 |
| Santeuil | " 1697 | Le Card. de Polignac | 1741 |
| Commire | " 1702 | Brumoi | " 1742 |
| Danet | " 1709 | | |

Although the cultivation of the arts of design is not the principal characteristic of the age of Louis XIV., yet it contributed to the splendour of this brilliant period. Architecture reflects on it the brightest lustre. Painting, at first cultivated with genius, experiences a decay, which must increase in the following century.

PAINTERS.

| | | | |
|---|---|---|---|
| Le Sueur | died im 1655 | Mignard | died in 1695 |
| Le Poussin | " 1665 | Jouvenet | " 1717 |
| Le Brun | " 1690 | Rigaud | " 1744 |

SCULPTORS.

| | | | |
|---|---|---|---|
| Puget | died in 1695 | Coysevox | died in 1720 |
| Girardon | " 1715 | Coustou | " 1733 |

ARCHITECTS.

| | | | |
|---|---|---|---|
| Fr. Mansard | died in 1666 | Claude Perrault | died in 1703 |
| Le Nôtre | " 1700 | H. Mansard | " 1708 |

ENGRAVERS.

| | | | |
|---|---|---|---|
| Gallot | died in 1635 | Audran | died in 1703 |
| Nanteuil | " 1678 | | |

MUSICIAN.

Lulli died in 1687.

## § II. ENGLAND, HOLLAND, GERMANY, ITALY, SPAIN.

England, Italy, and Spain follow France closely in the career of literature; the two former (with Holland) go beyond her in that of the sciences. Notwithstanding the appearance of some superior men, the development of Germany does not yet commence. Italy, in the first half of the seventeenth century, preserves the glory of painting, which Flanders shares with her.

1. *Literature.*—The names of Bacon and Shakspeare mark the first flight of English genius; but the religious wars for a long time arrest all speculation;* yet it is to religious wars that we must ascribe the phenomenon of *Paradise Lost* (notwith-

standing the late appearance of this poem, 1669). Under Charles II., England is subjected to the literary, as to the political influence of France; and this spirit of imitation exists in all the *classical* period of English literature (from the accession of Charles II. to the death of Queen Anne, 1661–1714). In this period England produced three great poets (Dryden, Addison, Pope), many witty and ingenious poets, and several distinguished prose writers.

ENGLISH POETS.

| | | | |
|---|---|---|---|
| Shakspeare | died in 1616 | Walter | died in 1687 |
| Denham | " 1666 | Dryden | " 1701 |
| Cowley | " 1667 | Rowe | " 1718 |
| Milton | " 1674 | Addison | " 1719 |
| Rochester | " 1680 | Prior | " 1721 |
| Butler | " 1680 | Congreve | " 1729 |
| Roscommon | " 1684 | Gay | " 1732 |
| Otway. | " 1685 | Pope | " 1744 |

ENGLISH PROSE WRITERS.

| | | | |
|---|---|---|---|
| Clarendon | died in 1674 | Addison | " 1719 |
| Tillotson | " 1694 | Steele | " 1729 |
| Temple | " 1698 | Swift | " 1745 |
| Burnet | " 1715 | Bolingbroke | " 1751 |

Italian literature has lost its brilliancy. An original and profound thinker (Vico, died 1744) founded at Naples the philosophy of history; we remark some respectable historians in Italy, but poetry is superseded by wit and affectation.

ITALIAN POETS.

| | | | |
|---|---|---|---|
| Marini | died in 1625 | Salvator | died in 1675 |
| Tassoni | " 1635 | | |

ITALIAN HISTORIANS.

| | | | |
|---|---|---|---|
| Sarpi | died in 1625 | Bentivoglio | died in 1644 |
| Davila | " 1634 | Nani | " 1678 |

Spanish literature exhibits a prodigy of philosophy and of humour; after the names of Cervantes and the two great tragic poets, follow those of several historians.

SPANISH WRITERS.

| | | | |
|---|---|---|---|
| Cervantes | died in 1616 | Lope de Vega | died in 1635 |
| Mariana | " 1624 | Solis | " 1686 |
| Herrera | " 1625 | Calderon | " 1687 |

2. *Philosophy.*—England, prepared by theological and political controversies, opens new roads to metaphysics and political science. Germany opposes a single man to all the metaphysicians and philosophers of England (Leibnitz). A Dutchman erects Atheism into a system (Spinoza), but another philosopher of the same nation (Grotius) gives to morals a scientific form, and shows that it ought to govern the interests as well of societies as of individuals. This new science, first resting upon erudition, is afterward supported by philosophy.

ENGLISH PHILOSOPHERS AND POLITICIANS.

| | | | |
|---|---|---|---|
| Bacon | died in 1626 | Locke | died in 1704 |
| Hobbes | " 1679 | Shaftesbury | " 1713 |
| Sidney | " 1683 | Clarke | " 1729 |
| Cudworth | " 1688 | | |

DUTCH PHILOSOPHERS AND POLITICIANS.

| | | | |
|---|---|---|---|
| Grotius | died in 1645 | Gravesande | died in 1742 |
| Spinoza | " 1677 | | |

GERMAN PHILOSOPHERS AND POLITICIANS.

| | | | | | |
|---|---|---|---|---|---|
| Puffendorf | died in | 1694 | Wolf | died in | 1754 |
| Leibnitz | " | 1716 | | | |

3. *Sciences.*—These had in Bacon a legislator as well as a prophet, but they received their true direction only from Galileo and Newton. A multitude of *savants* ranked themselves as followers of these great men.

ENGLISH.

| | | | | | |
|---|---|---|---|---|---|
| Bacon | died in | 1626 | The Gregories | died in | 1646, 75, 1708 |
| Harvey | " | 1657 | | | |
| Barrow | " | 1677 | Newton | died in | 1726 |
| Boyle | " | 1691 | Halley | " | 1741 |

ITALIAN.

| | | | | | |
|---|---|---|---|---|---|
| Aldrovandi | died in | 1615 | Borelli | died in | 1679 |
| Sanctorius | " | 1636 | Viviani | " | 1703 |
| Galileo | " | 1642 | Cassini | " | 1712 |
| Torricelli | " | 1647 | | | |

DUTCH.

| | | | | | |
|---|---|---|---|---|---|
| Huygens | died in | 1702 | Boerhaave | died in | 1758 |

GERMAN AND DANISH.

| | | | | | |
|---|---|---|---|---|---|
| Kepler | died in | 1630 | Kirkher | died in | 1680 |
| Tycho Brahe | " | 1636 | Stahl | " | 1735 |

4. *Learning.*—It exercises itself upon a greater variety of subjects.* The antiquities of the Middle Ages and of the East share the labours of the learned, who, until then, had been exclusively occupied with classical antiquities. *English scholars:* Owen, Farnaby, Usher, Bentley, Marsham, Stanley, Hyde, Pococke. *Scholars of Holland and the Netherlands:* Barlæus, Schrevelius, Heinsius, the Vossii. *Ger-*

*man scholars:* Freinshemius, Gronovius, Morhof, Fabricius, Spanheim. *Learned Italians:* Muratori, &c., &c.

5. *Arts.* — The decay of the arts followed in Italy the decay of literature; painting alone was an exception. Lombard school. Flemish school.

ITALIAN PAINTERS.

| | | | |
|---|---|---|---|
| Guido | died in 1642 | Guercino | died in 1666 |
| L'Albano | " 1647 | Salvator Rosa | " 1673 |
| Lanfranc | " 1647 | Bernin, sculptor, architect, and painter, | 1680 |
| Domenichino | " 1648 | | |

FLEMISH PAINTERS.

| | | | |
|---|---|---|---|
| Rubens | died in 1640 | Rembrandt | died in 1688 |
| Van Dyck | " 1641 | The young Teniers | 1694 |
| The elder Teniers | 1649 | | |

# PART II.—1715–1789.

---

## CHAPTER XXI.

### DISSOLUTION OF THE MONARCHY, 1715–1789.

In the interval between Louis the Great and Napoleon the Great, France descended a steep declivity, at the bottom of which the ancient monarchy, encountering the people, was shattered in pieces, and gave place to the new order of things which still prevails. The unity of the eighteenth century is found in a preparation for this grand event. First, the literary and philosophical war for religious liberty; then the great and bloody battle for political liberty, a ruinous victory over Europe, and, in spite of a transient reaction, the definite establishment of constitutional order and civil equality.

The house of Orleans appears at the commencement, and again at the close of this period.

*The Regent—Law.*—While the deceased king went alone and without pomp to St. Denis, the Duke of Orleans caused his will to be broken by the Parliament. The policy of the regent, his life, his manners, his whole person, were entirely opposed to those of the preceding reign. All the old barriers fell. The regent invited private persons to give their advice upon public affairs ; he proclaimed the maxims of Fénélon ; he had Telemaque printed at his own expense ; he opened the library of the king to the public. The financiers, who under the last reign had enriched themselves by the misery of France, were tried by a hot-headed chamber, and acquitted or condemned at random ; these violent measures against the financiers only increased the popularity of the prince. But it was not sufficient to condemn them ; it was necessary to replace them by other means, to look to this debt of three thousand millions which Louis XIV. had left. Then a grand scheme was tried ; a Scotch banker, named Law, a disciple, as he said, of Locke and Newton, came to make in France the first trial of credit. He opened a bank, substituted bills for money, and mortgaged those bills on an enterprise for collecting the immense revenues of the kingdom, and on the colonial riches of an unknown world. He created the Mississippi Company. For the first time men refused gold ; the value of the bills grew hourly. In the street Quincampoix, at the doors of the offices where they changed this inconvenient metal for paper, there were constant throngs of people. The regent becomes one of the directors of the enterprise, and makes himself a banker. Yet confidence was shaken; this idolatry of paper had its unbelievers; it fell rapidly. Wo to the last possessors! There was a strange change: the rich became poor, and the poor rich. Wealth, which had hitherto belonged to the soil, and stood immovable in families, for the first time took wings; she followed henceforth the wants of commerce and industry. An analogous movement took place all over Europe; the minds of men, if we may so speak, were detached from the earth. Law, making his escape from the kingdom in the midst of imprecations, left behind him, at least, this benefit (1717–1721).

*Alberoni.*—The regent, in his facility at adopting new ideas, in his scientific curiosity, in his loose manners, is one of the types of the eighteenth century. He enjoins the Bull* out of regard for the pope, but is not the less impious. His licentious friends are nobles; but his man, his minister, the true king of France, is the rogue Cardinal Dubois, the son of an apothecary of Brives-la-Gaillarde. The regent was naturally an ally of England, which, under the house of Hanover, also represented the modern principle, as in Germany did the young royalty of Prussia, and in the North, Russia created by Peter the Great. The common enemy was Spain, at whose expense the peace of Utrecht was

* The bull *Unigenitus*, &c.

made. Spain and France, enemies, although relations, regarded each other with a hostile eye. The Spanish minister, the intriguing Alberoni, undertook to restore the old principle over all Europe. He wished to give back to Spain all she had lost, to give the regency of France to Philip V.; he wished to re-establish the Pretender in England. To accomplish this, Alberoni counted on hiring the best swordsman of the time, on taking into pay the Swede, Charles XII.; this royal adventurer was to be paid by Spain, as Gustavus Adolphus had been by France. This vast project failed entirely. Charles XII. was killed; the Pretender failed in his attempts; the Spanish ambassador was taken in the act of conspiring with the Duchess of Maine, the wife of a legitimated son of Louis XIV.; this little and spirited princess had believed that, from her academy at Sceaux, she might change the face of Europe. The Mémoires of the Fronde, which had just appeared, excited her emulation. The regent and Dubois, who felt neither hatred nor friendship, found all this so ridiculous that they punished no one except some poor gentlemen from Brittany, who were the most conspicuous in the conspiracy (1718). France, England, Holland, the emperor, all united against Alberoni, and formed the quadruple alliance. Yet, in 1720, Spain obtained for her consolation Tuscany, Parma, and Plaisance, and the emperor, in giving her the investiture of these states, forced the Duke of Savoy to take Sardinia in exchange for Sicily. Europe was determined to have peace, and it was agreed for at any price.

*Ministry of the Duke of Bourbon and of Fleury,* 1725–45.—The oppressive and unskilful ministry of the Duke of Bourbon, who governed after the death of the regent (1723–26), was soon replaced by that of the prudent and circumspect Henry, ex-preceptor of the young king, who quietly seized both upon the king and the kingdom (1726–1745). Louis XV., who to his seventh year walked in leading strings, and to his twelfth year wore a waist of whalebone, was destined to be led during all his lifetime. Under the economical and timid government of the old priest, France was only troubled by the affair of the bull, the *convulsions* of Jansenism, and the remonstrances of Parliament. France, asleep under Henry, was united to England, asleep under Walpole; an unequal union from which France drew not the least advantage. England was at that time the admiration of the French; they went to study with the *free-thinkers* of Great Britain, as once the Greek philosopher did with the Egyptian priests. Voltaire went there to study Locke, Newton, and his tragedy of Brutus (1730). The president, Montesquieu, more circumspect since the publication of his *Persian Letters* (published in 1721), found in England a model for the imitation of all nations. No one thought of Germany, where Leibnitz was dead, nor of Italy, where Vico lived.

There were so many causes for war in the midst of this great calm, that a single spark from the North wrapped Europe in flames.

*France sustains Stanislaus — Stanislaus obtains Lorraine.* — Under the ministry of the Duke of Bourbon, a court intrigue had induced the marriage of the King of France to the daughter of a prince without a kingdom, Stanislaus Lesczinski, whom Charles XII. for an instant had made King of Poland, and who had retired to France. At the death of Augustus II. (1733), the party of Stanislaus arose in opposition to that of Augustus III., elector of Saxony, son of the deceased king. Stanislaus had sixty thousand votes. Villars and the old generals pushed into war; they pretended that they could not dispense with supporting the father-in-law of the King of France. Henry suffered himself to be driven into it; he did too little to succeed, but sufficient to compromise the French name. He sent three millions of money and fifteen thousand men against fifty thousand Russians. A Frenchman, who was accidentally present at the arrival of the French troops (the Count de Plelo, ambassador in Denmark), blushing for France, placed himself at their head, and was killed.

Spain declared herself for Stanislaus against Austria, that supported Augustus. This distant war in Poland was a pretext for her to recover her possessions in Italy; she succeeded partly, through the aid of France. While Villars was invading Milan, the Spaniards retook both Sicilies, and established there the Infant Don Carlos (1734–1735). They kept this conquest by the treaty of Vienna (1738). Stanislaus, as a recompense for the throne of Poland, received Lorraine, which at his death would belong to France; the Duke of Lorraine, François, son-in-law of the emperor, and husband of the famous Maria Theresa, had Tuscany in exchange, as a fief of the Empire. The last of the Medicis had died without posterity. Henry hastened to make a treaty to secure the two Sicilies to the Bourbons of Spain, in spite of the jealousy of the English. Add to this that ten thousand Russians had advanced as far as the Rhine. It thus became apparent, for the first time, that this European Asia could stretch her long arms beyond Germany, even to France.

Thus France, though superannuated with Fleury and Villars, under a minister of eighty years, and a general as old, had still gained Lorraine. Spain, renovated by the house of Bourbon, had gained two kingdoms from Austria. Austria, still under the house of Charles V., represented the old European principle, which was destined to perish in order to make room for modern principles. The Emperor Charles VI., full of fears like Charles II. of Spain in 1700, had, at the price of the greatest sacrifices, endeavoured to secure his estates to his daughter Maria Theresa, wife of the Duke of Lorraine, who had become Duke of Tuscany.

*Growing Strength of Prussia — Frederic II.*— In face of ancient Austria rose Prussia, a German, Slavonian, and French state, in the middle of Germany. No country had received more refugees after the repeal of the Edict of Nantes. Prussia was destined to renew the ancient Saxon opposition to the emperors. This state, though poor, and without any natural barrier, which could oppose to an enemy neither the canals of Holland nor the mountains of Savoy, had nevertheless grown and extended, a pure creation of politics, of war, that is to say, of will, of human liberty triumphing over nature. The first king, William, was a hard and brutal soldier, who had spent thirty years in amassing money, and in disciplining his troops with the blows of his cane. This founder of Prussia regarded the state as a regiment. He feared that his son would not continue the same policy, and was tempted to behead him, as the Czar Peter did his son

Alexis. This son, who was Frederic II., did not please his father, who valued only height and strength, and who everywhere collected men of six feet to compose regiments of giants. The young Frederic was small in stature, with broad shoulders, with a large hand and piercing eyes—a strange figure. He was a wit, a musician, a philosopher, with immoral and frivolous tastes, a great composer of trifling French verses; he had no knowledge of Latin, and despised the German language; a simple logician, who could neither attain the beauty of ancient art nor the depth of modern science. Yet he had something for which he merited his title of Great: he *willed*. He *would* be brave; he *would* make Prussia one of the first states of Europe; he would be a legislator; he would that his deserts of Prussia should be peopled; and he accomplished all. He was one of the founders of the military art between Turenne and Napoleon. When Napoleon entered Berlin, he only wished to see the tomb of Frederic; he took his sword for himself, and said, "This is mine."

Prussia was a new state, which owed its most industrious citizens to the revocation of the Edict of Nantes; it was sooner or later to become the centre of modern false philosophy. Frederic II. comprehended the part he had to play; he declared himself in poëtry and in philosophy the disciple of

Voltaire; this was to make court to current opinions: in this the frivolous tastes of Frederic served his most serious projects. The Emperor Julian had been the ape of Marcus Aurelius; Frederic was that of Julian. At first, in honour of the Antonines, whom Voltaire proposed to him as models, he wrote a sentimental and moral book against Machiavel. Voltaire, in his simple enthusiasm, revised the proof sheets, lauded the royal author, and promised a Titus to the world. At his accession, Frederic wished to destroy the edition.

*Maria Theresa and Frederic*, 1740.—The same year the Emperor Charles VI. died, and Frederic became king (1740). All the states that had guarantied the throne to Maria Theresa took arms against her. The moment seemed to have arrived to cut the great body of Austria in pieces. All hasten to the carnage. The most antiquated claims are revived: Spain claims Bohemia and Hungary; the King of Sardinia, Milan; Frederic, Silesia; France demands nothing save the Empire itself for the Elector of Bavaria, a client of her kings for more than half a century. The elector was chosen without difficulty, and, at the same time, was named general-in-chief of the King of France. Two brothers, named Belle-Isle, disturbed France with their chimerical projects. Fleury made war for the second time in spite of himself, and, as in the first, he caused it to miscarry. The French army was badly paid and badly fed, and after some easy successes, it dispersed itself in every place where it could subsist: it left Vienna on one side, and forced its way into Bohemia; on the other side, Frederic, conqueror at Molwitz, lays his hand on Silesia (1741).

Maria Theresa was alone; her cause seemed lost. With child at the time, she believed "that there would not remain a city for her to be confined in." But England and Holland could not see the triumph of France with indifference. The pacific Walpole falls, subsidies are given to Maria Theresa, an English squadron forces the King of Naples to neutrality. The King of Prussia, who has obtained what he wished, makes peace. The French, who wait in vain in Bohemia, lose Prague, and return with great difficulty over the snow. Belle-Isle, therefore, was at liberty to compare himself to Xenophon (1742).

The English land on the Continent, and place themselves at Dettingen, in the midst of the French army, which suffered them to escape and itself to be beaten (1743). The French troops were thrown back on this side the Rhine, and the poor Emperor of Bavaria was abandoned to the vengeance of Austria.

The King of Prussia did not count on this. Maria Theresa had again become so strong that she could not fail to retake Silesia from him. He placed himself, therefore, by the side of France and Bavaria, and returned to the charge ; he entered Bohemia, and assured himself of Silesia by three victories, invaded Saxony, and forced the empress and the Saxons to sign the treaty of Dresden. The Bavarian being dead, the Austrian caused her husband to be made emperor (Francis I., 1745).

In the mean time the French had the advantage in Italy. Seconded by the Spaniards, the King of Naples, and the Genoese, they established the Infant Don Philip in the dukedoms of Milan and Parma. In the Netherlands, under the Marshal of Saxony, they gained the battles of Fontenois and Raucoux (1745–6). The former, so celebrated, would have been lost without remedy, if an Irishman, named Lally, moved by his hatred of the English, had not proposed to break their columns with four pieces of cannon. An artful courtier, the Duke of Richelieu appropriated this conception and the glory of this success to himself. The Irishman, sword in hand, entered the English columns first. In the same year, France hurled on England her most formidable enemy, the Pretender. The Highlanders of Scotland welcomed him, rushed from their mountains with an irresistible impetuosity, swept cannons from their course, and demolished squadrons with their swords. This success was necessary for France. Her navy was reduced to nothing. Lally obtained some vessels, but the English guarded the sea; they prevented the Scotch from receiving succour. They had over the Scotch the advantage of numbers and wealth, a good cavalry and a good artillery. They conquered at Culloden (1745–46.)

*Peace of Aix-la-Chapelle*, 1748.—The Spaniards withdrew from Italy. The French were driven from it. They advanced in the Netherlands. England feared for Holland, and re-established there the stadtholdership. The success of France against Holland served at least to bring about peace. She had lost her navy, her colonies; the Russians for the second time had appeared on the Rhine. The peace of Aix-la-Chapelle gave back to France her colonies, assured Silesia to Prussia, Parma and Plaisance to the Bourbons of Spain. Against all hope Austria still maintained herself (1748).

*Philosophical and Literary France.*—France had had painful experience of her weakness, but she would not profit by it. The government of the old priest was succeeded by that of the king's mistresses. Mlle. Poisson, marchioness of Pompadour, reigned twenty years. Born a citizen, she had some feelings of patriotism. Her creature, the comptroller Machant, wished to impose taxes on the clergy; D'Argenson directed the administration of the war with the talent and severity of Louvois In the midst of the little war between the Parliament and clergy, false philosophy gained ground. At the court even, it had partisans; the king, enemy as he was to new opinions, had his small printing-press, and printed himself the economical theories of his physician, Quesnay, who proposed a tax to be levied upon land; the nobility and clergy, principal proprietors of land, must pay most of it. All these schemes only ended in vain conversations; the old corporations resisted; royalty, caressed by the philosophers, who wished to arm it against the clergy, experienced a vague terror at the view of their progress. Voltaire prepared a general antichristian history (Essay on Manners, 1756). By degrees, the new philosophy emerged from this polemical form, to which Voltaire had reduced it. In 1748, the President Montesquieu, the founder of the Academy of Natural Sciences at Bordeaux, gave, though in a disconnected and timid form, a materialist theory of legislation, drawn from the influence of climates; such is at least the predominant idea of the Spirit of the Laws: a book, so ingenious, so brilliant, sometimes so profound. In 1749 the colossal Natural History of Buffon appeared; in 1751 the first volumes of the Encyclopædia, a gigantic monument, which was to contain the whole of the eighteenth century, polemics and dogmatics, economy and mathematics, irreligion and philanthropy, atheism and pantheism, D'Alembert and Diderot. Condillac had briefly expressed all that the age comprises: Treatise of Sensations, 1754. In the mean time the religious war was continued by Voltaire, who had posted himself at the central point of observation in Europe, between France, Switzerland, and Germany, at the entrance of Geneva, and in the chief place of the ancient Vaudois, of Arnold of Brescia, of Zwingle, and of Calvin.

*Seven Years' War*, 1756.—This was the height of the power of Frederic. Since his conquest in Silesia he had lost all prudence. In his strange court at Potsdam, this witty warrior scoffed at God, at the philosophers, and at his brother sovereigns; he had used Voltaire ill, who was the principal organ of opinion; he assailed in his epigrams both kings and queens; he believed neither in the beauty of Madame Pompadour, nor in the poetical genius of the Abbé Bernis, the prime minister of France. The opportunity seemed favourable for the empress to recover Silesia. She excited all Europe, and the queens above all; she enlisted the Queen of Poland and the Empress of Russia; she courted the mistress of Louis XV. The monstrous alliance of France with Austria against a sovereign who maintained the equilibrium of Germany, seemed to unite all Europe against him. England alone aided him, and gave him subsidies. England was at that time governed by a gouty lawyer, the famous William Pitt, afterward Earl of Chatham, who raised himself by the power of his eloquence and his hatred towards the French. England desired two things: the preservation of the European equilibrium, and the ruin of the French and Spanish colonies. Her grievances were great; the Spaniards had ill treated some of her subjects who were engaged in contraband trade, and the French in Canada prevented them from building on their territory. In the Indies, La Bourdonnaie, and his successor Dupleix, threatened to found a great power in face of the English. The English, as a declaration of war, confiscated three hundred French vessels (1756).

It was amazing to behold in this war the little kingdom of Prussia, amid the masses of Austria, of France, of Russia, going from one to another, and confronting all. This is the second epoch of the military art. The simple adversaries of Frederic believed that he owed all his success to the precision of the manœuvres of the Prussian soldiers, to their skill in military tactics, in firing five times in a minute. Frederic had certainly perfected the soldier as a machine. But this could be imitated; the Czar Peter III., and the Count St. Germain, made automaton soldiers by a free use of the cane. What they could not imitate was the quickness of his manœuvres and his well-ordered marches, which gave him great facility in concentrating those rapid masses on the weak side of the enemy.

In this terrible chase which the great armies of the allies gave Prussia, we cannot avoid remarking the amusing circumspection of the Austrian tacticians, and the rash folly of the great lords who conducted the armies of France. The Fabius of Austria, the wise and sluggish Daun, limited himself to a war of opposition; he found no camp strong enough, no mountains inaccessible enough; Frederic always beat those paralytic armies.

*Rosbach*, 1757.—First, he rid himself of the Saxons. He did them no injury; he only disarmed them. Then he struck a blow at Bohemia. Repulsed, abandoned by the English army, which had decided at Closterseven to fight no longer, threatened by the Russians, conquered at Zaegerndorf, he went to Saxony, and there found the French and Imperialists united. Four armies surrounded Prussia. Frederic believed himself lost; he wished to put an end to his existence; he wrote so to his sister, and to Argens. He only feared one thing: that after his death the great distributer of glory, Voltaire, would not perpetuate his name; he wrote an epistle to appease him, thus imitating Julian, who, when mortally wounded, drew from his robe and pronounced a discourse which he had composed for such an occasion. "As regards myself," said Frederic, "as regards myself, threatened by shipwreck, it is my duty, facing the storm, to think, live, and die as a king!" The epistle finished, he defeated the enemy. The Prince of Soubise, expecting to see him fly, rashly pursued him; then the Prussians unmask their troops, kill three thousand men, and take seven thousand. They found in the camp an army of cooks, comedians, and hairdressers, a quantity of parrots and umbrellas, and I know not how many cases of lavender water (1757).

The tactician alone can follow the King of Prussia in this series of beautiful and scientific battles. The Seven Years' War, whatever the variety of its vicissitudes may be, was a war of policy and of strategy; it had not the interest of wars of opinion, nor of those wars for religion and liberty which occur in the sixteenth century, and in our own.

*Family Compact*, 1761.—The defeat at Rosbach renewed at Crevelt—great reverses, balanced by trifling advantages—the total ruin of the French navy and of the French colonies—the English masters of the seas and conquerors of India—the weakness, the humiliation of all old Europe before young Prussia—this is the Seven Years' War. It terminated under the ministry of M. de Choiseul. This minister, a man of spirit and talent, thought to strike a great blow by arranging the *family compact* between the different branches of the house of Bourbon (1761).

In the midst of the humiliations of the Seven Years' War, and even by means of these humiliations, the drama of the age makes rapid strides towards its development. Who had been conquered in this and the preceding war? France? No, but the nobility, who alone furnished the officers, the generals. The enemies of France could not question French bravery after Chevert and D'Assas. Had one not seen, in the combat of the exiles, French soldiers climbing the Alps under showers of grapeshot with which the cannons were loaded, and leaping on the cannons of the enemy even through the embrasures, while the pieces recoiled? As to the generals, the only ones that we can venture to name at this epoch are Saxe and Broglie, who were foreigners. He who appropriated to himself the glory of Fontenoi, the great general of the century, according to the saying of women and of courtiers, the *conqueror of Mahon*, the old Alcibiades of the old Voltaire, Richelieu, had shown sufficiently, during the five campaigns of the last war, what one ought to think of a reputation so skilfully got up. These campaigns were at least lucrative; he brought back enough from them to build on the boulevards of Paris the elegant pavilion of Hanover.

*J. J. Rousseau.* — Towards the end of this ignoble war of seven years, in which the aristocracy had fallen so low, the great plebeian mind burst forth. It was as if France had cried to Europe, "It is not I who am conquered!" In 1750, the son of a watchmaker of Geneva, John Jacques Rousseau, a vagrant, scribe, and footman by turns, had cursed all science in his hatred of a spurious philosophy, and of the caste of literary men; then he cursed all inequality in his hatred of a degenerated nobility (1754). This rage for levelling streamed in torrents through the letters of his New Heloise (1759). Naturalism is expounded in his Emily, Deism in the profession of the faith of the Savoyard Vicar (1762). In the Social Contract, finally, appeared the three maxims of the Revolution, traced by a fiery hand.

The Revolution advanced so irresistibly, that the king, who foresaw it with terror, worked for it in spite of himself, and opened its path. In 1763 he founded for it his temple, the *Pantheon,* which was to receive Rousseau and Voltaire. In 1764 he expelled the Jesuits; in 1771 he abolished the Parliament. A tractable instrument of necessity, he overthrew with an indifferent hand whatever yet remained standing of the ruins of the Middle Ages.

*Abolition of the Jesuits*, 1764.—The society of the Jesuits, which was believed to be so deeply rooted, was annihilated without a blow through all Europe. The Templars had perished in like manner in the fourteenth century, when the system to which they belonged had lasted its time. The Jesuits were given up to the parliaments, their deadly enemies. But, at the same time that the stones of Port Royal had fallen on the heads of the Jesuits, the downfall of the latter was fatal to the parliaments. These corporations, encouraged by their increasing popularity and by their recent victory, would move along the old paths. The imperfect balance of the old monarchy encountered the elastic opposition of the parliaments, who remonstrated, adjourned, and ended by respectfully yielding. Some courageous and decided men, among others Breton la Chalotais, undertook to lead them farther. In the trial of the Duke of Aiguillon they stood firm; they were broken up (1771). It was not to the judges of Lally, of Calas, of Sirven, of Labarre, that it belonged to achieve the Revolution, still less to the coterie that overthrew them. The spirited Abbé Terray, and the jovial Chancellor Maupeou, allies of the Duke of Aiguillon and Madame du Barray, were not honest enough to have the privilege of doing good. Terray, who had charge of the finances, remedied the disorder a little, but did it through bankruptcy. Maupeou abolished the venality of offices, and dispensed justice gratuitously, but no one would believe that it was gratuitous in the hands of the creatures of Maupeou. All the world ridiculed their reforms; no one more than themselves. Irrepressible laughter burst forth at the appearance of the Memoirs of Beaumarchais. Louis XV. read them, as did everybody, and was much amused with them. This egotistical monarch perceived the growing danger of the crown more clearly than any one, but he judged with reason, that, after all, it would outlast him (died in 1774).

*Louis XVI.*, 1774.—His unfortunate successor, Louis XVI., inherited all this danger. Many people had conceived sad forebodings on the occasion of his marriage fêtes, when several hundred persons were suffocated. Yet the accession of the honest young king, seating himself with his graceful queen on the throne, now happily purged of Louis XV., had excited in the country immense hope. For a society jaded and worn out, this was an epoch of happiness and genuine emotion. It cried, admired itself and its tears, and believed itself again young. The fashionable style was the idyl; at first, the insipidity of Florian, the innocence of

Gesner, then the immortal eclogue of Paul and Virginia. The queen built herself a hamlet, and bought a farm in Trianon. The philosophers conducted the plough by writing. "Choiseul is husbandman, and Voltaire is farmer." All the world interested itself for the people, loved the people, wrote for the people. Benevolence was fashionable; they gave small alms and great feasts.

While the higher circles enjoyed this sentimental comedy, that great movement of the world continued, which was about to sweep away everything in a moment. The true confidant of the public, the confidant of Beaumarchais, grew daily more bitter; he changed from comedy to satire, from satire to the tragical drama. Royalty, Parliament, nobility, all staggered with weakness; the world was as if intoxicated. Philosophy even sickened under the poison of Rousseau and Gilbert. Men believed no more in religion or irreligion; they wished to believe, however; strong minds went incognito to seek for creeds in the phantasmagoria of Cagliostro, and in the trough of Mesmer. In the mean time, the everlasting dialogue of rational skepticism resounded through France; the evident dogmatism of Kant responded to the nihilism of Hume, and over all rose the great poetical voice of Göethe, harmonious, immoral, and indifferent. France, in commotion and preoccupied, heard nothing of all this. Germany pursued the scientific epic poem; France worked out the social drama.

*Turgot — Necker.* — What gives a comic air to the gloom of these last days of the old society, is the contrast between great promises and complete inefficiency. Inefficiency is a common trait of all the ministers of that time. All promise, and can do nothing. M. de Choiseul would defend Poland, humble England, exalt France by a European war, when he could not defray the expenses of the day; if he had wished to execute his projects, the Parliament, who sustained him, would have abandoned him. Maupeou and Terray dissolved the Parliament, and could find nothing to replace it; they wished to reform the finances, and they had to rely on none but the robbers of the public treasury. Under Louis XVI., the great, the honest, the sanguine Turgot (1774–1776), proposes the true remedy—economy, and the abolition of privileges. To whom does he propose them? To the privileged party, who overthrow him. In the mean time, necessity obliged them to call to their aid an able banker, an eloquent foreigner, a second Law, but more honest. Neckar promises wonders: he encourages everybody, he announces no sweeping reform, he proceeds gently. He inspires confidence, he has recourse to credit, he finds money, he borrows. Confidence and a good administration would augment commerce — commerce would create resources. Short loans were made on the strength of casual, slow, and distant resources. Neckar finished by relinquishing his own plans and returning to the means proposed by Turgot—economy, and equality of taxes. The account which he rendered was an expressive acknowledgment of his weakness (1781).

*War of America*, 1778–84.—Neckar, we must confess, had had a double conflict to sustain. He had, besides the expenses of the interior, to defray those of the war which France carried on in favour of youthful America (1778–84). France contributed at that time to raise against England an English rival. Although the latter has shown that she does not care to remember the aid, never was money better employed. The country could not pay too much for the last naval victories of France and the creation of Cherbourg. There was then a rare season of confidence and enthusiasm. France envied America her Franklin; the young French nobility embarked in the crusade for liberty.

*Notables*, 1787.—The king, who had vainly tried the patriotic ministers, Turgot and Neckar, was now influenced by the queen and the court, and chose courtiers as ministers. One could not find a minister more agreeable than M. de Calonne, a guide more ready to encourage his master to plunge gayly into ruin. When he had exhausted the credit which the wise conduct of Neckar had created, he knew not what to do, and assembled the Notables (1787). He had to confess that the loans had been raised within a few years to 1646 millions of francs, and that an annual deficit existed of 140 millions. The Notables, who themselves belonged to the privileged classes, gave advice and accusations in place of money. Brienne, raised by them to the place of Calonne, had recourse to duties ; the Parliament refused to register them, and demanded the States-General, that is to say, their own ruin and that of the ancient monarchy.

*States-General,* 1789.—The philosophers had been overthrown with Turgot, the bankers with Neckar, the courtiers with Calonne and Brienne. The privileged would not pay, and the people could not any longer. The States-General, as an eminent historian said, only decreed a revolution, which had already taken place (opening of the States-General, May 5th, 1789.)

THE END.

www.ingramcontent.com/pod-product-compliance
Lightning Source LLC
LaVergne TN
LVHW021144110826
845150LV00005B/1123